International Payoffs

International Payoffs

Dilemma for Business

Yerachmiel Kugel
Gladys W. Gruenberg
Saint Louis University

Lexington Books
D.C. Heath and Company
Lexington, Massachusetts
Toronto

Library of Congress Cataloging in Publication Data

Kugel, Yerachmiel.
  International payoffs.

  Includes bibliographies references and index.
  1. Commercial crimes. 2. Corporations, American. I. Gruenberg, Gladys
W., joint author. II. Title.
HV6765.K84   364.1   76-48404
ISBN 0-669-01150-9

Copyright © 1977 by D.C. Heath and Company.

Published simultaneously in Canada.

Printed in the United States of America.

International Standard Book Number: 0-669-01150-9

Library of Congress Catalog Card Number: 76-48404

Contents

List of Figures

List of Tables

Preface

The international payoff scandal had broken early in 1975 with the United Brands tragedy and was followed by a steady stream of shocking news. Discussion of current business phenomena in the class in international business in the fall of 1975 at Saint Louis University School of Business and Administration stimulated the students to intense research. They were encouraged to apply the principles they were learning to a "now" happening. This research provided the seed from which this book grew.

To supplement readily available documents from governmental agencies and Congressional committees, the authors wrote to *Fortune*'s 500 for copies of codes of conduct, policy statements, and speeches of executives. Their response became a data bank for up-to-date knowledge about the effect of payoff disclosures on business operations and changes in business ethical perspectives.

What you read here is the result of this year-long research project supported by consecutive sabbatical leaves. We owe a special debt of gratitude to our respective spouses, Irit Kugel and Harold Gruenberg, for their tolerance of the long nights of burning the midnight oil in trying to complete the manuscript while the subject matter was still a current issue. It was a worthwhile sacrifice, we hope, since we have succeeded in bringing together in one place an historical account of what happened, an analysis of why it happened, and finally practical guidelines for both business executives and policymakers to aid in the resolution of the international payoff dilemma.

Special thanks go to students, David J. Batsch, Stanley D. Griffis, Yimin A. Huang, and Dennis Shannon, for their early assistance in this project. We also acknowledge the encouragement of our colleagues at Saint Louis University School of Business and Administration, especially that of Dean John Wagner, Associate Dean Leroy J. Grossman, and Director Seung Kim of the International Business Program. Departmental chairmen N.K. Kwak (Management Sciences) and Paul E. Merz (Economics) also provided moral support for the project.

Some material in this book first appeared in an article published in *Challenge*, September-October 1976, pp. 13-20. We express our special appreciation to *Challenge* editors and the International Arts and Sciences Press for permission to reproduce this material. The editors and staff at Lexington Books are also to be commended for their interest and efficiency in getting the publication off the press in record time.

No manuscript can become a publication without proficiency in typing, which was supplied in this case by Pat Feldmann and Eva Ruggeri and, on occasion, by other members of the Business School staff. If haste has caused errors, we are to blame. Scholarship too at times clashes with expediency. We have been goaded by our desire to lay the groundwork for stern and swift sanction of international payoffs to reduce subversion of the market system, for which we believe there is as yet no viable alternative.

-copyright 1976 by Herblock in *The Washington Post*

1 Introduction

The most immoral position of all is: perform, and we don't want to know how.
—The Wall Street Journal[1]

In the post-Watergate atmosphere of what has been termed "self-flagellation,"[2] the American people show signs of increased cynicism regarding the ethical standards of both politicians and businessmen.

Sparked by the suicide of United Brands' chairman and chief officer, Eli M. Black, who jumped to his death February 3, 1975, from his forty-fourth floor office in mid-Manhattan, the Securities and Exchange Commission (SEC) escalated its investigation into the questionable payments made by American multinational firms overseas.

The Facts

Although Black's suicide drew public attention to "corporate morality," the public concern about business conduct and its responsiveness to societal needs, it must be noted, is not new. Beginning in the 1960s, gaining momentum through the new era of social legislation and investigation of social and private institutions, and culminating in the current expose of international bribery, serious doubts about business integrity now exist in the public mind.

The uniqueness of Black's suicide, however, is its demonstration, even dramatization, to the public that individual, corporate, and societal corruption are inseparable. Real people with real consciences work in corporations. If corporate competitive conditions pressure real people to do what they otherwise would not consider doing and thereby trigger suicide or imprisonment, resulting in the suffering of families like ours, then corporate matters are surely public matters.

Although Ralph Nader and Mark Green seem to dispute this contention when they say . . .

many of these costs of corporate crime, to be sure, are often invisible to public's eye. There are no burned buildings or rioters to flash on the evening news . . .[3]

Black's suicide certainly signaled a turning point in the relationship between the corporation and society. The impact of corporate conduct suddenly became vivid, tangible, visible, and personal. Indeed, judging by the extent of news coverage on corporate misconduct both domestic and overseas since early 1975, the public has begun to reexamine its attitude toward business. Typical headlines read as follows:

Was Eli Black's Suicide Caused By Tensions of Conflicting World?

Putting the Clamps on the Multinationals

ITT: A Private Little Foreign Policy: Today Multinationals, Tomorrow the World?

Company Payoffs in U.S. Come Under New Scrutiny

Corporate Morality: Is the Price Too High?

SEC May Uncover More Domestic Bribes by Methods Developed in Overseas Cases

Payoff Triggering Wave of Stockholder Suits

Multinational Firms Under Fire All Over, Face a Changed Future

Multinationals Under Pressures to Change Their Ways

Never before have multinational firms been scrutinized as they are today.[4] The pressure comes from all directions. The scrutiny comes from both the United States and foreign governments of countries in which these corporations operate. It emanates from shareholders, academicians, activist groups, and lately even businessmen themselves.[5]

Implications of Current Uproar about Corporate Morality

What are the implications of this attack on business? Is it merely rhetoric or does it symbolize the beginning of the end of the American free enterprise system?

Unfortunately, the current uproar is more than just rhetoric. The following are examples of rising public concern:

1. The U.S. Senate adopted a resolution directing the executive branch to initiate multilateral negotiations on a code of conduct among governments to eliminate "the practices of bribery, indirect payments, kickbacks, unethical political contributions and other similarly disreputable activities."

2. In Paris, twenty-four OECD countries met with business leaders to discuss and express ideas for improving a draft of "Guidelines for Multinational Enterprise."

3. The UN's new Commission on Transnational Corporations is drafting a "code of conduct dealing with transnational corporations."

4. Almost one hundred significant institutional studies are underway on multinational corporations—by governments, associations, and academic authorities.

5. On March 27, 1976, President Ford in a TV campaign speech announced the formation of a special committee with cabinet-level authority to study the problem of American corporations' conduct overseas. Committee chairman Elliot Richardson issued a report in June 1976.[6]

6. Culminating year-long investigations by the Senate Foreign Relations Subcommittee on Multinational Corporations and the Senate Banking Committee, Bill No. 3664 was passed in the Senate on September 16, 1976, by a vote of 86 to 0.[7]

In short, the current concern about corporate conduct is beyond the rhetoric level. It has reached the executive, legislative, and judicial branches of governments. This situation is bound to result in real action with significant consequences both to business as an entity and to the people who work for business. The gap between individual life, corporate life, and societal life is now rapidly closing. All three groups work for the same ultimate common good and when the actions of any one of them seem to jeopardize that goal, they become the concern of all.

Purpose of the Book

This book is written in the hope that legislators, multinational firm executives, and the public at large will be motivated to delve beneath headlines and work together for a practical solution to the problem of international payoffs—that is, a solution geared to the realities of the market function.

More specifically, the purpose of this book is fourfold:

1. To present, as fairly and objectively as possible, the cases for and against international payoffs;
2. To delineate the gray areas relating to payoffs;
3. To develop a conceptual framework to facilitate the analysis of business ethics in general and business decisions relating to international payoffs in particular;
4. To contribute to the clarity of the measures that can be taken to control international payoffs and their implications for individual executives, business firms, and society as a whole.

Far from being in agreement with radical economists that payoff revelations are an indictment of government's failure to curb the growing power of multinational corporations, the thesis of this book is that there is a spectrum of activities in this field ranging from "white" to "black" and that blanket condemnation is not only unrealistic but may harm the ability of U.S. multinational firms to operate efficiently in the face of world competition.

Plan of the Book

After delineating the white, gray, and black areas and the various forms of international payoffs, the analysis focuses on the rationale of payoffs from the viewpoint of society, business, and the individual executive. Various studies of business behavior and attitudes, commissioned by business or initiated by various business-oriented publications, are used to illustrate the range of beliefs held by the business community on international payoffs.

This information is updated with the most recent reports of actual payoff cases in aircraft, oil, food, and drug industries. A chronology of events and reports appearing in the news media on the subject of international payoffs and business ethics mainly during 1975 and 1976 is also included to show the crescendo buildup of disclosure and public reaction.

Once the phenomenon of payoffs is analyzed, an attempt is made to develop a conceptual framework for formulation of decision-making criteria for international payoffs. A three-level analysis (society, business, individual) sets forth decision-making guidelines (legal, economic, and moral) designed so that the individual executive may base his decision on his own unique competitive situation in the global market.

Finally, a comprehensive proposal for measures needed to control international payoffs is presented; it involves four levels of activity: transnational (between nations), national (within nation-states), business (both as a market and as an institutional structure), and the individual executive (as a member of a profession, a family, and a community). At the transnational level the emphasis is on moral influence. At the national level the primary influence is legal, while at the business level it is economic. In each case the influence is directed at resolving the dilemma faced by the individual executive in opposition to international payoffs by making them increasingly incompatible with his individual self-interest.

This analysis is then applied to various present proposals for the control of payoffs to explain why emphasis on the individual executive represents a fruitful approach for dealing with international payoffs.

International payoffs are the current phenomenon that has given new life to the age-old debate about business ethics and social responsibility. Our hope is that this book will shed some light on this subject and serve as a guide through the maze of issues that have been raised and must be resolved both at the microeconomic level of the multinational firm and at the macroeconomic level of public policy determination. Preservation of our whole way of life may be the ultimate prize.

Notes

1. *The Wall Street Journal*, June 2, 1975.

2. David Eisenhower, *The Wall Street Journal*, December 4, 1975.

3. *The Wall Street Journal*, March 12, 1976.

4. For an excellent review of the content and evaluation of this attack on multinational firms, see, Neil H. Jacoby, *Corporate Power and Social Responsibility* (New York: Macmillan, 1973), pp. 3-20. Another viewpoint is expressed in Richard J. Barnet and Ronald E. Muller, *Global Reach, The Power of the Multinational Corporations* (New York: Simon and Schuster, 1974).

5. Cf. Leonard Silk and David Vogel, *Ethics and Profits* (New York: Simon and Schuster, 1976).

6. Richardson's letter dated June 11, 1976, to the Senate Banking Committee summarizes the report. See U.S. Congress, Senate, Committee on Banking, Housing and Urban Affairs, *Hearing*, Washington, D.C., May 18, 1976, Appendix, pp. 39-67.

7. The House took no action on the Senate Bill before adjournment for the November 1976 elections. S. 3664 is a compromise developed from three bills.

2

The Nature and Mechanics of Payoffs

Some were politicians on the take, generals for hire, "agents" of sordid influence, "consultants" in corruption. Other relationships, one would hope, were perfectly respectable and businesslike.

—Senator Clifford P. Case[1]

Just as the suicide of United Brands' Eli Black dramatized the personal trauma of international payoffs, so the multimillion-dollar amounts of such payoffs reported in the news media dramatized the extent of such payments. (See Table 2-1 for a list of the ten biggest spenders.) Slipping a $10 tip to a customs official is one thing; paying millions to a foreign intermediary to influence the purchase of public goods is something else. A California aerospace executive, reacting to the Lockheed disclosure, stated:

They overpaid. . . . They could have gotten by for maybe $100,000. There was no need to pay a million bucks to anyone. It reflects their lack of expertise.[2]

The payoff disclosures shocked the Securities and Exchange Commission (SEC) and Congress into demanding additional information to protect investors and consumers. As of April 1976 more than 95 companies in *Fortune*'s 500 had come under investigation and admitted expenditures of many millions of dollars in overseas payments. (See Chapter 4 for more details.)

Since subsequent disclosures have not produced the same exorbitant results as the first news, the current consensus in SEC and elsewhere is that continuing investigation may be counterproductive. The cost of discovery is beginning to outweigh the results achieved. For example, for International Business Machines Corporation, whose sales annually amount to many billions, discovery that in a seven-year period only $53,000 may have been improperly paid to foreign officials falls into the counterproductive category. Occidental Petroleum's chief executive officer, Armand Hammer, reported at the 1976 shareholders' meeting that a special committee looking into international payoffs had uncovered improper foreign payments of only $163,000 in seven and a half years: "For a company that's done over $20 billion in business in that period, that's an insignificant amount and was done without the knowledge of directors."[3]

Types of Payments

While the amount is important, the purpose of the payoff, to whom it is paid, and the nature of the quid pro quo that results give real clues for analysis of

7

Table 2-1
Ten of the Biggest Spenders

Ashland Oil, Inc.	Admits paying more than $300,000 to foreign officials, including $150,000 to President Albert Bernard Bongo of Gabon to retain mineral and refining rights.
Burroughs Corp.	Admits that $1.5 million in corporate funds may have been used in improper payments to foreign officials.
Exxon Corp.	Admits paying $740,000 to government officials and others in three countries. Admits its Italian subsidiary made $27 million in secret but legal contributions to seven Italian political parties.
Gulf Oil Corp.	Admits paying $4 million to South Korea's ruling political party. Admits giving $460,000 to Bolivian officials—including a $110,000 helicopter to the late President Rene Barrientos Orutno—for oil rights.
Lockheed Aircraft Corp.	Admits giving $202 million in commissions, payoffs, and bribes to foreign agents and government officials in The Netherlands, Italy, Japan, Turkey, and other countries. Admits that $22 million of this sum went for outright bribes.
McDonnell Douglas Corp.	Admits paying $2.5 million in commissions and consultant fees between 1970 and 1975 to foreign government officials.
Merck & Co., Inc.	Admits giving $3 million, largely in "commission-type payments," to employees of 36 foreign governments between 1968 and 1975.
Northrop Corp.	Admits in part SEC charges that it paid $30 million in commissions and bribes to government officials and agents in Holland, Iran, France, West Germany, Saudi Arabia, Brazil, Malaysia, and Taiwan.
G. D. Searle & Co.	Admits paying $1.3 million to foreign governmental employees from 1973 to 1975 to "obtain sales of products or services."
United Brands Co.	Admits paying a $1,250,000 bribe to Honduran officials for a reduction in the banana export tax. Admits paying $750,000 to European officials. Investigators say the payment was made to head off proposed Italian restrictions on banana imports.

Source: *Newsweek*, February 23, 1976, p. 30. Copyright 1976 by Newsweek, Inc. All rights reserved. Reprinted with permission.
Note: See Chapter 4 for update.

determinants, which is the purpose of this text. Labelling a payment as a bribe gives it an unsavory connotation, even though there may be no impropriety in fact. For example, does a donation become a bribe when it is made by a multinational sales agent to the favorite charity of a defense contract administrator? Similarly, multinational companies make contributions to local community projects, either voluntarily or under pressure, to preserve host country good will. Depending upon the viewpoint of the reviewer, such payment may be hailed as an example of social responsibility or it may be damned as corporate interference with host-country decision making.

At the outset, then, some standard for analysis must be determined so that international payoffs may be evaluated in a more or less objective manner. Various surveys have been made of the business community to ascertain how executives view such payments. They have classified payoffs by who receives them, what their purpose is, and the form of such payment.

The Conference Board survey of "unusual foreign payments" quotes one executive's listing by *receiver:*[4]

1. Bribes to customers;
2. Bribes to government officials to secure action or, in some cases, quicker action;
3. Bribes to tax authorities;
4. Illegal payments for overtime to employees in conflict with local labor laws.

Summarizing the results of the survey, The Conference Board states:

Of the various types of situations inviting unusual payments by U.S. companies abroad, the most frequently cited by participants in this survey are bribes and other payments to customers, and bribes to government workers to overcome red tape and get quicker action.[5]

The Investor Responsibility Research Center (IRRC) study of international payoffs corroborates this view by listing the following *purposes* of international payoffs:[6]

1. Avoiding harassment;
2. Obtaining advantage;
3. Influencing the political process;
4. Supporting the political process.

Harassment refers to such actions as refusal of lower-level government officials "to take routine actions on a timely basis." *Obtaining advantage* includes undervaluing shipments, inflating prices for products or services, or increasing profits through support by officials. Some Asian businessmen complain, according to the IRRC study, that

... their American partners often insist on paying a lot of money in bribes because they cannot be bothered to do things in the time-honored way of endless talk over tea. They therefore end up paying several times more in bribes than is necessary or even acceptable.[7]

Influencing the political process refers to payments to affect the outcome of elections in favor of a party or candidate, whereas *supporting the political process* is assistance to democratic governments for foreign policy purposes. Whether this type of payment did in fact help the company is doubtful but also immaterial.

A distinction can be made between cash and noncash payments, in classifying payments according to *form*. Noncash payments may be listed as follows:[8]

1. Gifts: paid vacations, home rental, gift certificates, scholarships for children, country-club dues;
2. Privileges: use of automobiles or aircraft, unsecured loans, dummy brokerage accounts, special discounts;
3. Special opportunities: buying from businesses run by relatives, putting relatives on the payroll as consultants, rigging of company contest so relative can win;
4. Other gratuities: paying for auto rentals, free samples, unlimited use of credit cards.

Another neglected classification of payments focuses on their *legality*. We present this classification for its usefulness in determining the appropriateness of the various payments made by multinational firms and in providing guidelines to international executives considering their use:

1. Bribery and extortion (the black area);
2. Kickbacks, political contributions, and donations (the gray area);
3. Sales, commissions, wages, and gratuities (the white area).

This range of black to white highlights the legal and ethical involvement of executives in the decision-making process with reference to international payoffs. The black and white payments are quite easy to decide; the gray area is the problem. Here is where the need to adjust personal conduct to different customs and laws of different countries presents the executive with his economic and moral dilemma. The guidelines that are developed later in this book are designed to help him to arrive at a decision. As was stated in the introduction, moralizing is no help because every executive must make up his own mind by considering the environment within which he is operating. But before a decision can be made, he must be aware of the alternatives and their consequences.

Bribery and Extortion—The Black Area

In West Africa a bribe is known as *dash*. In Latin American it is *la mordida* (the bite); in Italy, *la bustarella* (the little envelope); in France, *pot de vin* (jug of wine); and in the United States, *grease*. By whatever name, bribery includes all outright payoffs to clerks and customs inspectors as well as the hiring of government officials as consultants with a view toward *improperly* influencing their decisions.

Since bribery clearly stands in the black zone of international payoffs and is unlawful in most of the countries of the world, the legal definition is most appropriate:

The offering, giving, receiving, or soliciting of any thing of value to influence action as official or in discharge of legal or public duty. The receiving or offering any undue reward by or to any person concerned in the administration of public justice or a public officer to influence his behavior in office.[9]

At common law the emphasis is on the perversion of justice or improperly influencing actions of public officials. Although the term was originally meant to apply to judicial actions, it has now been extended to cover voters, cabinet ministers, legislators, sheriffs, and other classes of public officials.

In *Wharton's Criminal Law and Procedure*, bribery is discussed in terms of the giver's intent, purpose, and his defenses in rebuttal thereof. Definitions are somewhat ambiguous and different degrees of bribery exist. Accepted rules are:

Mental state—Bribery must be committed with a corrupt intent, that is, with the intent of influencing official action to obtain a result which the party would not be entitled to as a matter of right. A corrupt intent need not be shown as to both parties of the transaction, only the defendant in the trial. Thus, the payment of money to an official with the intent to influence his action in a matter pending before him is bribery. Here again, there is difficulty of proving a corrupt agreement.

Purpose—The general rule is that the purpose or object sought by the bribe may be anything within the scope of official action. The scope or the purpose of bribery is now as broad as the duties of the officer that accepts the bribe.

Defenses—The defendant may disprove the existence of the corrupt intent essential to bribery by proving that he believed the payment was reimbursement for proper expenses, or that it was received as a loan in good faith.[10]

History of Bribery. Historically, the documentation of bribery is part of human activity. The Code of Hammurabi, king of Babylon, provided that "if a man [in a case] bear witness for grain or money [as a bribe], he shall himself bear the penalty imposed in that case." Another edict promulgated 1300 years before Christ by a king of Egypt prescribes capital punishment for the official or priest who accepts a bribe in the performance of his judicial functions.[11] References in the Bible, as well as Greek and Roman codes, show that bribery, when discovered, was harshly dealt with.

Later historical examples continued to involve activities to influence legislative or administrative action. In seventeenth-century England, Sir Francis Bacon's admission that as Lord Chancellor he had accepted bribes to influence his judgment involving the grant of patents and monopolies was denounced by Parliament. Steps were immediately taken to remove him from office. He was fined, imprisoned for a few days, and excluded thereafter from holding other governmental offices.[12] Later, in reviewing a new edition of Bacon's work that appeared in 1837, Lord Thomas B. Macaulay neatly summarized the argument against bribetaking while at the same time indicating its prevalence:

That these practices were common, we admit. But they are common, just as all wickedness to which there is a strong temptation always was, and always will be common. They are common, just as theft, cheating, perjury, and adultery have always been common. They were common, though prohibited by law. They were common, though condemned by public opinion. They were common, because in that age law and public opinion united had not sufficient force to restrain the greediness of powerful and unprincipled magistrates. They were common, as every crime will be common *when the gain to which it leads is great, and the chance of disgrace and punishment small.* But though common, they were universally allowed to be altogether unjustifiable; they were in the highest degree odious; and, though many were guilty of them, none had the audacity publicly to avow and defend them [emphasis supplied].[13]

In the United States, bribery in connection with business activities was aimed at financial manipulation and market control. One example is the Credit Mobilier Union Pacific Railroad scandal of 1872.[14] Not only had a great deal of money been realized from Union Pacific's construction, but it also appeared to have been used for the corruption of Congress. Before the end of the year two House investigating committees were calling witnesses and taking testimony. Congressman Oakes Ames, brother of Union Pacific's president Oliver Ames, was censured for offering bribes (no one was punished for taking them). The strain proved too much and within a few weeks he died of a stroke.

The westward movement and the growth of industrial markets were equally conducive to payoffs. The robber barons have been cited for such activity.[15] Notably the building of railroads after the Civil War involved bribery of legislators, falsification of corporate records, extortion and theft. Famous names such as Carnegie, Drew, Fisk, Gould and Rockefeller were involved. It was not unusual for financial trusts to buy out competitors under threat of bankruptcy. Famous men stated: "I will not sue you for the law takes too long. I will ruin you" and then proceeded to do so.[16]

The threat of ruin and bankruptcy is an important factor in the current discussion of international payoffs. Northrop Corporation's board member, Richard Millar, clearly makes this point in his testimony before the Senate Subcommittee on Multinational Corporations:

Senator Church. [to elicit information about the "necessity" of international payments] . . . necessary in the sense that unless the money was paid, Northrop might fail to make the sales it hoped. Was that the reason the money was paid?
Mr. Millar. . . . I think you must assume that they felt that the ongoing program and prospective sales were imperiled if the payment was not made.
Senator Church. So this really was a form of blackmail, was it not? . . .
Mr. Millar. Yes.[17]

Blackmail, of course, is synonymous with extortion. Extortion is the unlawful obtaining of money from another. The coexistence of extortion and bribery is understood in law:

Bribery consists in the offering a present, or receiving one, if offered; extortion, in demanding a fee or present, by color of office. To constitute extortion the wrongful use of fear must be the operating cause producing consent.[18]

An exaction is still another variation; it compels payment of a fee for services where no payment is due. Thus, the difference between extortion and exaction is that in the former case the officer extorts more than his due when something is due; in the latter, he exacts something when there is nothing due. In both cases, however, use of an official position for personal gain is involved.

While extortion and bribery are usually considered mutually exclusive, there are elements common to both. In fact, economic power may determine whether the influence is on the offering or receiving end. For example, when the initiative comes from the receiving end with a threat to interfere with the multinational firm's activity in the host country, as was the case in South Korea according to the report of Gulf Oil's special task force,[19] it is labelled extortion. When the initiative comes from the offering end as inducement to influence judicial, legislative, or administrative action, as appeared to be the case with United Brands' export tax case in Honduras,[20] it is called bribery. The roles may change from time to time, however, especially when the briber can no longer justify the continued outlay and the "bribee" does not agree to discontinue it. Once the black-bag operation starts, the roles become so enmeshed that it is difficult to determine where bribery ends and extortion begins.

In summary, then, there are two necessary elements for unlawful bribery at common law:

1. The receiver must be in some governmental position;
2. The thing of value must be offered to improperly influence official action.

Whether the action is ever taken or whether it is harmful to the host country is immaterial in determining the legality of international bribery.

This common-law view is the black area of international payoffs. This black area is what some companies refer to when they state that they have been guilty of doing nothing illegal. Most people, however, feel that the boundaries of illegality should be extended to other types of payment.

Once the definition is expanded to include other persons besides governmental officials (such as purchasing agents and trustees) and to apply to attempts to influence improperly actions that fall within a wide scope of responsibility of any official, public or private, the gray area of payoffs begins to appear. Some of these are already unlawful in the United States by reason of specific legislation or regulations under the jurisdiction of various public agencies such as SEC, Internal Revenue Service (IRS), Federal Trade Commission (FTC), and Interstate Commerce Commission (ICC). Most are acceptable in other countries provided there is disclosure.

Kickbacks, Political Contributions,
Donations—The Gray Area

Whenever a sale or purchase is made that involves a corporation or governmental agency, the agents on both sides of the transaction are tempted to manipulate the documentary evidence of the price and quantity (such as invoices, bills of lading, accounting entries) to include rebates to the purchaser or the supplier. This practice is sometimes the result of a reciprocal arrangement, but it may also depend on who is in a stronger market position. Such payments, known as kickbacks, are one segment of the gray area of international payments.

Kickbacks may imply a conflict of interest wherein the executive personally gains at the expense of the company he works for, but this is not necessarily the case when the money received is turned over to the firm. The main purpose of SEC regulations in demanding disclosure of kickbacks is that they hide true information about the business transactions involved, whereas bona fide discounts or price increases are properly recorded. Such falsification may also constitute tax fraud under IRS regulations and is a kind of "unfair competition" under the surveillance of the FTC. The market system requires knowledge of true price and quality to operate effectively. Kickbacks interfere with this knowledge. Fair trade laws are designed to prevent such undisclosed price adjustments.

It is important to realize, however, that this concept of fairness in no way implies that the businessman has a responsibility to charge what the consumer considers a fair price. Every market implies a basically adversary relationship wherein the supplier (the firm) and the demander (the consumer) have diametrically opposite goals. The former wants a higher price to increase his profits; the latter wants a lower price to increase his standard of living. In a free market prices are determined by this interaction. In no sense is the businessman acting in the consumer's interest. He merely reacts to market demands.

Consumers who feel that business firms should act primarily in their interest are not only naive; they are not interested in the preservation of free markets. As soon as a market is designated as one in which the consumer interest is paramount, it is logical to insist that the government should control or operate the productive resources that supply that market. Utilities are a case in point, as are railroad transportation, public education, and the postal service. None of these can be characterized as a free market.

The role of public agencies in the private marketplace is to improve communication by insisting that the consumer and the investor have available all the information they need for economic decision making. That is why the SEC is hitting hard on disclosure of international payoffs, since they may reduce the firm's profit potential and increase prices for reasons unrelated to the true costs of doing business.

The same reasoning applies to political contributions. While these payments are legal in a number of foreign countries, they are illegal in the United States. Corporations are in hot water not because they made the payoffs but because they were concealed from stockholders and deducted for income tax purposes.[21]

In general, commissions paid to distributors or sales agents are acceptable international payments unless they are excessive. As we get into payment for services rendered, the white area of international payments appears.

Sales, Commissions, Wages, Gratuities—
The White Area

In the United States, the white area includes all payments to which the receiver is entitled, such as wages, fringe benefits, and commissions. More specifically, if payment is the result of an internal relationship that exists between the multinational company and the individual who is receiving it and it is not meant to influence an outsider to help the company at the expense of his own responsibility, then the payment is in the white area.

Clearly, however, any of the payments[22] discussed above are acceptable in a particular country if they are consistent with that country's customs and laws. Thus, the customs and laws of a country determine what is "acceptable" conduct. The problem arises when decisions must be made in the face of different customs and laws of different countries. This situation is the heart of the dilemma confronting the international executive. This risky area can be resolved in the same way that other business decisions are made: By balancing the costs and benefits based on his own conscience, the business executive is able to determine whether the payment he makes is for the sale or purchase of goods or services or is to exert undue influence on the outsider. The need to adjust personal conduct to the different customs and laws of different countries is not riskless, but then neither are most business actions.

As economies moved from the agricultural, underdeveloped stage to the developed, industrial stage, adjustments in business decision making had to be made along national economy lines. Now that international concerns face the multinational firm, similar adjustments must be made. Hopefully, the various national economies will ultimately come to some general terms on the problem of international payoffs. In the meantime the businessman must provide his own guidelines for temporary use until such international agreement is reached and implemented. This book is designed to help in developing those guidelines.

Mechanics of Payoff

The types of payments discussed above are implemented by various mechanisms and at various levels of command. Table 2-2 summarizes the mechanics that are used for international payments depending upon the channels available to the multinational corporation.

Direct Channel

The direct method is obviously the simplest of the payoff procedures. An official of the paying organization deals directly with the individual who wields the desired amount of influence. However, the gain from simplicity is grossly offset by the degree of risk involved when the officials deal directly with each other. The risk of discovery is usually too great with this method of transacting business. Furthermore, when utilizing in-house personnel, the company may be

Table 2-2
Mechanisms for Distribution of International Payoffs

Level of Command	Mechanism
Direct	Company to recipient
Indirect	1. Subsidiary corporation
	2. Dummy corporation
	3. Sales agent

severely lacking in knowledge as to whom payment should be made or how much to pay.

Indirect Channels

Payments made through intermediaries, then, are the most common mechanism used in international payoffs. In many host countries, multinational corporations are represented by agents since they maintain no physical plant or employees upon whom they can draw for such services. Working through agents is acceptable in the same way that dealerships are normally established by corporations in remote and urban communities to promote products.

1. *Subsidiary corporations* permit more stringent control over operations than the use of independent distributorships. However, even when the multinational corporation maintains such inside control, some go astray (the most notable example being the Exxon subsidiary, Esso Italiana). Tightening up internal auditing controls can solve cash drains, but the fact that they occur at all is indicative of an environment that provides a breeding ground for payoffs. Distributorships without production facilities (beer, oil, automobiles, franchises of various sorts) call for a brand of manipulation that few individuals can survive unscathed because pressures build up from both sides of the market: from the producer to push the product or suffer the loss of the franchise, from the consumer to enhance the flow of goods or suffer the loss of favored status. Shortages and surpluses cause distributors problems that are adjusted on a case-by-case basis. Forming personal relationships eases the burden of market competition.

On the other hand, a subsidiary corporation may be used just to take care of payoffs, such as Gulf's Bahamas Exploration Corporation.[23] Periodically, the parent company makes a capital contribution to the subsidiary to allow it to repay other units that are making payoffs. The subsidiary accounting records are not consolidated with the parent company, and more importantly the payoffs are not deducted for income tax purposes. Therefore, at least one legal problem, with the IRS, is sidestepped. Checks are cashed (in Gulf's case) at one bank, and the cash deposited and accumulated in a safety deposit box in another bank. When a sufficient amount is available, an official acts as a courier and moves the cash, via suitcase, from the subsidiary to another official of the multinational corporation who takes possession of the currency and distributes the payoffs. The cash channels back to the United States, and bookkeeping transactions involve funnelling the funds ($5 million in Gulf's case) into political activities abroad.

With this method the parent company retains control of the money until it is passed on to the individual being paid off. Along with the control, the parent company is able to disguise the payoff as an expense for services or goods that are never received or shipped. As in Gulf Oil's case, the subsidiary gradually became a dummy corporation when exploration was ended.[24]

2. Another indirect mechanism is the establishment of a *dummy corporation* with only a payoff function. For example, Northrop established a Swiss firm, Economic and Development Corporation (EDC), as a vehicle to channel commissions to influential foreigners who helped the U.S. planemaker sell its jet fighters. The dummy corporation operates with the understanding that the parent company asks no questions about how it functions or how it obtains contracts. The parent corporation pays the dummy corporation sales commissions, and the latter in turn passes some or all of the commissions to independent agents. With this arrangement, the paying company does not know to whom the payments are made and cannot be linked directly to any payoffs. Conversely, the company cannot be sure of the amount of money actually required and whether or not it is actually paid.

3. The *sales agent* is the most usual mechanism for channeling payments, but it is also the most controversial since most companies who employ sales agents do so for legitimate purposes. Executives who have replied to questionnaires for studies already cited[25] insist that the use of sales agents is a matter of good business practice since opening a permanent branch office in each country in which the product is marketed is prohibitively expensive. While the dollar amount of such payments can be quite large due to the sales volume for a product such as aircraft, percentagewise the commissions are quite low when compared with fees paid in other professions such as real estate brokerage.

The justification for sales agents is strongly pointed out by Northrop's Thomas V. Jones:

We have similarly utilized the services of sales agents and commission agents in those countries where they appeared to be a necessary adjunct to our own marketing organization. In many cases, an established sales agent in the country is the most efficient means of achieving the necessary understanding of how to structure and present our programs.[26]

The lack of a permanent company-controlled production and distribution facility in the host country is what forces a multinational firm to rely on foreign agents to handle transactions. Such agents are a most versatile breed of entrepreneur in a complex world economy. They deal in products ranging from drugs to tanks, from construction equipment to washing machines. As facilitators of the market, they profit from expediting transactions. They know to whom to go for what kind of service. They have contacts, and they maintain these contacts by personal favors. Whether it is a special vacation at a Nice villa or a special gratuity such as a private plane, they know what is required and they know the channels through which the payment must flow.

There is nothing wrong with sales agents or their commissions, provided a real service is rendered and the price is right. However, use of sales agents has been criticized by another multinational executive on the ground that they are employed mainly by new international companies, mostly American based, for whom sales overseas are a small element in their overall operations. This use of sales agents gives the older "true" multinationals a bad name, according to Unilever's chairman, E.G. Woodroofe. He registers his resentment at being "lumped in with the rest" and claims that a truly multinational firm has no trouble surviving in the global competitive market because its storehouse of knowledge and experience puts it in a unique position vis-à-vis local competition even with the latter's lower overhead and advantages given by local government. He adds:

The only real power of any multinational company . . . is the power not to invest, not to start new ventures or gradually to run down the old ones. . . . The key to success is to be able to recognize what parts of the central storehouse of knowledge and experience are relevant to a particular local problem, and to be able to dovetail them into the knowledge and experience which is purely local in such a way as to produce the optimum solution. . . . two major advantages to being multinational which outweigh all the disadvantages: (1) stability that comes from investments spread across many countries, and (2) economies in using knowledge over and over again, everywhere adapting its use to local needs.[27]

As a payoff scheme, the use of sales agents results in paying unusually large commissions, part of which are turned over to third parties, who allegedly aid the company in securing the contracts. The company may not deduct the commission as a tax-deductible expense. This practice satisfies the IRS (unless some unusually deep and detailed tax audit research is accomplished) but leaves the company in trouble with the SEC, since the rule of disclosure is violated.

Since the mechanics that are used to take care of international payoffs are closely related to why they are made, the next chapter discusses the rationale of international payoffs so that the purposes may be related to the moral, legal, and economic aspects of our study of multinational behavior.

Notes

1. U.S. Congress, Senate, Foreign Relations Committee, Subcommittee on Multinational Corporations, *Hearings*, Washington, D.C., May-September, 1975, Part 12, p. 109. (Hereafter referred to as Senate Hearings.)

2. *Newsweek*, February 23, 1976, p. 33. The table of payments that accompanied this special report is reprinted in Table 2-1. A similar list was reported in the AFL-CIO *American Federationist*, October 1975, p. 6. A final list of "big spenders" is given in Chapter 4 of this volume.

3. *The Wall Street Journal*, May 24, 1976; IBM, April 27, 1976. Occidental's notoriety came from domestic political contributions rather than international payoffs.

4. The Conference Board, *Unusual Foreign Payments: A Survey of the Policies and Practices of U.S. Companies*, New York, 1976, pp. 6-12. Reprinted with permission.

5. Ibid.

6. Investor Responsibility Research Center, Inc., *The Corporate Watergate*, Special Report 1975·D, Washington, D.C., October 1975, pp. 64-66. Reprinted with permission.

7. Ibid.

8. Cf. "Kickbacks as a Way of Life: How Widespread in U.S.," *U.S. News & World Report*, October 29, 1973, pp. 38-40.

9. *Black's Law Dictionary* (St. Paul, Minn.: West Publishing Co., 1968), p. 239. Reprinted with permission.

10. *Wharton's Criminal Law and Procedure* (Rochester, N.Y.: Lawyers Co-op Publishing Co., 1975), pp. 773-89. Reprinted with permission.

11. For additional references, see *Encyclopaedia of Social Sciences* (New York: MacMillan, 1930), v. III, pp. 690-92.

12. Harvey Matusow, "Scandal, Impeachment, Conviction, 1621," *Horizon*, Winter 1974, pp. 34-36.

13. Thomas B. Macaulay, "Lord Bacon," *Edinburgh Review*, 1837; reprinted in *Essays, Critical and Miscellaneous* (Philadelphia: A. Hart, late Carey and Hart, 1850), p. 267. Macaulay quotes Bishop Hugh Latimer, who called bribery "a princely kind of thieving."

14. Cf. James McCaque, *Moguls and Iron Men* (New York: Harper & Row, 1964), pp. 352-61; and Robert Athearn, *Union Pacific Country* (New York: Rand McNally, 1971), pp. 124-27.

15. Cf. Matthew Josephson, *The Robber Barons* (New York: Harcourt, Brace, 1934); and Peter d'Alroy Jones, ed., *The Robber Barons Revisited* (Lexington, Mass.: D.C. Heath, 1968).

16. Ibid.

17. Senate Hearings, p. 121.

18. *Black's Law Dictionary*, pp. 696-97. Reprinted with permission.

19. Securities and Exchange Commission, *Report of the Special Review Committee of the Board of Directors of Gulf Oil Corporation*, Washington, D.C., December 30, 1975, pp. 93-122. (Hereafter referred to as the Gulf Report.)

20. "The Great Banana Bribe," *Newsweek*, April 21, 1975.

21. Cf. Eldon S. Hendricksen, *Accounting Theory* (Homewood, Ill.: Richard D. Irwin, Inc., 1965). Few people realize that the Labor Management

Relations Act, 1947 (Taft-Hartley Act) prohibits political contributions in federal elections by *corporations* as well as labor unions (Section 304, amending Section 313 of the Federal Corrupt Practices Act). Criminal penalties are applicable to both the giver and the receiver.

22. Throughout this book the distinction is made between *payment* and *payoff*. Payment refers to all international transactions of whatever nature, including even those designated in this chapter as the white area. Payoff, on the other hand, has a distinct connotation of wrong-doing and refers to those transactions clearly in the black area and those that are in the questionable gray area. This distinction becomes especially important when measures for reform are discussed in Chapter 7. Only payoffs are considered a proper target for legislation.

23. Cf. IRRC, *The Corporate Watergate*, pp. 66-67; also Gulf Report, pp. 31-61.

24. *The Wall Street Journal*, November 17, 1975.

25. Cf. The Conference Board, *Unusual Foreign Payments*.

26. Senate Hearings, p. 151.

27. Speech at a company annual general meeting, London, May 8, 1972. Reprinted with permission.

3 The Rationale of International Payoffs

... those who have succeeded have done so because they have mastered the American system of organized irresponsibility.

—John W. Clark, S.J.[1]

Before we discuss whether a businessman should engage in international payoffs and what policy measures, if any, should be adopted to control them, we need to clarify the rationale for such payoffs. This rationale, as it has unfolded in the news media, Senate hearings, and reports to the Securities and Exchange Commission, involves ethical and economic elements. In this chapter we delve beneath the surface of both these elements to discover the motivation of the executive who makes such payments—that is, the why of international payoffs.

As is discussed in the preceding chapter, some international payments (that we have labelled *white*) are completely moral and legal and therefore cause no ethical problem for the executive who pays them. Those payoffs that raise ethical dilemmas are in the *gray* and the *black* areas.

Basically, the reason a person engages in an action that is ethically questionable is a function of the perceived net gain that is expected to result from such action. Thus, the pragmatic businessman risks his ethical image only if circumstances dictate that such a gamble is worth taking.

To understand the ethical considerations of the businessman, it is important to assess the influences that shape his general ethical beliefs and values.

Attitudes toward Ethics in General

Sample Studies of the 1960s

Two major studies have highlighted the moral dilemma of businessmen. Both were written by Jesuit scholars whose background and training have uniquely equipped them for such research. John Clark's book was published in 1966, while Raymond Baumhart's appeared in 1968.[2]

Clark attempts to assess the ethical *standards* of American businessmen[3] whereas Baumhart concentrates on their ethical *behavior*. That individuals are often reluctant to admit the truth about their ethical behavior is evidenced by the great disparity in Baumhart's findings between an executive's self-image and his appraisal of his counterparts' ethical behavior. Therefore, what Baumhart's executives say about others should approximate what Clark's respondents consider to be businessmen's ethical standards.

Baumhart used *Harvard Business Review* (HBR) readers as his source for questioning businessmen about their ethical beliefs and practices. Clark questioned members of the Executive Training Program at the University of California at Los Angeles. Thus, to the extent that both groups of businessmen represent the more progressive segment of the business community, we can conclude that error, if any, would tend toward higher standards and more ethical practices than in business as a whole. In addition, those who subscribe to HBR or who attend classes are more likely to be younger and/or more aggressive executives. This conclusion is borne out by the fact that more than 50 percent of the sample in each case were college trained and under forty-five years of age, whereas the average for the business community as a whole is under 50 percent in each category.[4]

Both studies found that an individual executive is guided in his business decisions by his perception of what is right. In Baumhart's study 807 executives indicated that such "right" decisions are influenced by the following factors in order of decreasing importance:[5]

1. A man's personal code of behavior;
2. Formal company policy;
3. The behavior of a man's superiors in the company;
4. Ethical climate of the industry;
5. The behavior of a man's equals in the company.

On the other hand, in explaining why he makes the "wrong" decision, the executive reverses that order somewhat as follows:[6]

1. The behavior of a man's superiors in the company;
2. Ethical climate of the industry;
3. The behavior of a man's equals in the company;
4. Lack of company policy;
5. Personal financial needs.

Clark's study of 103 businessmen gives a similar profile of positive influences:[7]

1. Family training;
2. Conduct of superiors;
3. Religious training;
4. Conduct of peers;
5. Practices in industry;
6. School and university training.

In both studies it is interesting to note the influence of coworkers and supervisors on individual behavior and the lesser importance of education and religion in influencing behavior. The first point shows the significance of the attitude of being "other" directed that was prevalent in the 1960s, while the latter point is explained by the upheaval in educational and religious traditions during the 1960s, particularly among the youth of the United States. (Society and government role are discussed more fully in Chapter 7 where measures for reform are analyzed.)

Other major conclusions of the Baumhart study are:[8]

1. Good ethics in the long run is good business.
2. Most businessmen feel it is harder to live by ethical standards at work due to pressures of competition.
3. Competition is the factor of greatest influence on behavior.
4. Managers of multinational companies, in regard to handling of culture-related differences, disagree about what constitutes ethical behavior abroad.
5. Though most businessmen oppose increased governmental involvement in business, many feel it has improved U.S. business practice.

The following represents Clark's pyramid of ethical standards that he developed from the empirical responses:[9]

Primary Guides:
1. Social institutions;
2. Respect for others;
3. Individual integrity.

Middle Guides:
1. Official legislation;
2. Representative authority;
3. Parity between authority and moral responsibility;
4. Private enterprise.

All of these ultimately lead to the kind of value judgment that results in moral or immoral business decisions.

Who Is Likely To Have Higher Ethical Standards? Baumhart's study classifies individual ethical standards by age, income, and occupation. It concludes that managers typically become more ethical as they grow older, partly because of financial security. More importantly, the reason cited for the fact that older businessmen are more ethical is that "experience teaches."[10]

As far as occupation is concerned, Baumhart finds that some occupations provide more temptations than others. In summing up the evidence, Baumhart concludes:

It appears that there are more temptations in jobs involving competitive relationships, like the salesman's or purchasing agent's than in those involving fiduciary relationships, like the accountant's or engineer's. In a limited sense, then, it is easier to be ethical in some occupations than in others.[11]

Sample Studies of the 1970s

The studies of the 1970s emphasize more recent developments that have expanded the experience of business executives with ethical questions. In 1972 the American Management Associations (AMACOM) surveyed 7,200 American businessmen enrolled in its general management division. In the 2,821 usable replies, the following are listed as the most influential factors in determination of personal goals and aspirations:

1. Personal life experiences;
2. Parents;
3. Educational background and training;
4. Peer group standards;
5. Religious background and training.[12]

While specific questions relating to business conduct as such are missing so that comparison with earlier studies is somewhat hampered, family and personal considerations are clearly prime indicia in determining values. Peer group standards, however, fall below education.

Three-quarters of the AMACOM respondents think that attitudes toward success are changing. They place a happy home life first, with a more perfected religious faith outranking, as a primary life objective, the traditional goal of acquiring wealth. Thus, there may be some cause for believing that individual executives, especially the younger breed, have been influenced by the "student-led cultural revolution" of the 1960s.[13]

This change in values is reflected in the fact that younger executives are not satisfied with their progress nor are they too optimistic about their future opportunities. Executives over age sixty show more satisfaction with career advancement and a sense of personal fulfillment than any other age group, as follows:[14]

Under 30	28% satisfied
30-39	26% satisfied
40-49	29% satisfied
50-59	32% satisfied
60 and over	39% satisfied

As indicated, the younger age group is the least satisfied with career advancement and with personal fulfillment.

Regardless of age, a majority of lower management and supervisory employees are not satisfied with their career advancement and personal fulfillment. They feel that their organization is incapable of providing them with opportunities to improve this situation in the future.

About 70 percent of AMACOM respondents admit to compromising personal principles to conform to organizational or superior's standards. While a scant majority feel that this pressure is increasing or at least not improving, the fact that 47 percent feel that these pressures are decreasing is a sign away from the prognosis of *The Organization Man.*[15]

The University of Georgia study evolved from the Watergate scandal and discusses business morality versus Watergate morality. The size of the response was 238 of a sample of 400. The study is in the form of propositions taken from magazine and newspaper articles. Examples of responses to these propositions are given below:[16]

1. Managers today feel under pressure to compromise personal standards to achieve company goals.

Disagree	24.6%
Somewhat Disagree	11.0
Somewhat Agree	43.2
Agree	21.2

2. I can conceive of a situation where you have good ethics running from top to bottom, but because of pressures from the top to achieve results, the person down the line compromises.

Disagree	15.1%
Somewhat Disagree	6.7
Somewhat Agree	34.5
Agree	43.7

Thus, Baumhart, Clark, and the Georgia studies, although not to the same degree, see the impact of supervisory pressure for results on executive ethical standards and/or behavior.[17]

Some conclusions of the Georgia study are:

1. Managers are under strong pressure to adhere to their superiors expectations of them.
2. Managers today experience pressure to compromise their moral standards to satisfy the organization.[18]

Attitudes toward International Payoffs

A noteworthy aspect of the surveys of the 1960s is that international payoffs were not considered a problem of any great significance although subsequent disclosures date payoffs back to that time. Baumhart's survey indicates that only 11 percent of the sample consider "buying business, e.g., bribes, entertainment" as a problem for ethical judgment. On the other hand, 22.5 percent cite "bribes, excessive gifts and favors, call girls" as "the one practice I would most like to see eliminated."[19]

While Clark used cases instead of direct questions to elicit his responses, only two cases can be considered applicable to the international payoff situation, "auditor's report conceals bribe" and "expensive Christmas gifts," both of which had 40 percent of the replies emphasizing profit or personal advantage at the expense of ethical value or social goal. Clark concludes:

Apparently they are motivated by the conviction that large gifts do not necessarily imply moral suasion to practice favoritism.[20]

In answer to the question about "the one practice I would most like to see eliminated" 14 percent cited gifts and bribes, including bribery and expensive entertainment. Clark concludes that "this is an area where it is most difficult to set ironclad boundaries of propriety; yet many of the respondents were troubled by the practices of their companies."[21]

Current Studies

This attitude is corroborated by the latest questionnaires on business ethics in general and on international payoffs in particular.

The *Business and Society Review* study, conducted in 1974 among 500 presidents of large corporations, resulted in 50 replies. While general ethical questions on stealing, whistle-blowing, and political contributions predominate, one question dealing with bribing a tax assessor resulted in a 98 percent "no" response to the question: "Do you pay the fee?"[22] Kenneth R. Andrews of Harvard University points out the problem with such inquiries:

. . . it is much easier to recognize the appropriate response than to know what one would actually do facing the specific dilemma described under the pressure of some urgent competitive pressures.[23]

In another study for the American Management Associations,[24] this time among lower supervision, data collected from 121 managers attending executive development programs indicates that accepting and giving gifts (bribes?) for preferential treatment is rated unethical, but not as unethical as outright cheating and stealing. This study also confirms the attitude exhibited in all of the previous studies that respondents think others not only act less ethically than they, but that others do not live up to their own ethical standards. According to the AMA study, this attitude not only encourages the "everybody else is doing it" philosophy but also brands the ethical person as a "sucker."

The survey conducted by the Opinion Research Corporation for Pitney Bowes indicates that 50 percent of the 531 participants have not changed their ethical views due to international payoff disclosures and would continue to make such payments for economic reasons.[25] Of the 73 executives who participated in The Conference Board survey, only 25 percent consider international payoffs a problem. Hence, in discussing the reasons for making such payments, the survey relies on responses of fewer than 20 who made such payments, with the others conjecturing about the consequences of their refusal to do so.[26] Further justification for payoffs can be found in statements of business executives in public hearings, the press, and other studies.

Our own data bank has replies from more than 50 multinational firms, but nowhere is there evidence favoring international payoffs. They are always mentioned in terms of experiences and opportunities refused or conjectures of what others are doing and why they may be doing it.

Those Who Condone Payoffs

International payoffs are condoned, in general, to maintain and enhance the multinational company's position in international competition. Specifically, executives who feel that there is some justification for payoffs may be classified as follows:

1. Those who feel that U.S. firms should not attempt to control their nationalist counterparts who have different standards and customs;
2. Those who see payoffs as a means of preventing delays and expediting acceptable action and therefore less costly and more effective and/or with no viable alternative;
3. Those who predict that without payoffs U.S. firms will lose foreign business, thereby jeopardizing the continued viability of the multinational enterprise and eventually the U.S. economy.

Sample statements are set forth below in each of these categories.

1. Difference in Standards and Customs

Bob Dorsey, Gulf Oil Corporation:

There is no universal ethical absolute. . . . You know that mores, customs, standards, values, principles, and attitudes vary all over the world. What is immoral to some, is perfectly correct to others. What is onerous to one culture, may be perfectly proper to another. ... We are sometimes subject ... to political pressures which we cannot always successfully resist.[27]

Richard Millar, Northrop Corporation:

We assumed that these were standard, typical, and in conformance with the best practice.[28]

James McDonnell, McDonnell Douglas Corporation:

People in other parts of the world don't look on this as being wicked. They just grew up that way. They do it as a matter of routine.[29]

2. Overcoming Red Tape

Food products executive:

After committing resources to the project and setting schedules, it can be difficult to move the necessary papers without small presents.[30]

C. Wolcott Parker II, Interamerican Consultants, Inc.:

The lubrication of low-level bureaucrats to keep your documents on top of their "get done today" basket is a normal procedure in many countries.[31]

Industrial equipment executive:

Our overseas managers operate under the same moral constraints as our domestic managers. This type of constraint does not eliminate small gifts often extended to minor government officials who have expended efforts to expedite matters beneficial to both the company and the country.[32]

3. Loss of Busines

Daniel Haughton, Lockheed Corporation:

We only say the practice exists, and that in many countries it appeared, as a matter of business judgment, necessary in order to compete against both U.S. and foreign competitors.[33]

Publishing executive:

I think it is axiomatic that in Rome you do as the Romans do. To do otherwise weakens an American company's competitive position vis-à-vis local firms.[34]

Rubber company executive:

Whatever your moral viewpoint may be, the fact is that, if you are going to do business in those countries and remain competitive, some such payments must be made.[35]

Since all these reasons condoning payoffs relate to the business firm rather than the individual executive, they are discussed more fully below in our consideration of the market conditions that form the environment for international payments. As is explained in Chapter 7 on measures for reform, business environment affords the temptation but does not force unethical behavior on the individual executive.

Those Who Oppose Payoffs

Our data bank suggests that many businessmen agree with this evaluation of the ethical dilemma. Businessmen who are opposed to payoffs can be grouped into three major classifications:

1. Those who decry the lack of moral leadership among top executives and see the need for improving communication of moral precepts to subordinates;
2. Those who consider that the social costs of disclosure outweigh the business benefits of international payoffs and that ethical conduct pays;
3. Those who feel that payoffs are a sign of moral decay and decry the double standard used by some business executives who are normally moral in their private lives.

Examples of statements that have been received in our data bank are shown below.

1. Need for Moral Leadership

John J. McCloy, Gulf Oil Special Review Committee:

It is hard to escape the conclusion that a sort of "shut-eye sentry" attitude prevailed on the part of both the responsible corporate officials and the recipients as well as on the part of those charged with enforcement responsibilities.[36]

W.H. Conzen, Schering-Plough Corporation:

I am pointing up the fact that managements who are committed to the principle of ethical business conduct have perhaps assumed too readily that this principle was understood clearly throughout far-flung international organizations.[37]

2. Social Costs Outweigh Business Profits

Howard Blauvelt, Continental Oil Co.:

Some of these bribes may not be illegal under the laws of the U.S., and perhaps were not unlawful where accepted. But they were wrong! . . . No matter what the context, that type of conduct will in final account not benefit the corporation or you. . . . Let your conscience be your guide. In gray areas comply strictly with company policy.[38]

Robert D. Stuart, The Quaker Oats Company:

Legal behavior is not difficult to define. . . . Ethical behavior may be somewhat harder to define, since to some extent it is governed by personal princi-ples . . . (it should be such that it is) not embarrassing to you, your family or our company if it were revealed publicly and that behavior which would seem right to those who live by the best standards of morality. . . . We are not interested in advantage at the expense of principle.[39]

H.B. Schacht, Cummins Engine Co., Inc.:

Seek out and populate our company with people who have a heightened "sense of outrage" at any wrong . . . and unquenchable determination to right the wrong . . . don't let our pressure for business turn somebody else's head either.[40]

3. The Temptation and The Double Standard

William H. Wendel, The Carborundum Company:

Morality varies with time and place. It is a moving target. . . . Yet I wonder how frequently management unwittingly creates a climate that tempts subordinates to cheat, not directly in their own behalf, but on behalf of the company and the company's measurement of performance.[41]

Thomas C. MacAvoy, Corning Glass Works:

Some business leaders who I know personally to be men of high personal integrity, accept a lower standard of behavior for their business life. It must be recognized at the same time, however, that the nature of management and business life thrusts a person into ethical problems which are sometimes different in kind, and often different in degree from the ethical considerations of private life.[42]

Fred T. Allen, Pitney Bowes:

When a company fails to take strong action against an employee at whatever level—most people think the employee had the implicit—if not the explicit—

consent of management. They assume that unethical acts are accepted standards of corporate behavior. After all, why should you fire a man for doing his job?[43]

Effect of Business Moral Climate

Since the individual executive acts in accordance with what he perceives as the firm's self-interest, it is important to consider the appropriateness of international payoffs as a means to achieve business goals. To understand this problem, it is useful to clarify, first, whether a firm should resort to any means to achieve its business economic goals.

Before analyzing economic market conditions, let us view the various studies that have attempted to classify business social conduct and the role of the individual executive. The philosophical or conceptual framework of the social responsibility debate is reserved for Chapter 5. Here we concentrate only on empirical analysis of business moral climate that influences the rationale for international payoffs.

First, there is the question of how worthy are the means the business firm uses to achieve its goals. Are the means to achieve economic ends less worthy than the means to achieve noneconomic ends? As Paul Heyne states: "Business is associated with materialism, amorality, selfishness, academic time-serving, pornography (?), and cultural impoverishment. Small wonder if the businessman sometimes feels defensive."[44] But Heyne continues: "Business is *not* a matter of satisfying materialistic human wants but of satisfying *any* human wants—for pork chops, classical records, museums, or this book . . . viewed in another way *no* human want is materialistic, but only the means through which a want is satisfied."[45]

Then there is the question of the ethics and morality of business means. In this regard, there is the view that ethics is not a branch of economics. Thus, to achieve economic goals, business (as an institution) should not be concerned with ethics.

Exemplification of this belief is Albert Carr's comparison of business decision making to a poker game. Like poker players, businessmen should seize any opportunity to win so long as it does not involve outright cheating. Bluffing, for instance, is not only permissible but respected if done successfully.[46] In line with this philosophy is Carr's question: "Can an executive afford a conscience?"[47]

Another problem related to the morality of business means is the freedom to act. As William Hocking states: "There is no sense in 'I ought' unless 'I can!' The moral law is invalid unless man is free."[48] Similarly, business freedom is its ability to compete. In the most extreme case is it wrong for business to act unethically (for instance, to pay bribes) in order to avoid bankruptcy?

While the ethics of self-defense or warfare permit the use of the most extreme means, Thomas Garrett, S.J., notes that such ethics "demand that the attack be unjust and that all normal means of defense, such as the courts, should have been tried before extreme measures are taken."[49]

But morality and ethics are often ignored in less extreme choices. The whole philosophy of this business view dictates the use of means that work—not necessarily those that are moral or ethical. It has been said that since pragmatism was born in America, the country of business, we should expect it to be the philosophy of the businessman.

The freedom to act or be ethical depends, by and large, on business competitive conditions. In his classical study of business ethics, Raymond Baumhart, S.J., found:

The most important influence on an industry's ethical practices is competition, both the amount and the kind. . . . Beyond a certain point (call it the ethical optimum of competition), as competition increases, so do unethical practices.[50]

He depicts this theme as shown in Figure 3-1.

On the other hand, the view that business practice must be ethical regardless of mitigating circumstances holds that competition (the "everybody else doing it" argument) does not justify unethical practices. For instance, if a business firm controlled by the underworld uses criminal practices to achieve its goals, does that justify an ordinary businessman's following suit to meet such competition?

As one code of ethics in our data bank states: "The law is a floor. Ethical

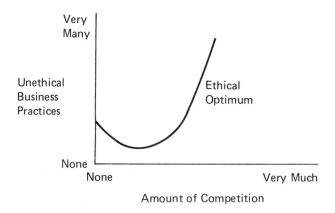

Source: Raymond Baumhart, S.J., *An Honest Profit* (New York: Holt, Rinehart and Winston, 1968), Exhibit 13.1, p. 122. Reprinted with permission.

Figure 3-1. The Ethical Optimum of Competition.

business conduct should normally exist at a level well above the minimum required by law."[51] Such a precept assures business against "economic Darwinism" and the rapid deterioration of the environment in which business operates.

Many businessmen object to Carr's analogy of business and the poker game, and their typical comments are quoted by Timothy Blodget as follows:

Deception does not succeed. It yields short run rewards. The economic system would collapse without mutual trust.

Business is not a closed society, free to operate by special rules as long as all the players understand them ... responsible businessman recognizes a great responsibility to non-players in Mr. Carr's game.

The analogy of business and the poker game would be excellent except for the fact that the consumer on whom business depends will prefer the non-players.[52-]

Finally, there is the question of where to draw the line. If every businessman tends to be just a little less moral, the end result is a gradual decline of business morals and an eventual state of complete anarchy. Blodget offers a similar, bleak comment: "If the players in Mr. Carr's poker game shoot it out among themselves and thereby endanger the lives of the people living next door, someone is going to call the police and break up the game for good."[53]

In summary, these studies imply that there are various alternatives available to the business executive in determining whether or not to adopt international payoffs. They can be resolved into one basic question: Do the benefits outweigh the costs? Those who oppose the payoff insist that morality pays and that costs outweigh benefits in the long run. Those who condone the payoff are equally adamant in their contention that the payoff is necessary to obtain and retain business viability in the countries where it is common practice. This difference of opinion brings us to the discussion of the specific economic elements that create a climate for international payoffs.

Why do some firms engage in payoffs while others do not? Is the answer merely a difference in moral attitude or is it inherent in the market structure? The disclosures to date seem to follow a pattern, and multinational corporations that have made such payments can be grouped according to certain economic characteristics:

1. Type of industry and market;
2. Economic relationship with the host country.

Influence of Industry and Market

No small company has been cited for international payoffs, not because they are more ethical but simply because there are no small multinational companies.

Investments in the billions are the rule, and oligopoly, where a few large companies divide the pie, is the model market structure. Also, the customers involved in international markets are not nickel-and-dime consumers for retail goods. The retail-trade type of international venture has not been involved in international payoffs. To expand consumer markets, such firms deliberately follow a policy in the host country of buying supplies for retail outlets from native manufacturers if at all possible. Permission for imports from the home country is not a continuing problem.

Companies involved in international payoffs, on the other hand, are dealing in multimillion-dollar commodities (airplanes, tanks, power generators) that are not normally exchanged at the retail level. Most are bought by governments rather than private corporations or individuals, which means that the negotiators of sales contracts are government officials. Influencing their judgment on whether to purchase a Lockheed or a Northrop plane or to contract for the services of a U.S. management maintenance or construction firm is the only way of selling such goods or services.

While simple economic comparison of the price and quality of the product or service would seem to be the best method for determining such decisions, some government officials are not averse to taking gratuities as an added inducement, especially when the available products are so much alike in price and quality. Since oligopoly markets are characterized by lack of price competition, international payoffs become a kind of nonprice competition, at least on the surface. While advertising and tie-in maintenance and parts sales are permissible methods to influence purchases, kickbacks to purchasing agents are not generally acceptable business practices.

International payoffs are just such kickbacks in another form. They are paid to government officials to influence their decisions in the purchase of public goods for the host country. This practice is the same phenomenon as payments to purchasing agents of private business firms who make similar decisions for their organizations. In fact, it would come as no surprise if the corporations that have been cited for international payoffs are engaged in similar activities among private companies who make large purchases or among U.S. agencies who make decisions for billions of dollars in public purchases. Political contributions to the party in power serve the same purpose.

United Brands' activities in Honduras give another clue as to the industries that are more susceptible to international payoffs. Multinationals dealing in a natural resource of the host country, especially one on which its national economy is dependent and one that is continually in jeopardy from an extraction or export tax in the host country, are likely to find themselves in an environment for such payments.

Influence of Economic Relationship with Host Country

Analysis of the multinational corporation's relationship with the host country is illuminating. Exploitation of the natives is a simplistic way of describing the

MNC's relationship with the host country, but *paternalism* is a better term, with all the positive and negative aspects that the father image implies. Treating the native population as children results in many manipulative policies that gradually evolve over the years, including allowances as a regular procedure for agents with whom the multinational does business or who are relied on for expediting official actions. In this historical context, as the host country becomes more independent and more demanding of its inheritance as it matures, the balancing of the firm's investor concerns with host country demands becomes an ad hoc, day-to-day decision-making process for the executives involved. As in the case of United Brands, once the die was cast and the company decided to go for broke in maintaining a friendly export tax mechanism in Honduras by payoffs, there was no way to turn back without disclosure, which (as subsequently developed) resulted in damage to the company's image and embarrassment to the host country. Refusal to continue such payoffs after they have become standard operating procedure is unthinkable. Maintenance of the status quo is the safest way to play the game. The fact that eventual disclosure comes is not in the game plan.

In connection with oil interests in the Middle East, similar problems exist, but the response has been different. Since several companies are involved in the Aramco pool, it is more difficult to prevent disclosure and therefore no widespread practice of payoffs has been uncovered there. However, in South Korea, Gulf Oil was alone, and in addition, it was supported by the U.S. government's attempt to influence host-country politics.

Therefore, two additional factors in the environment contribute to the propensity for international payoffs. They tend to occur where (1) the MNC is flying solo, and (2) the U.S. government is giving at least tacit support to promote larger foreign policy goals.

At the end of Chapter 2, in the discussion of payoff mechanics, Unilever's former chairman, E.G. Woodroofe, emphasized the point that the true power of any multinational firm is its power to not to invest. Thus, the MNC with host-country production facilities (i.e., with investment) has greater power to resist pressure for international payoffs than has the firm with only distribution facilities.

Without permanent company-controlled production or distribution facilities in the host country, the multinational corporation is forced to rely on foreign sales agents. Employment of such agents requires a contractual arrangement for payments in the form of sales commissions. Whether the sales agent merely acts as a conduit for payment to government officials is the thorny problem raised by the international payoff disclosures. How much responsibility should the MNC take for the final destination of such payments? The answer rests with each executive in the form of the cost-benefit analysis presented in Chapter 6.

Briefly, if the disclosure of such arrangements can hurt the MNC image, then corporate officials responsible for the company's future relations with the host country must be aware of the existence and dangers of such arrangements.

But even with subsidiary corporations, it is not certain that the problems of international payoffs will be avoided, as Esso Italiana suggests. For the purposes of this chapter, it is necessary only to point out that the host-country economic relationships play a significant part in determining whether or not international payoffs will be made and under what circumstances.

If sales are in question, influencing the purchaser is involved. If investment is threatened, influencing the ruling power applies. If taxes and licensing fees or price controls are about to impinge on profits, influencing legislators or administrators is considered. Political influence and economic success go hand in hand in most host countries (as they do in most parent countries, we might add), and the methods that the multinational corporation takes to accomplish its objectives depend on how closely these political and economic activities are allied. Understanding these factors is important in analyzing the international payoff dilemma.

The MNC can adjust to whatever controls are enacted, especially if they apply equally to all in the industry. It cannot plan if no guidelines are provided. The purpose of this book is to offer such guidelines so that individual executives may have the necessary input for arriving at a resolution of the international payoff dilemma.

Before offering such guidelines, however, let us examine the application of the above rationale to various published accounts of international payoffs to see what led to the crescendo of public demand for control of such activities.

Notes

1. John W. Clark, S.J., *Religion and the Moral Standards of American Businessmen* (Cincinnati: South-Western Publishing Co., 1966), p. 78.

2. Ibid.; and Raymond Baumhart, S.J., *An Honest Profit* (New York: Holt, Rinehart and Winston, 1968).

3. Clark, *Religion and the Moral Standards*, p. 47.

4. U.S. Department of Labor, Bureau of Labor Statistics, *Educational Attainment of Workers*, Special Labor Force Report 186, Washington, D.C., March 1975, p. A-19.

5. Baumhart, *An Honest Profit*, p. 47. Reprinted with permission.

6. Ibid.

7. Clark, *Religion and the Moral Standards*, p. 118. Reprinted with permission.

8. Baumhart, *An Honest Profit*, pp. 4-5. Reprinted with permission.

9. Clark, *Religion and the Moral Standards*, Chapter 7, pp. 149-77. Reprinted with permission.

10. Baumhart, *An Honest Profit*, p. 75 (age), p. 76 (income).

11. Ibid., p. 101 (occupation). See also Table 6-1 (Chapter 6) of this volume for a similar comparison.

12. American Management Associations, *The Changing Success Ethic* (New York: AMACOM, 1973), p. 19. Reprinted by permission of the publisher from *The Changing Success Ethic*, p. 19. © 1973 by AMACOM, a division of American Management Associations.

13. Cf. Daniel Yankelovich, "The Real Meaning of the Student Revolution," *The Conference Board Record*, March 1972. See also note 9 in Chapter 5 of this volume on the social activists survey.

14. Cf. American Management Associations, *The Changing Success Ethic*, p. 29. The items in the age group career satisfaction listing are reprinted by permission of the publisher from *The Changing Success Ethic*, p. 29. © 1973 by AMACOM, a division of American Management Associations.

15. Ibid., p. 27; cf. William H. Whyte, Jr., *The Organization Man* (New York: Simon & Schuster, 1956).

16. Archie Carroll, "A Survey of Managerial Ethics: Is Business Morality Watergate Morality?" *Business and Society Review*, Spring 1975, pp. 58-60. Copyright 1975 Warren, Gorham and Lamont, Inc., 210 South Street, Boston, Mass. All rights reserved. Reprinted with permission.

17. Baumhart, *An Honest Profit*, p. 82; Clark, *Religion and the Moral Standards*, p. 102 (Case B).

18. Archie Carroll, "A Survey of Managerial Ethics," p. 60. Copyright 1975 Warren, Gorham, and Lamont, Inc., 210 South Street, Boston, Mass. All rights reserved. Reprinted with permission.

19. Baumhart, *An Honest Profit*, pp. 26-27.

20. Clark, *Religion and the Moral Standards*, p. 107.

21. Ibid., pp. 121-22.

22. Business and Society Review Survey, 'Business Executives and Moral Dilemmas," *Business and Society Review*, Spring 1975, pp. 51-57.

23. Ibid., p. 57.

24. William A. Ruch and John W. Newstrom, "How Unethical Are We," *Supervisory Management*, November 1975, pp. 17-21.

25. Opinion Research Corporation, Caravan Surveys, *Executive Attitudes Toward Morality in Business*, Princeton, N.J., July 1975, p. 5.

26. The Conference Board, *Unusual Foreign Payments: A Survey of the Policies and Practices of U.S. Companies*, New York, 1976, p. 13.

27. U.S. Congress, Senate, Foreign Relations Committee, Subcommittee on Multinational Corporations, *Hearings*, Washington, D.C., May-September, 1975 (Part 12), p. 8. (Hereafter referred to as Senate Hearings.)

28. Ibid., p. 132.

29. *St. Louis Post-Dispatch*, April 27, 1976.

30. The Conference Board, *Unusual Foreign Payments*, p. 10.

31. C. Wolcott Parker II, President, Interamerican Consultants, Inc., speech delivered before the Commonwealth Club of California, San Francisco, California, January 23, 1976, in *Vital Speeches*, February 15, 1976, p. 283. Reprinted with permission.

32. The Conference Board, *Unusual Foreign Payments*, p. 17.

33. Senate Hearings, p. 346.

34. The Conference Board, *Unusual Foreign Payments*, p. 28.

35. Ibid., p. 2.

36. Securities and Exchange Commission, *Report of the Special Review Committee of the Board of Directors of Gulf Oil Corporation*, Washington, D.C., December 30, 1975, p. 4.

37. W.H. Conzen, Chairman and Chief Executive Officer, Schering-Plough Corporation, Kenilworth, N.J., speech delivered at Annual Meeting of Shareholders, April 1976. Reprinted with permission.

38. Howard Blauvelt, Chairman and Chief Executive, Continental Oil Company, Stamford, Conn., in *Conoco Conscience*, 1976, p. 18. Reprinted with permission.

39. Robert D. Stuart, President and Chief Executive Officer, The Quaker Oats Company, Chicago, Ill., speech delivered at Annual Meeting of Shareholders, October 2, 1975. Reprinted with permission.

40. H.B. Schacht, President, Cummins Engine Co., Inc., Columbus, Indiana, speech delivered at Planning Conference, June 1975. Reprinted with permission.

41. William H. Wendel, President, The Carborundum Company, Niagara Falls, N.Y., speech to Chemical Buyers' Group of the Purchasing Management Association, October 16, 1975. Reprinted with permission.

42. Thomas C. MacAvoy, President, Corning Glass Works, Corning, N.Y., speech delivered at University of Notre Dame, South Bend, Indiana, November 1, 1973. Reprinted with permission.

43. Fred T. Allen, Chairman of the Board and President, Pitney Bowes, Stamford, Conn., speech before American Chamber of Commerce in Switzerland, October 16, 1975. Reprinted with permission.

44. Paul T. Heyne, *Private Keepers of the Public Interest* (New York: McGraw-Hill, 1968), pp. 17-18. Reprinted with permission.

45. Ibid.

46. For an excellent presentation of this view, see: Albert Z. Carr, "Is Business Bluffing Ethical?" *Harvard Business Review*, January-February 1968, pp. 143-53.

47. Albert Z. Carr, "Can an Executive Afford a Conscience?" *Harvard Business Review*, July-August 1970, pp. 58-64.

48. William E. Hocking, "What Pragmatism Is," *Types of Philosophy* (New York: Charles Scribner's Sons, 1959), p. 98.

49. Thomas Garrett, S.J., *Business Ethics* (New York: Appleton-Century-Crofts, 1966), p. 98.

50. Baumhart, *An Honest Profit*, p. 121. (Figure 3-1 is reprinted with permission.)

51. Caterpillar Tractor Co., *A Code of Worldwide Business Conduct*, Peoria, Ill., October 1, 1974, p. 8. Cf. Chapter 5, note 4.

52. Timothy B. Blodget, "Showdown on Business Bluffing," *Harvard Business Review*, May-June 1968, pp. 162-70. Copyright © 1968 by the President and Fellows of Harvard College; all rights reserved. Reprinted with permission.

53. Ibid.

"MY, THERE ARE A LOT OF IMPORTANT PEOPLE HERE TONIGHT"

—copyright 1976 by Herblock in *The Washington Post*

4 Empirical Evidence: Case Studies

Beginning in 1973, following disclosures of political contributions by the Special Watergate Prosecutor, the Securities and Exchange Commission decided that use of corporate funds for undisclosed or illegal purposes had significance to public investors. Therefore, on March 8, 1974, the SEC began an inquiry into the possible violations of federal securities laws and had occurred and discovered falsifications of corporate financial records designed to disguise or conceal the source of corporate funds, as well as secret funds (so-called slush funds) disbursed outside the normal financial accountability system. Since these practices cast doubt on the integrity and reliability of corporate accounting, they represented a threat to the disclosure system established by the federal securities laws to protect investors. The United Brands incident on February 3, 1975, brought this activity to the headlines.

SEC Disclosures

As a result of injunctive actions brought against nine corporations during 1974,[1] it became clear to the SEC that the potential magnitude of the problem required an additional disclosure mechanism to supplement the enforcement action already undertaken. Therefore, a voluntary disclosure program was instituted for questionable or illegal payments, whereby companies were encouraged to conduct their own investigations under the supervision of outside experts and make the findings available to the SEC, their boards of directors, stockholders, and other interested persons through interim 8-K reports or annual 10-K reports.

In its report on questionable and illegal corporate payments and practices, submitted to the Senate Committee on Banking, Housing and Urban Affairs in May 1976, the Securities and Exchange Commission gave the following two purposes for its voluntary disclosure approach:[2]

1. To insure that investors and shareholders receive material facts necessary to make informed investment decisions and to assess the quality of management;
2. To establish a climate in which corporate management and the professionals who advise them become fully aware of these problems and deal with them in an effective and responsible manner.

45

In accordance with Rule 3(a) of the SEC's informal procedures,[3] companies were also encouraged to discuss the question of disclosure with the SEC's staff before filing. The SEC report analyzes the public disclosures filed by 95 corporations as of April 21, 1976. (See Appendix 4A at the end of this chapter for the list of 95 companies.)

It is important to keep in mind at the outset that the SEC report is interested in all questionable payments—domestic as well as foreign. The coverage in this book, however, is confined to foreign payments. Some of the most notorious accounts of payoffs, therefore, have not been chosen as case studies because they were part of the domestic Watergate scandal and did not involve international payoffs. For this reason, also, there is some discrepancy between SEC data and that set forth in this chapter.

According to the SEC report, of the 95 companies admitting payments (domestic and foreign), 66 are in manufacturing. The two largest identifiable groups are drug manufacturers and oil companies, with each having twelve companies involved. The SEC report singles out payments to foreign officials for special mention by stating that 54 companies engaged in such activity. However, for our purposes all three categories of foreign transactions—foreign political contributions, foreign sales-type commissions, and foreign payments to officials—are considered international payments. Therefore, we arrive at a total of 66 companies (see Table 4-1) reporting *foreign* payments, as of April 21, 1976, the closing date of the report.[4]

Subsequent to the SEC report, disclosures were made by 41 additional companies between April 21, 1976 (the SEC closing date) and August 29, 1976 (our closing date); these bring the total number of reporting companies to 136 (95 in the SEC report and 41 added later).[5] Table 4-2 indicates that of these 136 companies reporting *any* payments, 32 made *overseas* payments of more than $1 million (27 in the SEC report and 5 later). While more than 25 percent of the reporting companies were in the million-dollar group before April 21, 1976, only 12 percent of companies reporting after that date paid over $1 million overseas. Table 4-2 also shows that four companies reported over $20 million in overseas payments (3 in the SEC report and 1 later). Viewed in that perspective, there is some justification for labelling the SEC voluntary disclosure activity as a "sputtering" investigation.[6] There have been no new spectacular disclosures of international payoffs since August 29, 1976.

In summary, the total of firms reporting any type of questionable payment (domestic or foreign) between February 3, 1975, and August 29, 1976 (our period of investigation) is 136, of which 32 made more than $1 million in foreign payments (23 percent of those reporting). The 1974 revenue data in Table 4-1 makes apparent that even for the million-dollar group, there is little materiality in SEC terms since these payments were usually spread over a four- or five-year period and amount to less than 5 percent of the firm's total revenue in any one year in even the most notorious cases.

It must be emphasized that both the failure to disclose and the questionable accounting practices (rather than the amount of the payment) are of greater significance for purposes of this book and the measures for reform presented in Chapter 7.

The payoff picture, therefore, is not as appalling as the initial headlines about United Brands and Lockheed portended. Nevertheless, it is important to trace the development of disclosures in these critical headline cases so that fact may replace whatever fiction still remains in the minds of policymakers and the public. As each case study of specific company operations unfolds, the why and how of international payoffs appears in a real-life situation. Student and practitioner alike can thus apply the decision-making process suggested in Chapter 6 in hindsight and discover whether each company involved made a rational business decision.

Introduction to Case Studies

As noted in Chapter 3, where the rationale of international payoffs is discussed, certain industries and economic relationships are tempted to use payoffs more than others. The SEC report cited the drug and oil industries in this connection. We have added the aircraft and food industries to this list since Lockheed and United Brands provided the spark for the investigation and headlines.

Table 4-2 supports this selection in that of the 32 companies spending more than $1 million in overseas payments, half are in these four industries:

Aircraft	4
Oil	3
Food	2
Drug	7
Total	16

It should be noted that the aircraft, oil, and food industries provide extensive case studies of individual companies due to their coverage by the news media and the congressional hearings. The drug industry, on the other hand, did not receive such notoriety, hence there is less detailed individual company coverage. Our consideration of this industry is due exclusively to the fact that it was singled out for special mention by the SEC. The case studies below are classified as follows:

Industries	Companies
Aircraft	Lockheed and Northrop
Oil	Gulf and Exxon
Food	United Brands
Drug	(Industry as a whole)

Table 4-1

Companies Reporting Foreign Payments, by Type and Amount of Payment, as of April 21, 1976

Name of Company and 1974 Revenue ($000)	Industry (if relevant)	Type of Foreign Payment			Total Amount of Payment
		Political Contribution	Sales Type Commissions	Payments to Officials	
1. Abbott Labs $765,415	Drug	n.i.	$538,000	$142,000	$680,000
2. Allergen Pham. $25,396	Drug	n.i.	13,399	23,500	36,899
3. Amer. Cyanamid $1,779,872	Drug	$100,000	$1,150,000[a]		1,250,000
4. Amer. Home Prod. $2,048,741	Drug	n.i.	$3,442,000 govt. $2,982,000 ind.[a]		6,424,000
5. Amer. Standard $1,676,973		500/yr.	c	266,000	291,000[e]
6. Ashland Oil, Inc. n.i.	Oil	125,000	362,000	30,000	517,000
7. Baxter Labs $466,284	Drug	420	1,971,600	174,200	2,146,220
8. Boeing $3,778,000	Aircraft	n.i.	b	b	n.i.
9. Bristol Myers n.i.	Drug	n.i.	b	d	n.i.
10. Burroughs $1,510,835		n.i.	$1,500,000[a]		1,500,000
11. Butler National $1,489		n.i.	n.i.	102,000	102,000
12. Carnation $1,889,353	Food	n.i.	n.i.	1,261,000	1,261,000
13. Carrier Corp. $984,681		none	2,161,000	453,000	2,614,000
14. Castle & Cook $753,131	Food	30,000	n.i.	80,000/yr.	430,000[e]

15. Cities Service $2,806,300	Oil	30,000	n.i.	n.i.	30,000
16. Coastal States Gas $1,315,265	Oil	none	$8,000,000a		8,000,000
17. Coherent Rad. $14,469		n.i.	20,388	n.i.	20,388
18. Colgate-Palmolive $2,615,448	Oil	none	n.i.	865,000	865,000
19. Core Labs $24,202	Oil	none	n.i.	184,485	184,485
20. Del Monte $1,274,000	Food	n.i.	d	d	n.i.
21. Dresser Ind. $1,397,970		n.i.	n.i.	24,000	24,000
22. Electronic Associates n.i.		n.i.	n.i.	83,000	83,000
23. Exxon $45,792,858	Oil	46,031,000	n.i.	761,000	46,792,000e
24. Gardner-Denver $423,000		n.i.	b	69,200	69,200
25. Gen. T. & E. $2,841,850		182,000	176,000	7,813,455	8,171,455
26. Gen. Tire & Rubber $1,756,646		n.i.	$1,430,000a		1,430,000
27. B. F. Goodrich $1,975,244		none	31,000	93,000	124,000
28. Goodyear Tire & Rubber $5,256,247		n.i.	$820,000a		820,000
29. Gulf Oil Corp. n.i.	Oil	6,900,000	n.i.	n.i.	6,900,000
30. Honeywell $2,600,000		b	n.i.	1,040,000	1,040,000

Table 4-1 (cont.)

	Industry (if relevant)	Type of Foreign Payment			Total Amount of Payment
Name of Company and 1974 Revenue ($000)		Political Contribution	Sales Type Commissions	Payments to Officials	
31. ITT $11,154,401		64,300	$3,800,000[a]		3,864,300
32. Johnson & Johnson $1,967,885	Drug	none	$990,000[a]		990,000
33. Koppers Co. $914,184		b	1,500,000	none	1,500,000
34. Kraftco $4,500,000	Food	8,500	n.i.	200,000	200,000
35. Levi Strauss $4,500,000		n.i.	n.i.	75,000	75,000
36. Lockheed[f] n.i.	Aircraft	n.i.	200,000,000	50,750,000	250,750,000
37. McDonnell-Douglas $897,700	Aircraft	n.i.	$2,500,000[a]		2,500,000
38. Merck & Co. $1,329,550	Drug	157,684	$3,603,635[a]		3,761,319
39. Minnesota M & M n.i.		n.i.	n.i.	52,000	52,000
40. NCR Corp. $889,787		none	300,000	n.i.	300,000
41. Northrop Corp. n.i.	Aircraft	n.i.	30,000,000	454,000	30,454,000
42. Northwest Ind. $103,700		n.i.	n.i.	582,000	582,000
43. The Offshore Co. $133,400		none	none	15,000	15,000
44. Ogden Corp. $1,858,119		n.i.	b	175,000	175,000

	Company	Industry				
45.	Pfizer, Inc. $1,571,887	Drug	43,500	n.i.	218,500	262,000[e]
46.	Pullman, Inc. $1,425,587		none	125,665	2,150,000	2,275,665
47.	Rockwell Int. $4,408,500	Aircraft	8,300	n.i.	668,000	676,300
48.	Rohm & Haas Co. $1,021,736		none	n.i.	592,000	592,000
49.	Rollins, Inc. $193,297		n.i.	none	127,000	127,000
50.	Santa Fe Int. $255,912		b	n.i.	66,140	66,140
51.	Schering-Plough $726,872	Drug	n.i.	$207,000[a]		207,000
52.	G. D. Searle & Co. $621,310	Drug	none	$1,303,000[a]		1,303,000
53.	Smith Int. $199,501		n.i.	n.i.	13,349	13,349
54.	Standard Oil (Indiana) $2,016,710	Oil	652,000	$690,000[a]		1,342,000[e]
55.	Stanley Home Products, Inc. $164,521		none	n.i.	50,000	50,000
56.	Sterling Drug $899,787	Drug	b	103,000	252,000	355,000
57.	Sybron Corp. $495,093		n.i.	n.i.	76,500	76,500
58.	Tenneco, Inc. $5,001,470	Oil	n.i.	n.i.	535,000	535,000[e]
59.	UOP, Inc. $615,046	Oil	none	n.i.	90,000	90,000
60.	United Brands $2,841,850	Food	n.i.	n.i.	1,250,000	1,250,000

Table 4-1 (cont.)

Name of Company and 1974 Revenue ($000)	Industry (if relevant)	Type of Foreign Payment			Total Amount of Payment
		Political Contribution	Sales Type Commissions	Payments to Officials	
61. United Tech. n.i.	Aircraft	b	1,950,000	90,000	2,040,000
62. Upjohn Co. $805,744	Drug	none	c	2,736,000	2,736,000
63. Warner-Lambert $1,946,063	Drug	15,300	1,664,100	576,000	2,240,100
64. Westinghouse Elec. Co. $5,838,118		n.i.	150,000	93,000	243,000
65. White Consol. Industries $1,016,621		none	1,180,000	10,000	1,190,000
66. Whitaker Corp. $778,246		n.i.	133,425[a]		133,425

Source: Compiled from data of Securities and Exchange Commission, *Report on Questionable and Illegal Corporate Payments and Practices*, Exhibits A and B, submitted to U.S. Congress, Senate, Committee on Banking, Housing and Urban Affairs, May 12, 1976.

n.i. = not indicated in SEC report.

[a]Foreign sales commissions and payments to foreign officials listed together.

[b]Possible payments but not illegal.

[c]Questionable payments but no amount given.

[d]Payments indicated but not material.

[e]Estimate based on SEC report.

[f]Lockheed is omitted from SEC data analysis.

Table 4-2
Final List of Big Spenders Overseas

Name of Company[a]	Industry (if relevant)	Amount of Overseas Payment[b]
1. American Cyanamid	Drug	$ 1,250,000
2. American Home Products	Drug	7,424,000
3. Anderson, Clayton & Co.		2,600,000[c,d]
4. Baxter Labs.	Drug	2,146,220
5. Burroughs		1,500,000
6. Carnation	Food	1,261,000
7. Carrier Corp.		2,614,000
8. Celanese Corp. (5/26)		2,200,000[c,e]
9. Cleveland Harris (8/10)		1,800,000[c]
10. Coastal States Gas	Oil	8,000,000
11. Exxon	Oil	27,761,000
12. Gen. T & E.		8,171,455
13. Gen. Tire & Rubber		3,000,000[c]
14. Gulf Oil Co.	Oil	6,900,000
15. Honeywell		1,040,000
16. ITT		3,864,000
17. Ingersoll-Rand Co.		1,600,000[c]
18. Koppers		1,500,000
19. Lockheed	Aircraft	250,750,000
20. Loews Corp.		1,500,000
21. McDonnell-Douglas	Aircraft	2,500,000
22. Merck & Co.	Drug	3,761,319
23. Northrop	Aircraft	30,000,000
24. Pullman, Inc.		2,275,665
25. Raytheon (7/6)		23,000,000[c]
26. G.D. Searle & Co.	Drug	1,303,000
27. Sperry Rand Corp.		2,000,000
28. United Brands	Food	1,250,000
29. United Technologies (5/24)	Aircraft	7,040,000[e]
30. Upjohn Co. (8/5)	Drug	4,100,000[e]
31. Warner Lambert	Drug	2,240,100
32. White Consol. Ind.		1,190,000

Sources: Taken from Table 4-1 and from *The Wall Street Journal* (on dates indicated).

Note: Only companies reporting over $1 million in overseas payments by August 29, 1976, are listed. Cf. *Newsweek* table, Chapter 2.

[a]Date of disclosure in ( ) if later than SEC list (i.e., after April 21, 1976).

[b]Total estimated from SEC report unless otherwise indicated.

[c]Total estimated from *The Wall Street Journal* report.

[d]Not listed by SEC; payments reported in *The Wall Street Journal* prior to April 21, 1976, but probably not illegal or material.

[e]Made additional disclosures on date indicated.

Due to space limitations, we have not presented all the factual evidence on international payoffs that was disclosed in SEC reports and other published accounts on the cases covered in this chapter. However, we have provided sufficient information to make an analysis possible in the application of the rationale in Chapter 3 and the guidelines for decision making in Chapter 6.

We emphasize that our selection implies no moral or legal judgment on our part. The case studies are provided only to permit application of the principles and guidelines to real-life situations.

Aircraft Industry Case Studies

Sales in the aircraft industry depend on a relationship between the MNC and foreign governments. There are two major reasons for this. First, the large sums involved in aircraft purchases require the capital that only governments in small countries can amass. Second, products of the aircraft industry are defense related, which also requires government control of air transportation.

A physically large and economically wealthy country like the United States can afford the luxury of regulated competition in its air transportation industry. Smaller countries, however, have neither the private capital nor the inclination to allow the uncertainties of the market system to determine the productivity and availability of aircraft products. Therefore, even economically strong countries like Japan and The Netherlands have nationalized the airline industry or at least control purchases of aircraft so that military and commercial operations are under similar government supervision. Therefore, the only way to make a sale in those countries is to influence government agents. The means chosen to accomplish this influence are subject to question if they go beyond the price and quality of the product.

When the host-country environment is coupled with an oligopoly market, as pointed out in Chapter 3, the lack of price competition gives rise to international payoffs as a kind of nonprice competition, similar to the kickbacks to purchasing agents in the private sector. International payoffs are used to influence government decisions in the purchase of public goods for the host country.

Foreign Military Sales (FMS). Another important consideration in connection with the aircraft industry applies to military sales generally. Before a foreign government buys a U.S. military item, it usually consults with the Military Assistance Advisory Group, which is maintained by the U.S. Defense Department in the host country.[7] Although this advisory group does not actually make the purchase, its influence is such that U.S. manufacturers use foreign national sales agents, not only to assist with host-country officials, but also to act as middlemen with U.S. advisors, since direct activities on the part of the U.S. multinational to exert such influence are unlawful.

After consultation with the U.S. State Department to be certain that there is no conflict with broader foreign policy objectives, the U.S. Defense Department places the order with the MNC and then resells it to the host country. Since some countries, notably in the Middle East,[8] require foreign nationals to complete the final details of the sales contract, reasonable commissions are readily accepted as part of the cost in negotiating with the U.S. Defense Department. On this point Richard Millar of Northrop testified:

In the case of FMS sales the amount of commission has to be approved by our Government and they are spelled out.[9]

For this reason multinationals are somewhat justified in their insistence that foreign payoffs are made with the knowledge and consent of both the U.S. State and Defense Departments.

Military purchases involve a further problem in connection with penalties to control payoffs. Since aircraft companies produce sophisticated hardware that cannot easily be duplicated, individual companies cannot be replaced as government contractors in the short run. Therefore, the U.S. Defense Department is in no position to use its own purchases as a weapon in any battle to control payoffs. Unless a viable substitute can be found for a particular company's product or service in the foreseeable future, government retaliation in the form of product boycott is not feasible.

To illustrate these factors in real life, we have chosen Lockheed Aircraft Corporation and Northrop Corporation as case studies. Other aircraft companies, such as Boeing, McDonnell Douglas, and Rockwell, have been mentioned in connection with international payments, but Boeing denies any wrong doing and Rockwell's payoffs have been largely confined to domestic political activities. Besides, the two companies we have chosen for case studies provide all the empirical evidence necessary for application of the principles and guidelines presented in this text. We emphasize again that our selection implies no moral or legal judgment.

Lockheed Aircraft Corporation

As one of the largest suppliers of aircraft in the world, particularly fighter planes and other military hardware, Lockheed Aircraft Corporation, based in Burbank, California, was a likely target for investigation as soon as SEC decided to go that route. Senate investigating committees had already been on the corporation's trail due to its financially troubled operations, which surfaced with a threatened bankruptcy in 1971. When the government stepped in to provide a $250 million guarantee for Lockheed's loans, all of its operations were open to scrutiny. It soon became apparent that there were more than a few questionable activities involving international payoffs.

In the course of hearings before the Senate Banking Committee at the time Congress was considering the Lockheed loan guarantee, Senator William Proxmire, one of the opponents of the guarantee, heard evidence that Lockheed had been paying off foreign officials to win aircraft contracts.[10] These hearings also revealed that overseas agents had been used for laundering funds to hide the identity of both the giver and the receiver. When the story first broke, Lockheed compounded its notoriety by appearing to declare its right to bribe and refusing to disclose the information sought by Congress and the SEC, unless ordered to do so by court injunction.[11] That there was something to hide became quite clear as subsequently, in hearings before the Senate subcommittee on multinationals, the following story was disclosed:

Agents and Commissions. As Lockheed's business setbacks developed, its corporate management began to grasp at straws for salvaging the wreck. If the company's product could not survive the competitive market, foreign sales might be augmented by payments to officials who were responsible for making purchase decisions for their governments. Or, in the alternative, contacts close to these foreign officials could be persuaded to act as middlemen in the transfer of funds. It is clear from the Senate testimony that top corporate officers of the company were involved in the payoff operation. There is even a record of disagreement among them as to how and to whom payments should be made.[12]

When the company's profit position improved, however, things got a little out of hand. As the then board chairman Daniel J. Haughton stated before the Senate subcommittee, when Lockheed was selling abroad in the range of $150 million a year, the 5 percent commission payments seemed "small and relatively insignificant" when compared to corresponding sales and profits. He adds:

But when we got to the 1975 range of about $900 million overseas sales per year, the dollar amounts, based on the same commission percentages, of course, grew very large. The overseas profits and associate advance payments on these contracts provided great financial benefits to our company and its shareholders—and a great many jobs for our employees.

However, these commission payments tended in some cases to breed serious and unfortunate side effects including direct or indirect payments to foreign officials.[13]

These side effects are what brought about the continuing investigation of Lockheed not only in the United States but in many countries of the Western, Middle Eastern, and Far Eastern world as well.

For example, Triad, Adnan Khashoggi's marketing firm, received $9.7 million in commissions from Lockheed, of which $450,000 went to two Saudi Arabian generals for Tristar promotion.[14] In typical chauvinistic style, U.S. investigators did not get too excited when disclosures involved developing countries in the Middle East such as Saudi Arabia and Iran, since payoff practices were thought to be a "way of life" in those parts of the world.[15] But when developed countries like Japan and The Netherlands got into the act, the payoff problem began to take on a more shocking and even unethical tinge, since it was perceived as an interference with trade in the free world market. Also, other U.S. aircraft companies, who were already miffed at Lockheed's government support, pointed out that international payoffs were additional evidence that Lockheed could not survive the heat of the competitive market kitchen.

Military Orders. Some countries were not averse to cancelling Lockheed orders. Japan promptly discontinued purchase negotiations, and although Canada gave financing problems as the reason for calling off its contract talks, it appears that Lockheed's image was also involved. Canada's decision was later reversed with prodding from the U.S. Defense Department in the form of a promise of financial help.[16]

As mentioned earlier, the U.S. Defense Department is opposed to using boycott of companies furnishing military supplies as a tool in controlling payoffs. This fact is especially true in this case since Lockheed produces some of the most sophisticated military hardware and cannot be easily replaced as a government contractor.[17]

Subsequent to the payoff disclosures, as Table 4-3 shows, Lockheed continued to receive multimillion-dollar orders from various branches of the U.S. military establishment, and no amount of bad press seemed to diminish the continuing improvement of the company's profit position.[18] Since Congress had voted to guarantee Lockheed's loan, there was no support for withdrawal of government contracts as a sanction for misconduct since any action that diminished Lockheed's profitability automatically made it less likely that the loan would be repaid.

Penalties. Lockheed suffered retaliation from other sources, however, and penalties apply to both the corporation and individual executives who were responsible for the foreign payoffs. Such actions include the following:

1. Daniel J. Haughton, then chairman of Lockheed's board, was forced to retire with an annual corporate pension of $65,000. He was kept on as a consultant under a ten-year contract calling for fees of $750,000. This consultant contract was subsequently suspended pending a report from the special committee investigating Lockheed's illegal corporate payments.[19] This special review committee resulted from the SEC consent decree and court injunction, agreed to on April 13, 1976.

2. A. Carl Kotchian, former vice-chairman of Lockheed's board, was retired with a consultant contract, which was subsequently suspended. SEC had charged both Kotchian and Haughton with violating antifraud, reporting, and proxy solicitation provisions of the Securities Exchange Act of 1934. Both have resigned from other company directorships.[20]

3. A suit was filed by the nonprofit Center for Law in the Public Interest on behalf of stockholders, as a class action suit. It charged that Lockheed violated federal securities laws relating to disclosure, recordkeeping, and proxy materials and asked the court to overturn the election of directors and other restitution by and damages against individual officers who were involved.

4. Reversing an earlier decision, the Federal Trade Commission decided that

Table 4-3
Selected Contracts Awarded to Lockheed

U.S. Agency or Government	Type of Purchase	Amount ($ millions)
Air Force	C130H cargo planes	16.7
	C-5A transport repair	7.9
	Study and analysis	3.6
	Satellite test center	14.7
	C-5A lock systems	3.0
	F104 maintenance	30.0
Army	Aircraft maintenance	5.2
Navy	S3A antisubmarine warfare planes	17.2
	P3C antisubmarine warfare aircraft	9.7
	P3C antisubmarine warplanes	8.0
	P3C patrol planes	4.9
	S3A antisubmarine warplanes	13.9
	P3C patrol planes	5.0
	Engineer gunfire control system	4.0
	S3A antisubmarine warplanes	13.6
	S3A patrol planes	15.0
	Trident missile activation	19.4
	S3A antisubmarine warplanes	11.6
	P3C submarine warplanes	6.5
	Trident parts and flight training	7.1
Navy & Air Force	S3A patrol plane parts & C130H transport planes, etc.	1,030.0
Navy & Army	Antisubmarine warfare patrol planes & Artillery fuses	23.2
Defense Dept.	C130H transports for Egypt	41.4
Australia	C130H Hercules aircraft	115.0
Canada	Orion long-range patrol aircraft	697.0
	CP 140 aircraft	1,030.0
Egypt	C130 transports	65.0
Saudi Arabia	Air traffic control system	625.0

Source: Compiled from *The Wall Street Journal*, various dates.
Note: Sample from news accounts of contracts during first eight months of 1976.

Lockheed payoffs to obtain contracts are an unfair practice within the meaning of the federal fair trade law. This decision permits other U.S. aircraft companies to sue Lockheed and its former officials for interfering unfairly with competition in the market. (See chart of potential individual penalties in Chapter 7.) Damages, court costs, and restitution could result in permanent harm to Lockheed.

Japanese Experience. Others who felt sharp retribution were officials in Japan's transportation ministry and corporate officers of both All Nippon Airways and the Marubeni Trading Corporation, the latter of which had acted as a go-between for Lockheed's operation. Japanese involvement with Lockheed goes back to post-World War II years, when the United States was helping Japan rebuild its military strength. As stated earlier, foreign military sales normally require the employment of influential sales agents under a commission arrangement. For example, one of Lockheed's contracts with Yoshio Kodama, a free-lance sales agent with considerable behind-the-scenes political power in Japan, started out with an annual retainer of $130,000, with regular additions on the following sliding fee scale for sales to any major airline in Japan:[21]

3 to 6 planes	$4,000,000 (fixed fee)
7 to 15 planes	$ 130,000 each
16 and over	$ 60,000 each

What the agent did with the money was his business. Lockheed was interested only in results.

As it developed, only All Nippon Airways placed an order for Lockheed Tristar aircraft. Although negotiations were conducted with Toa Domestic Airways and Korean Air Lines, neither of these was successful and no commissions were paid. However, if the P-3C Orion sale for the Japanese Air Force had gone through, Kodama's commission was scheduled to be $9 million. Subsequent payoff disclosures caused cancellation of this deal. As of September 15, 1976, eighteen individuals had been arrested in Japan for foreign currency manipulation, tax evasion, and perjury as result of Lockheed involvement.[22]

The Netherlands Experience. Across the Atlantic, Lockheed's activities also came to light in the form of negotiations with The Netherlands Prince Bernhard to promote the sale of Lockheed Starfighters. As a NATO partner, Holland, like Japan across the Pacific, was assisted in building up military potential by U.S. Defense Department personnel. When the Dutch Navy decided it needed a new long-range patrol plane in 1973, Lockheed's P-3C Orion came into the competition along with Hawker Siddeley (British) and Breguet (French). The total contract involved between $150 and $200 million for 13 planes and equipment. The contact with Prince Bernhard was an ex-KLM (The Netherlands national airlines) agent who had been employed by Lockheed as a salesman. When Prince Bernhard requested a commission of $4 to $6 million, however, Lockheed officials balked because this amount was considerably larger than the $1 million previously discussed.[23]

As soon as these disclosures had been made at the hearings of the Senate Subcommittee on Multinational Corporations, Dutch officials set up their own investigating committee whose report was published on August 29, 1976. While there was no recommendation for prosecution of Prince Bernhard since no payment was made when the sale fell through, there was enough damaging confirmation of his involvement with Lockheed to warrant his removal on behalf of Queen Juliana from all public activities ranging from inspector general of the Dutch Armed Forces to honorary president of the World Wildlife Fund. He was replaced by Princess Beatrix to present the 1976 Erasmus Prize awarded annually by the Erasmus Foundation in Amsterdam for notable contributions to European culture and science.

Other Countries. In Indonesia and Saudi Arabia, however, where similar disclosures about Lockheed's payoff activities were made involving Indonesian Air Force officials and the Arab Triad trading firm run by Adnan Khashoggi, no host country investigations have occurred.

Conclusion. On the whole, the Lockheed corporation and individuals involved with it suffered from what both parent country (United States) and host countries (Japan and The Netherlands) considered improper conduct, even though it seemed to be in accordance with "normal" practice. These individual penalties are compatible with our proposal in Chapter 7, namely, that individuals bear the full burden of their acts. The only problem is that these sanctions are being imposed with hindsight. For the future it is imperative that executives be made aware of the potential penalties in advance so that these costs can be used in calculating the risk of international payoffs and hence act as a preventative. It is unlikely that international payoffs will ever be made by Lockheed Aircraft Corporation on such a wholesale basis again.

The chronology in Chapter 8 contains a complete history of Lockheed payoff disclosures, and it is interesting to note that of the 485 items in the total chronology, over 100, or more than 20 percent, refer to Lockheed activities. Thus, it appears that Lockheed was responsible in no small measure for keeping the news media in a constant state of shock over the continuing series of disclosures that shook governments as well as individuals. The Lockheed payoff experience vindicates Senator Frank Church's remark when he opened the hearings of the subcommittee on multinationals:

It is no longer sufficient to simply sigh and say that is the way business is done. It is time to treat the issue for what it is: a serious foreign policy problem.[24]

Northrop Corporation

There is no need to repeat what has been said about the aircraft industry and military sales in the discussion of Lockheed exploits, but it is important to realize that Northrop, a Los Angeles corporation, is in the same ball game. Its F-5 Freedom and Cobra II fighter planes are sold in almost twenty countries.[25] Adnan Khashoggi of Saudi Arabia and his Triad organization were involved in handling accounts for Northrop, similar to such activities for others, in part due to the host country's insistence on a national sales agent to complete contract details. Again, however, it was not the practice itself that created the worldwide furor but the methods used to hide its existence.

Dummy Corporation. Northrop developed a dummy corporation in Switzerland called the Economic and Development Corporation (EDC), ostensibly to act as a sales organization but in reality to act as the conduit for funds kept in Swiss bank accounts. Although Northrop achieved more notoriety for its domestic political contributions and the hunting lodge recreational facilities made available to various U.S. government officials than it did for EDC foreign payoffs, the latter give us an example of how company operations can escape detection of accounting and auditing controls.[26]

The following exchange at the Senate hearing serves to explain EDC operations:

Senator Case. Was it just a dummy? Was it just an entity created for various purposes of the kind that you have been talking about to the chairman?

Mr. Jones. In a sense it was, as I understand it to be, an office through which a contract could be held and the services would then be performed by individuals who would either be consultants to this organization, they could be owners. . . .

Senator Case. By this organization you mean, too, EDC?

Mr. Jones. Yes sir. It was a way to be able to employ individuals on a contingent fee basis as they were required to be employed to make sales of our airplanes. . . .

Senator Case. How did you figure on the percentage rate?

Mr. Jones. It followed the practice of several other service-type commissions that we learned about: 1½ percent for the first $15 million, 1 percent for the next $35 million, then 3/4, then it ended up anything over $70 million was a half percent. On a typical sale of 50 airplanes, $100 million which might take 5 years, EDC would get say $1 million, $200,000 a year, which incidentally is half the cost of an office in that country. It was the economics of having people willing to work on a commission basis rather than us have to spend money in the marketing department. This was one of the main reasons for setting up.[27]

While Northrop's activities were not on as grand a scale as those of Lockheed, nevertheless they touched many well-known figures, according to disclosures made before the Senate Subcommittee on Multinational Corporations:[28]

1. A former French national assemblyman was alleged to have been on Northrop's payroll.
2. Retired military officers and other influential persons like Kermit Roosevelt were retained to take advantage of relationships that had been created in various host countries.
3. Many recreational and other gratuities were supplied for international as well as local politicians, such as football tickets, the hunting lodge, sponsored vacations, and fund-raising dinners.

The chronology in Chapter 8 contains additional items.

On April 13, 1976, Northrop reached a final settlement with the U.S. Defense Department on improper billings for payments to foreign agents. It agreed to withdraw some charges and make repayments of $2.3 million.

Penalties. As for penalties, officials of Page-Europa S.p.A., an Italian subsidiary, were asked to resign after improper payments in five countries were turned up. All agreements with consultants were terminated, which caused Adnan Khashoggi to file a complaint against Northrop for collection of the commissions due him. However, no action was taken against corporate officers.[29] In fact, Thomas V. Jones was reelected chairman of the Northrop board on February 19, 1976.

Neither did the company suffer unduly from the misadventure. For example, on March 11, 1976, Saudi Arabia agreed to pay Northrop $1.8 billion for modernizing its air force, and on May 12, 1976, Thailand announced that it was purchasing $50 million worth of F-5 jet fighters from Northrop. A sampling of contracts awarded to Northrop Corporation after the payoff disclosures appears in Table 4-4. These are evidence of the fact that Northrop, like Lockheed, is considered indispensable to defense since no other corporation possesses comparable capability for specific items of military hardware.

Conclusions on the Aircraft Industry

In summary, these two corporate case studies point up both the temptations and the difficulties involved in shaping solutions for the international payoff dilemma in the aircraft industry. Lack of its own sales force in the host country requires the MNC to employ foreign sales agents. Since these agents are independent contractors largely outside the control of the multinational corporation, what happens to the large commissions that are warranted by the multimillion-dollar purchase price for aircraft is also largely outside the MNC control. It is difficult to find serious fault with the executive decision to retain sales agents since it is based on a true business calculation and is not inherently improper. It is the methods used for preventing proper disclosure of such payments, however, that are open to question.

In the case of Northrop, the creation of a dummy corporation (EDC) to make international payments is an example of failure to disclose. While foreign currency fluctuations are usually given as the reason for maintaining Swiss bank accounts, this reason is more an excuse than a cause. The desire for secrecy to escape tax liability on the part of both the giver and the receiver motivates this arrangement. It has no acceptable place in accounting practice, however, and neither the business community as a whole nor the accounting profession approves it.[30] There was nothing inherently wrong with contracting with Adnan Khashoggi to promote airplane sales. What was indefensible was hiding this and other transactions through EDC operations and off-the-books accounts.

Similarly, most of Lockheed's commissions were reasonable and legitimate considering the amount of sales and practices in the industry. However, it was Lockheed's failure to disclose foreign payments that resulted in continuing temptation to falsify the transactions.

Another area for possible censure lies in attempts to influence sales directly

Table 4-4
Selected Contracts Awarded to Northrop

U.S. Agency or Government	Type of Purchase	Amount ($ millions)
Air Force	F15 fighter countermeasure sets	4.8
	F5 development program	11.8
	F5 FMS contract	29.6
	Pilot training	3.2
	F5E fighters	56.8
	Trainer wings & F5E fighter gear	8.1
	F5 fighters	10.1
	F5 aircraft	50.7
	F5E fighters	6.9
	Ground equipment	9.4
	A15 fighters, electronic devices	4.5
Army & Air Force	Beam-Reder missile & F5E fighters	10.3
E.P.A.	Air pollution training institute	3.2
Norway	Mark 37 torpedo	5.9
Saudi Arabia	Construction & training services	1,500.0
Saudi Arabia, Iran & Chile	F5E planes	85.8
Switzerland	Fighter planes	460.0
	F5 fighters	135.0
Kenya	F5 warplanes	70.0

Source: Compiled from *The Wall Street Journal*, various dates.
Note: Sample from news accounts of contract awards during first eight months of 1976.

through political contributions to the host country or payments to public officials. The reason that such practice is not acceptable in the United States is equally applicable to the host country. When the political payoffs are initiated by host-country officials, there is no cure that can substitute for publicity. Knowing that disclosure is required in the United States is likely to reduce the demand for such payments in host countries.

In the final analysis, international payoff practices in the aircraft industry were carried on as a result of deliberate executive decisions. Under our proposal for reform in Chapter 7, the individuals responsible for those executive decisions are to be held accountable and in most instances have already been removed from their executive positions.

We now move to the oil industry where similar payoffs were made but for different reasons.

Oil Industry Case Studies

As is pointed out in Chapter 3, certain extractive industries have special problems in maintaining a profitable relationship with the host country. Especially in developing countries, initial bargaining power is mostly on the side of the multinational corporation being wooed to invest huge sums of capital in the host country. However, after the installation is completed, the bargaining power shifts somewhat. In economic terms, this is the shift at the margin from consideration of opportunity costs to a consideration of sunk costs. Getting a return on investment before unforeseen and unfortunate changes occur in the host country's political power structure is the name of the game.

Political Uncertainty. A 1974 study the authors made among multinational companies to determine the positive and negative factors that influence MNCs in their overseas investment decisions indicates that a major negative factor is uncertainty, involving threats of nationalization, new taxes, or other host-country regulations that upset projected plans.[31] The inability to plan effectively ultimately leads the MNC to emphasize short-run profits and interferes with its desire to stabilize investment in the host country. One chief executive officer put it this way:

Businessmen don't mind trying to forecast economic conditions. They evaluate the risks and weigh the rewards and they make decisions based on this appraisal. Government action, on the other hand, is unpredictable. There is no way to forecast it. And it is this environment of uncertainty, where there's no rationale that can be developed as to what direction the government will move, that makes businessmen unwilling to make commitments.[32]

Thus, for petroleum refining and related products and services, such as tankers and pipelines, international payoffs are considered not so much to promote sales contracts as to prevent harsh legislation designed to coerce MNCs to transfer a greater share of ownership or profits to the host country. To illustrate this point we now examine two corporate case studies in the oil industry:

1. Gulf Oil Corporation, with special reference to its relationships with a developing country (South Korea) and a developed but politically unstable country (Italy);
2. Exxon Corporation and its activities (also in Italy).

Gulf Oil Corporation

Like most of the payoff disclosures, Gulf Oil Corporation's involvement emerged during the Watergate investigation into domestic political contributions. Early in August 1973, when Nixon campaign officials were required to release the list of donations from corporate funds, Gulf's name was there to the tune of $100,000. By November of that year both the corporation and one of its vice presidents, Claude C. Wild, Jr., had pleaded guilty to U.S. Justice Department charges of violating the Corrupt Practices Act, which forbids political contributions in federal elections. By the time the SEC got into the act in March 1974, the amount involved was up to $10 million in contributions (both domestic and foreign) between 1960 and 1973.

Political Contributions. In March 1974 the SEC filed suit against Gulf and Wild, not only because the domestic political contributions had not been properly shown on the company's books, but also because an additional $4 million had been delivered to President Park Chung Hee in South Korea. Gulf settled the SEC case by agreeing to refrain from similar violations in the future and to establish an outside review committee to investigate and report back to the board of directors. This committee's report to the SEC, issued on December 30, 1975, forms the basis for the following story about Gulf payoffs.[33]

Late in the 1950s, after the fighting in Korea had ended, U.S. multinationals were invited to participate in the new government's attempt to expand the country's industrial base, as part of the U.S. commitment to the security of *South Korea*. In 1963 and 1964 Gulf made its first investments in South Korea's petroleum refining industry. This action was a mutually advantageous venture since Gulf was anxious to obtain an outlet for its Kuwait crude oil. A refinery at Ulsan was completed in 1964, and $25 million was invested in the Korean Oil

Company (KOCO), which Gulf jointly owned with the Korean government. With the plastic and fertilizer plants that followed, Gulf's investment grew to $200 million or more. The Korean government was an active partner in all the operations.

Meanwhile the U.S. government was assisting the Korean government to stabilize its power base under the leadership of President Park Chung Hee and his Democratic Republican Party. Gulf was encouraged to support his election and contributed $1 million in the 1966 campaign. According to company president Bob Dorsey, the approach was so strong that

... there were veiled threats of what—you know—threats that if you want to survive and do well—if you want to continue the role you're in and prosper in this country you had best do this.[34]

The $1 million came from funds held in accounts in the Bahamas by a defunct subsidiary known as Bahamas Ex. (Bahamas Exploration Company, Ltd.), which had been organized in 1944 when it appeared that a new petroleum law would make oil exploration in the Bahamas a profitable endeavor. Although this legislation never materialized, Bahamas Ex. remained part of Gulf's exploration division from 1944 until 1960 with no apparent function except to hold some exploration licenses. In 1959 assistant comptroller William C. Viglia took over the Bahamas Ex. operation and later became the courier for almost 200 cash transfers from an off-the-books bank account in amounts ranging from $10,000 to $100,000.[35] This black-bag operation occurred, on average, twice a month between October 1961 and July 1973, when Bahamas Ex. was liquidated.

Between January 1960 and July 1972, a total of more than $5 million was transferred to the Bahamas Ex. account, of which $4.5 million was returned to the United States for domestic political activities, and $108,000 was used to purchase a helicopter for a Bolivian general. Apart from these funds, another $4.4 million was partially recorded on Bahamas Ex. books but never received. These transfers were traced to a foreign destination as follows:[36]

1966	$1,004,000 Korea
1969	140,030 Bolivia
	100,000 Switzerland
1970	3,000,000 Korea
	110,000 Bolivia
1971	50,000 Beirut

The $3 million transfer to South Korea was the result of direct negotiations between Gulf's president Bob Dorsey and S.K. Kim, a representative for the Korean government, who had originally asked for $10 million that Dorsey refused. But when Kim suggested that Gulf's continued prosperity depended on the political contribution, negotiations continued and resulted in agreement on $3 million.

Thereafter the funds were booked to Bahamas Ex. and disbursed from a Swiss bank account in the following manner:[37]

9 checks of $200,000 each	$1,800,000
Cash aggregating	1,199,790
Bank commission	210
Total	$3,000,000

Dorsey's failure to disclose these payoffs to the Gulf board of directors is explained in his own words:

... the matter being rather delicate, and recognizing that any revelation of this would be both embarrassing to Gulf and embarrassing to the party to whom the payment was made, I simply decided that the better course was not to tell them.[38]

Gulf's political contributions in *Italy* follow a similar pattern, but since the entire petroleum industry was involved, we postpone discussion of the Italian political payments until the next case study, Exxon Corporation. Both Gulf and Exxon had extensive refinery and marketing networks in Italy, and payments were made by Gulf to Italian newspaper publishing firms that were owned, controlled by, or affiliated with two political parties, namely, the Christian Democratic Party and the Socialists. In the Gulf report, Esso Italiana is identified as the initiator of these contributions.[39]

Although Gulf Oil Corporation made political contributions in *other countries*, there was no illegal element involved in them. For example, political contributions made in Sweden and Canada are lawful in those countries. Hence, Gulf's payments there were considered acceptable from the standpoint of the host country. Also, information about these payments was readily available in host-country records.

Secret Funds. Other payments made in *South Korea* include those usually referred to as "grease." J.K. Darden, a Gulf employee who spent considerable time in Korea, explained the process in a memo as follows:

When an application for a permit or license was received by the agency, it went to the desk of the lowest clerk in the section. He put his "chop" (name stamp) on it and passed it to the next higher clerk for his chop and so on until the application finally reached the section chief or other person authorized to approve it. The journey of this application up the chain of command might take days, weeks or sometimes months or even become "lost" in the process.

In order to speed up the flow of a document, it was necessary to pay for the accelerated service. Most of these payments were small, ranging from $50 to $200, depending on the level of approval needed. My Korean managers told me that these "contributions" were used to supplement the meager salaries of the governmental workers.[40]

A substantial portion of such expenditures were charged on the books of KOCO and KORGOC (Korean Gulf Oil Company, a wholly owned Gulf subsidiary), as entertainment expenses, which averaged over $1 million annually from 1970 through 1974.

An off-the-books fund, however, known as the "Gray Fund," was also used to dispense gratuities to South Korean governmental officials to ease access to agencies and expedite Gulf government business through a tightly controlled bureaucracy. Other questionable practices that aided the Korean ministry included kickbacks from KOCO distributors and insurance carriers as well as transfers of stock and equipment at below-cost prices.

In *Italy* Gulf Oil Corporation maintained a similar off-the-books account known as the "Black Fund." Payments from this fund amounted to $422,604.80 for the twelve-year period from 1962 to 1974. Table 4-5 is a reproduction of the categories of payments that were made from this special account. They range from political contributions to merit bonuses and run the gamut from black to white as such payments are defined in Chapter 2.

There are accounts of various other payments in the Gulf report, most of which fall in the category of "transactions to comply with the spirit of the Undertaking [under the SEC agreement] rather than to express any doubts on the part of the Committee as to its propriety."[41] But the report warns:

In any event, regardless of the propriety of motives and legality under local law, the maintenance of off-the-books corporate accounts, wherever located, cannot be justified in a publicly owned company. There is no control or accountability to the company or its outside auditors for either receipts or disbursements, and the true state of financial affairs of the company may be obscured, if only minimally, as in the case of a large company such as Gulf. Moreover, the possibilities of abuse are manifest.[42]

From similar off-the-books funds, Gulf made payments to various individuals in the following *other countries:* Bolivia, Turkey, Switzerland, Kuwait, Venezuela, Nigeria, Gabon, Angola, Ecuador, and The Netherlands. To detail these activities further is unnecessary for our purposes since the methods and sources were the same and recounting them would be unduly repetitious.

Other Payments. One other method that Gulf Oil used to accomplish international payoffs was through rebate of part of the purchase price, in other words, kickbacks. These fall within the gray area of the payoff definition in Chapter 2. Rebates paid to the Korean Ministry of National Defense by KOCO are listed below:

1971	$166,468
1972	477,585
1973	472,718
1974	455,360
1975 (8 mos.)	264,425
Total	$1,836,556

At the rate of 15 to 17 cents per barrel, it is evident that Gulf's total sales to the ministry over this period amounted to a very large sum. When a Gulf official

Table 4-5
Gulf in Italy: Schedule of Categories of Payments from Special Account, 1962-1974

Category	U.S. Dollars[a]	Number of Items[b]
Political Contributions or Payments	235,886	22
Payments for Consulting Services, Professional Fees, Commissions, Etc.	60,959	17
Payments in Connection with Gasoline Station Marketing Development	23,538	34
Payments for Services re Ragusa Tax Claims	38,462	2
Payments to Newspapers, Editors, Journalists	10,815	11
Payments to Bassiano and Terranova Communes	15,385	2
Payments to Consulting Firms for Gasoline Marketing Studies	9,076	15
Business Gifts	8,545	3
Payments in the Nature of Charitable or Goodwill Contributions	8,769	7
Payments to Professional Manufacturing or Trade Associations	4,333	5
Payments in Connection with Union or Dealer Association Problems	2,308	2
Approved Merit Bonus Paid to Gulf Employee	1,538	1
Bank Fees	1,474	7
Total	422,526	

Source: Securities and Exchange Commission, *Report of the Special Review Committee of the Board of Directors of Gulf Oil Corporation*, Washington, D.C., December 30, 1975, p. 139.

[a]These dollar amounts are based on the lire amounts converted to dollars at the rate of L.650/$1.

[b]Numbers refer to the number of transactions or withdrawals that are included in the particular category.

tried to stop the practice, he was immediately told that the Korean defense ministry would not hesitate to take its business elsewhere.[43]

Penalties and Remedial Action. Although the Gulf special review committee points out that no officer, director, or employee of Gulf Oil Corporation benefited personally by reason of international payoffs,[44] after the SEC consent decree several corporation officers found it necessary to resign or were dismissed. The following are examples:

1. Claude C. Wild, Jr., a former Gulf vice president, pleaded guilty in November 1973 to charges involving *domestic* political contributions uncovered by the Watergate Special Prosecutor. He was acquitted in this case on a technicality growing out of the U.S. Justice Department's failure to file the suit on time. The lawsuit under the SEC complaint is still pending, and he refused to appear before Gulf's special review committee.

2. William C. Viglia, comptroller of the Bahamas Exploration Company, Ltd., was indicted on charges of perjury in connection with his testimony to a federal grand jury. He was also charged with lying to U.S. customs agents in connection with his black-bag operations at the Miami transfer point. The Gulf special review committee was unable to interview him because he refused to testify on the ground that such testimony might tend to incriminate him (in other words, he "took the Fifth"). On August 5, 1976, at seventy-one years of age, he was sentenced to one year in federal prison for perjury.

3. Bob Dorsey, chief executive officer of Gulf Oil Corporation, held various executive positions in the company during the period under investigation. The special review committee was concerned primarily with his culpability in connection with *domestic* affairs:

If Dorsey did not know of the nature and extent of Wild's unlawful activities, he perhaps chose to shut his eyes to what was going on. Had he been more alert to the problem, he was in a ready position to inquire about and put an end to it.[45]

Subsequent to the committee's report, Dorsey was forced to resign. He was awarded the same retirement benefits, however, that he would have received without the resignation. He took payment in a lump sum of $1.6 million that reduced his yearly pension from $244,000 to $48,000.[46]

4. Also ousted from their positions on January 14, 1976 were William Henry, executive vice president; Fred Deering, senior vice president; and Herbert Manning, vice president and secretary. Manning was retained but demoted to a position as an employee on the general counsel's staff. He alleged that his involvement in the payoffs was merely following orders. Henry, on the other hand, was found to be personally involved in the transfers from Bahamas Ex. and in the determination of the amounts and persons to whom the cash payments were to be delivered. The special review committee felt that his

inability to reveal who authorized him to transfer $871,000 of corporate funds to a defunct exploration subsidiary in the Bahamas was "scarcely credible."[47] Deering was also intimately acquainted with the Bahamas Ex. operation, and the committee concluded that he did not "act in a manner consistent with the responsibilities of his office" since he made transfers totalling $1.6 million of corporate funds to an off-the-books Bahamas bank account while he was comptroller from 1968 through 1972.[48]

The company too was involved in "corporate therapeutics," as it has come to be called.[49] Eight lawsuits, filed against nineteen present and past officers and directors of the corporation, were settled by agreement on September 30, 1976. Although the company received $2 million from North River Insurance Company as result of insurance covering directors and officers (D&O insurance), this amount was hardly a drop in the bucket considering that the special review committee cost $3 million to cover the cost of hearings, affidavits, transcripts and reports and that $100,000 was paid to each member of the three-man committee. However, to recover some of the costs the company took additional action against the above-mentioned executives:

1. Stock options were rescinded for Bob Dorsey (due 200,000 shares, got 100,000), William Henry (due 43,700, got 7,450), and Fred Deering (due 10,000, got 7,500). At the time Gulf shares were worth $17.81 each.

2. Executive incentive pay for 1975 was reduced by the following amounts: Bob Dorsey, $250,000; William Henry, $45,000; Fred Deering, $50,000; and Henry Manning, $25,000. Past executives suffered similar losses: Royce Savage (former general counsel), $100,000; E.D. Brockett (former chairman and director), $150,000; and Joseph E. Bounds (former executive vice president), $4,000 per year. Thus, a total of eight individuals of the nineteen mentioned in the suit were penalized for their responsibility in the Gulf payoff scandal (including Wild). The other eleven were not identified and to date no one except Viglia has been given a prison sentence.[50]

There remains pending a stockholder lawsuit for damages of $500,000 filed by Project on Corporate Responsibility, Inc., which refused the request to be included in the settlement. Under the terms of the settlement, Gulf was also required to pay all attorneys' fees (both defendants' and plaintiffs') except those of Wild and Viglia. Plaintiffs attorneys' fees amounted to $600,000.

Conclusion. A recurrence of the international payoff phenomenon at Gulf Oil Corporation appears unlikely. Immediately after the special review committee's report, Gulf established a new Board Committee on Business Principles and made changes in its policy manual to prohibit political contributions and require disclosure of funds for foreign political propaganda. A change in top officers and directors has brought a new moral climate to the executive suite. Whether this change is pervasive and permanent or will eventually lapse into a public relations, image-building happening remains to be seen. The fact that individuals at Gulf

Oil Corporation were made to bear the burden of their improper actions squares with our proposal for reform in Chapter 7. Stricter penalties are needed, however, to tip the scales on the cost side of the calculation.

Exxon Corporation

Exxon Corporation has been chosen as a case study in international payoffs mainly for its involvement in the oil industry's political contributions in Italy. Both in the Senate hearings and in the Gulf report, Exxon's subsidiary, Esso Italiana, is charged with providing the leadership in payments to Italian political parties in the years from 1964 to 1972 under the direction of its general manager, Vincenzo Cassaniga. It is not the payments themselves but the devious methods used to cover them up that are of interest here.

Italian Experience. In 1964 several oil subsidiaries of Standard Oil Company of New Jersey (Exxon's previous name) based in Europe agreed to set up a special budget for political contributions. To make the payments tax deductible as a business expense, the funds in Italy were paid to various political party newspaper publishing companies, as payments for advertising, with dummy invoices issued for accounting purposes.

Another method of payment was through secret bank accounts. Cassaniga had forty such accounts through which $29 to $32 million in Esso funds flowed without corporate control. Payments under the special budget grew from $760,000 in 1963 to more than $5 million in 1968.[51]

It was not until suspicious activities relating to oil contracts and real estate deals surfaced in 1972 that Cassaniga's activities were put under investigation at Exxon headquarters, and he was subsequently discharged. It developed that Cassaniga had generated part of the funds in his secret bank accounts by rebates from suppliers, customers and banks. He had total personal control over the bank accounts, which thus made it impossible for auditors to detect their existence.

Table 4-6 shows the recipients of Esso Italiana funds from the special budget for the years 1963 to 1972. These political contributions were considered legal in Italy, but the methods used to raise the money and to disburse the funds were questionable.

The fact that the internal accounting system of the corporation did not discover the special budget or any of the secret bank accounts of Cassaniga is attributed to lax management, according to the report submitted to the audit committee of Exxon's board of directors on October 17, 1972:

We believe that the "mind and management" philosophy, which led to a "mild coordination" approach in overseeing operations in the European affiliates, has been over-emphasized to the detriment of management control. As a result of this audit, it is our opinion that the regional headquarters groups have not had sufficient indepth involvement with the activities of the affiliates to properly carry out the necessary surveillance and guidance.[52]

The audit report goes on to condemn the "bogus documentation and false accounting" that were accepted at all levels of management, thereby subverting the entire control system and making it virtually impossible to verify the validity of financial transactions.

Vincenzo Cassaniga was also president of Unione Petrolifera Italia (UPI), a trade association of the oil industry in Italy. Since Esso Italiana held a seventeen percent share of the oil market in Italy, it was second in size only to the Italian National Oil Company, known as ENI-AGIP, which owned 26 percent. All aspects of oil production and pricing in Italy are controlled by the national government. Although there is no direct evidence of quid pro quo in connection with the political contributions made by the oil industry from June 1969 through December 1972, it was during this time that the Italian government was considering the following measures:

1. Rebates for costs incurred when the Suez Canal was closed;
2. Favorable interest rate of 4.5 percent on deferred taxes;
3. Offset of OPEC price increases through excise tax decreases;
4. Deferral of the proposed shift to nuclear power generation.

All these measures affected the fate of the oil industry, and Esso Italiana acted

Table 4-6
Recipients of Esso Italiana Special Budget, 1963-1972

Name of Political Group	Amount of Payment (dollars)
Democrazia Cristiana (DC)	11,948,046
Socialista Democratico Italiana (PSDI)	5,160,952
Socialista Italiano (PSI)	1,245,028
Liberale (PLI)	591,531
Socialista Italiano d'Unita Proletaria (PSIUP)	71,111
Sociale Italiano (MSI)	236,106
Republicana Italiano (PRI)	267,521
Others (Unknown)	1,096,344
Total	$29,616,639

Source: U.S. Congress, Senate, Foreign Relations Committee, Subcommittee on Multinational Corporations, *Hearings*, Washington, D.C., May-September 1975, p. 301.

as the collection agent for the industry. Each company was advised of its pro rata share, although it could decide which party was to get the funds.[53]

The Reaction. All of the foregoing information was available to Exxon management in 1972. It took until 1975 for the matter to be publicized and then only as result of Senate hearings. Gulf exonerates its own general manager, Nicolo Pignatelli, an Italian national on whom Gulf relied to carry on its Italian operations with little interference from the MNC home office. The Gulf report, however, blames Cassaniga, acting in his capacity as president of UPI, for transferring $1.5 million in political funds to ENEL (Italy's government-owned electric utility) in anticipation of the May 1972 elections. He had gotten an advance on the funds from Italcasse, the national savings association, and had already incurred the indebtedness when he approached the other members of UPI for their payment, according to the Gulf report. They all ultimately paid their share. Gulf's general manager was in complete agreement with Cassaniga of Esso Italiana that the payment should be made. He regarded the contributions as an act of "good citizenship" to support the existing political system in Italy and in particular the center-left democratic political parties in their efforts to retain control against the radical right and left.[54]

Immediately after the disclosure of the UPI contributions, the Italian government set up a Special Parliamentary Commission to investigate the matter. A determination of the legality of the payments under Italian law has not yet been made. The question has been rendered moot, however, by a new law passed by the Italian Parliament in 1974, which prohibits corporate political contributions unless, in the case of private corporations, such contributions are authorized by appropriate corporate action and so recorded on the company's books.[55]

Conclusion. The obvious embarrassment to Exxon occasioned by the Esso Italiana escapade makes it quite certain that such international payments are a thing of the past. This conclusion is especially true since Exxon lost sight of some $90 million in total funds during the period when Vincenzo Cassaniga was general manager in Italy. For SEC purposes, however, the failure to report such contributions and the "shut-eye sentry" attitude that also characterized Gulf activities during this period[56] permitted large sums to go unrecorded and constitute "materiality" of interest to investors under Securities and Exchange Commission regulations.

It is also clear that the SEC voluntary disclosure policy has resulted in the kind of public accounting that was the original purpose of the program. While discharge of Cassaniga constitutes a personal sanction, there is no indication that any other Exxon officers have been censured for their negligence in maintaining fiscal control. The damage to the company's image is summarized in the statement before the Senate subcommittee:

We are concerned and embarrassed by the fact that these irregularities occurred on such a scale and for several years in one of our affiliates. This is particularly distressing because we believe we have built a reputation for lawful ethical conduct worldwide ... when the full situation was disclosed by our own investigators, we stopped all questionable activities promptly and decisively, on our own initiative, over 3 years ago.[57]

Other Oil Companies

Other oil companies mentioned in connection with international payments are listed in Table 4-1. They include Ashland, Mobil, and Occidental about whom news accounts have appeared from time to time. Both Ashland and Occidental were deeply involved in domestic political contributions, and their officers have been cited for illegal payments under the Corrupt Practices Act. Mobil Oil Company was part of the Italian caper.

Conclusions on the Oil Industry

In summary, the oil industry's main interest in international payments was to protect investments in refineries and distribution facilities once they had been established in the host country. The record disclosed in this account, however, does not indicate that such payments had any direct effect in this connection. Whether the companies involved would have engaged in international payoffs had they seriously considered all the pros and cons suggested in the guidelines presented in Chapter 6 is problematical. We feel that they would not, and hindsight shows that overseas payoffs in the case of the oil companies were not a rational executive decision.

The Food Industry (Bananas) Case Study

Three major companies have been involved in banana export in Latin America almost since the Panama Canal was built. They are Standard Fruit Company, a subsidiary of Castle & Cooke, Inc.; Del Monte Corporation, and United Brands, which recently acquired the long established banana firm known as United Fruit Company. The SEC report mentions all three companies as having engaged in international payoffs, but we have chosen United Brands as our major case study in this industry because of its notoriety.

United Brands

United Brands, as United Fruit Company, has long been synonymous with bananas in Central American countries under the Chiquita label. The White Fleet is welcomed or resented depending on whether it is considered a job provider or an exploiter.[58] As we point out in Chapter 3 in our discussion of host-country relationships, the father image is a two-faced one, and paternalism of companies like United Brands is a welcome target for nationalistic slogans. When United Brands took over the banana operations of United Fruit Company in Honduras, it inherited this paternalistic background. As with any swift change in a traditional society, however, the United Brands' takeover resulted in a break-down of many informal and personal relationships that United Fruit had cultivated. The new top management's seeming lack of expertise in bananas, coupled with increased nationalism in the host country, augmented pressure to obtain a larger share of the banana pie.

Del Monte confirms these pressures involved in overseas investment. It admits that it has greased the channels of communication in order to effect swifter government decisions—by using proper accounting methods and regular SEC reporting, however. As an example, Del Monte cites its frustration in getting Guatemalan approval for purchase of 55,000 acres of new banana lands. Finally after eighteen months of delay, it made a $500,000 payment to a "consultant" for his good offices. The favorable decision came through almost immediately. Whether such payment is "for services rendered" or whether it is an attempt to obtain improper concessions is an open question involving goals and means.

The Buildup. The situation came to a head in 1973 when seven Central and South American countries formed the Union of Banana Exporting Countries (UBEC), a consortium similar to that of OPEC in the oil-producing countries. UBEC's first act was to propose an export tax of $1.00 for every forty pounds of bananas shipped from member ports. Ecuador, the largest banana producer in Latin America, refused to go along with the proposal and it fell through. But in 1974 Honduras did enact a 50 cent tax on each box of bananas for export, which was later reduced to 25 cents, apparently in response to a United Brands payoff.[59] This action reduced United Brands' taxes from about $15 to $7.5 million.[60]

United Brands was worried that passing this tax on to consumers in the form of a price increase would reduce demand for the product, especially during an inflationary period. Since other banana-producing countries had not as yet enacted a similar tax (and some, as in Ecuador's case, did not intend to do so), competition from other companies in the industry might force absorption of the tax, thereby reducing company profits. Of the seven banana-producing countries only Panama and Costa Rica enacted a similar tax.

U.S. State Department officials in Tegucipalpa got wind of the $1.25 million payment to a high-level Honduran government officer and passed the information along to superiors in Washington, who in turn sparked SEC investigation.[61] When Eli Black, United Brands' board chairman, jumped to his death from his office window forty-four stories above Manhattan, the cat was out of the bag. There had been no love lost among United Brands' top officers ever since Black had trod on a few toes to make it up the corporate ladder, and now they were only too glad to blame the whole mess on him. However, SEC was satisfied that he was in on the decision, so that for its purposes United Brands had violated the disclosure and materiality regulations of the Securities Exchange Act.

The Reaction. Although the payment cannot be traced to any specific Honduran government officials,[62] President Oswaldo Lopez Arellano's government was at once challenged by opposition forces on the ground that his integrity had been sufficiently compromised to warrant his removal from office. He was removed as the army's commander-in-chief, and a commission was appointed to investigate the charges. Thus, as we have seen in the cases involving Japan and Italy, there is some justification for the Senate Subcommittee on Multinational Corporations to feel that the impact of MNC activities on U.S. foreign policy is sufficiently strong to warrant investigation and control.

As result of the United Brands incident, the SEC decided to issue a new directive warning U.S. corporations of their obligation to disclose foreign payments and offering to let them off the hook if they voluntarily came forward with such information. The flood of 8-K and 10-K reports to stockholders and the SEC showed that United Brands was only the tip of the iceberg and that the SEC was right in its decision to force disclosure. Officials in the SEC enforcement division are convinced that when a company receives substantial benefit from large international payoffs, investors have a right to know about it.[63]

As for United Brands, most previous top executives were replaced, and a special review committee was appointed by the board of directors to investigate all international payments including some in Costa Rica and Panama, as well as outside the Western Hemisphere, notably in Italy, which were thought to be in the neighborhood of $750,000. SEC filed a suit against the company alleging violation of the antifraud and reporting provisions of the federal securities law. The case was subsequently settled by consent decree on January 28, 1976. Under the terms of the settlement, the company is required to make full disclosure of all unlawful payments to foreign government officials, and the SEC is granted access to company books and records in perpetuity. The special review committee composed of outside directors is set up on a permanent basis with Dean Michael Sovern of Columbia University Law School as the overseer.

Since the consent decree, there has been no further disclosure involving United Brands, but at the stockholders meeting on May 13, 1976, there were still many questions on international payoffs. Future payoffs, according to present management, are to be considered on a case-by-case basis, but it is unlikely that an incident similar to the Honduran one will recur.

Conclusions on the Food Industry

The problems involved in the one-crop developing countries are similar to the oil-producing countries in that foreign investment has been relied on to provide economic development. Coffee in Brazil, tin in Bolivia, copper in Chile, bananas in Honduras, and crude oil in Saudi Arabia are examples. The developing countries with natural resources need MNC technology and export facilities for efficient production and sale of their products in world markets.

In Honduras and other Central and South American countries, nationalism in recent years has clashed with long established economic tradition, and foreign investors have been placed in the ambivalent status of necessary evils. Government officials in these countries, faced with satisfying their constituencies in the desire for independence and at the same time for increases in the standard of living, are also in a dilemma.

To resolve this dilemma, the ruling power in the host country has the alternative of increasing taxes on MNC profits or nationalizing the industry by expropriation, which is limited by the host-country dependence on MNC capital resources and technology. In either case the temptation for the MNC is strong to use influence on government officials in the firm's self-interest.

Del Monte's example of the payment to expedite a real estate deal, however, is quite different both in kind and degree from United Brands' outright bribe of a high government official to reduce the export tax. The effect on the host country is different as is the long-run economic result both to the host country and the MNC. The individual executive, however, is still faced with the problem of choosing means to accomplish proper business goals. This dilemma must be resolved according to the legal, moral, and economic considerations of each individual executive who faces it. Our international payoffs guide in Chapter 6 provides the suggested tools for such decision making.

The Drug Industry Analysis

The drug industry was singled out by the SEC in its report because twelve companies had made voluntary disclosures, which was the highest number for any industry equal only to the oil industry. Our investigation shows that no one company can be singled out for special treatment because the pattern for all is the same, namely, that certain improper payments were made but the companies are not required to tell who received them under the SEC voluntary disclosure program. Under those conditions the facts are hard to come by, and we must rely on meager news releases for our information. Nevertheless, the amounts paid are substantial enough to warrant analysis.

Reporting Companies. 1. The G.D. Searle case gives an example of how the SEC amnesty program works. Searle does business in 125 countries and has manufacturing facilities in 41 countries.[64] It reported $1.3 million in foreign payments. An audit committee of its board investigated and found that some questionable foreign payments had mistakenly been treated as "marketing expenses (commissions)" and had been deducted from income tax returns. Therefore, Searle owed the U.S. Treasury $84,000 in additional taxes. The company also adopted a new code of conduct requiring employees to refrain from making such payments again on penalty of discharge. There was no formal SEC action taken to seek a permanent injunction against such activities in the future, however. Under the voluntary disclosure program only the amounts must be made public, not the recipients, so that they are saved embarrassment and the company avoids the risk of losing future foreign contracts.

2. Merck & Co., a New Jersey-based firm, reported $3.6 million in questionable payments to employees of foreign governments between 1968 and 1975. Merck paid an additional tax bill of $264,000 as result of these disclosures, and the IRS is continuing investigation for additional violations of the Internal Revenue Code. Merck blamed its auditor for failing to follow up on information about questionable foreign payments, and the special board committee of outside experts set up to investigate the matter blames the chairman of the board for ignoring warning signals.

3. Warner-Lambert Company uncovered payments in 14 of the 140 countries in which it does business. In the five years from 1971 to 1975, its payments averaged $450,000. The funds were mostly commissions on pharmaceutical sales to foreign governmental agencies. Top management officials were aware of such payments but did not do anything to stop them. The payments were made in cash or through intermediaries and were recorded in the books as promotional expenses and thus deducted for tax purposes.[65]

4. Johnson & Johnson investigated all of its 135 companies in 45 countries and came up with improper payments totaling $990,000 between 1971 and 1975.

5. Upjohn Company[66] admitted that nearly $4.1 million was paid to employees of foreign governments or their intermediaries in 22 countries between 1971 and 1975. During the same five-year period sales had totaled $3.28 billion, which thus makes the materiality of the international payoffs highly doubtful under SEC regulations.

6. Bristol-Myers Company[67] told the SEC that its investigation by Price, Waterhouse & Company had turned up instances of questionable payments. It did not state the amount or in what countries such payments were made.

7. Sterling Drug Company reported payments in nineteen foreign countries between 1970 and 1974. It stated that most of the funds had gone to low-ranking government employees in small amounts totaling between $103,000 and $180,000 annually.

Conclusion. As result of these disclosures in the drug industry the IRS opened tax fraud investigations to see whether additional taxes were due on the payments which had been deducted as business expense.[68]

Because of the worldwide marketing program that most drug companies have, coupled with the fact that most health activities in developing countries as well as some developed countries of Western Europe are under the control and budget of the government, it is not unusual that drug companies should be dealing with governmental officials in arranging purchases of its products. In addition, most countries control drug entry very strictly, and like the U.S. Food and Drug Administration, they require that drug companies get permission from the government to market a drug beforehand. With the volume of governmental paper work involved, small payments to get the necessary stamp are not considered unusual. However, here again, given the changes in business environment, the individual executive must decide whether such payments are justifiable.

Summary

In this chapter the case studies presented give flesh and blood to the international payoff dilemma. Each company considered as a case study was part of the peculiar economic and political environment that shaped its decision to make payoffs. Whether the same decisions would be made today is doubtful since that environment has surely changed. However, in Chapter 6 we provide guidelines for decision making in international payoffs that are timeless and can take account of any changes. Each executive can work out the payoff dilemma for himself, not only for today but for the future as well.

Before the executive moves through this labyrinth, however, it is important that he sees how his decision on international payoffs fits into his role as individual, businessman, and member of society. This is the purpose of the next chapter.

Notes

1. This group of nine companies includes four of the corporation case studies chosen for this chapter (Gulf, Lockheed, Northrop, and United Brands). The other company reported on here made voluntary disclosures (Exxon).

2. U.S. Congress, Senate, Committee on Banking, Housing and Urban Affairs, *Report of the Securities and Exchange Commission on Questionable and Illegal Corporate Payments and Practices*, Washington, D.C., May 1976. (Hereafter referred to as SEC Report.)

3. Securities Act Release No. 4936 (December 9, 1968).

4. This number includes Lockheed Corporation, which is excluded from SEC's voluntary disclosure list because information was obtained from Lockheed by court order rather than voluntarily.

5. Both the SEC list and our supplementary list of reporting companies appear in appendixes to this chapter.

6. *The Wall Street Journal*, July 9, 1976. The SEC report also makes the point that some 9,000 companies file information on their activities every year.

7. About ninety countries are eligible for U.S. military purchases, with limitations in some cases on their degree of sophistication (*The New York Times*, April 15, 1975).

8. *The New York Times*, May 9, 1975.

9. U.S. Congress, Senate, Foreign Relations Committee, Subcommittee on Multinational Corporations, *Hearings*, Washington, D.C., May-September, 1975, p. 128. (Hereafter referred to as Senate Hearings.) Senator Church is chairman of this subcommittee.

10. *The New York Times*, August 11, 1975.

11. "Lockheed's Defiance: A Right to Bribe?" *Time*, August 18, 1975, pp. 66-67. This was subsequently denied by D.J. Haughton, Lockheed official; see Senate Hearings, p. 346.

12. *The Wall Street Journal*, November 17, 1975. See also Senate Hearings, pp. 362, 375-76.

13. Senate Hearings, p. 347. At the 5 percent rate a commission of $45 million is due on $900 million in sales.

14. *The Wall Street Journal*, October 14, 1975.

15. Senate Hearings, p. 382. See also statement of McDonnell Douglas executive in *St. Louis Post-Dispatch*, April 27, 1976. Middle Eastern government officials retaliated by claiming that they were following U.S. customs, and the Shah of Iran immediately moved to outlaw the practice (*The New York Times*, September 9, 1975).

16. Japan cancelled its $1.3 billion order for 100 Lockheed P-3C Orion antisubmarine airplanes, worth $13 million each (*The New York Times*, February 11, 1976). The Canadian order was for $750-$950 million of the Orion planes (*The Wall Street Journal*, March 2, May 20, and July 22, 1976).

17. Such economic sanction against the corporation is recommended in our reform proposal only in the case of recidivism. Lockheed is a good example of how difficult it is to implement a boycott in real life. Such dependence on Lockheed can be illustrated by a list of Lockheed's foreign military sales (FMS) contracts from 1968 to 1973 (Senate Hearings, p. 366). The following countries use Lockheed products: Taiwan, Turkey, Greece, Norway, Denmark, Germany, Belgium, Italy, Netherlands, Japan, and Jordan.

18. It was reported that Lockheed repaid $35 million on its loan in two months (*The Wall Street Journal*, June 25, 1976).

19. *The Wall Street Journal*, August 6, 1976. See also *Parade* magazine, May 23, 1976, wherein Haughton insists that he had done nothing wrong.

20. *The Wall Street Journal*, March 10, 1976.

21. *The New York Times* (news service), March 4, 1976.

22. *St. Louis Post-Dispatch*, September 15, 1976.

23. Cf. *International Herald Tribune* (Paris), September 2, 1976.

24. Senate Hearings, p. 2.

25. "Lifting the Lid on Some Mysterious Money," *Time*, June 23, 1975, p. 50.

26. *The New York Times*, June 6, 1975.

27. Senate Hearings, pp. 157-64, testimony of Thomas V. Jones, president and chairman of the Northrop board, before Senator Clifford Case.

28. *The New York Times*, June 7 and July 1, 1975.

29. Both President Jones and Vice President James Allen agreed to make restitution for the amount of domestic political contributions in which they had been involved. Jones was indicted for this activity and paid a $5,000 fine to settle the case. There were no indictments involving international payoffs.

30. Cf. Larry B. Godwin, "CPA and User Opinions on Increased Corporate Disclosure," *CPA*, July 1975, pp. 31-33.

31. Yerachmiel Kugel and Gladys W. Gruenberg, "Attitude of Multinational Firms Toward Overseas Investment," paper presented at meeting of Academy of International Business, Dallas, Texas, December 28-30, 1975. See also *The New York Times*, October 16, 1976.

32. "Howard Blauvelt Looks Ahead," *CONOCO '75*, December 1975, p. 6. Reprinted with permission.

33. Securities and Exchange Commission, *Report of the Special Review Committee of the Board of Directors of Gulf Oil Corporation*, Washington, D.C., December 30, 1975. (Hereafter referred to as Gulf Report.) An interesting account of Gulf activities based on this report appears in *Fortune*, June 1976, pp. 121-24, 206-10. Chelsea House Publishers in New York also published the report in paperback as "The Great Oil Spill."

34. Gulf Report, p. 100. This illustrates the link between bribery and extortion made in Chapter 2.

35. Gulf Report, Appendix D.

36. Gulf Report, p. 53. The report itself is not too clear on the source or destination of these funds. Apparently, even the special review committee had trouble determining what happened.

37. Gulf Report, p. 103.

38. Gulf Report, p. 105.

39. Gulf Report, p. 128.

40. Gulf Report, p. 106.

41. Gulf Report, p. 160.

42. Gulf Report, p. 146.

43. Gulf Report, p. 121.

44. Gulf Report, p. 216.

45. Gulf Report, p. 279.

46. *The Wall Street Journal*, March 22, 1976.

47. Gulf Report, p. 258.

48. Gulf Report, p. 265.

49. *The Wall Street Journal*, September 30, 1976.

50. Ibid.

51. Senate Hearings, pp. 242, 246.

52. Senate Hearings, p. 275.

53. Gulf Report, pp. 128-129.

54. Gulf Report, p. 132.

55. Gulf Report, p. 126, footnote **.

56. Gulf Report, p. 297.

57. Senate Hearings, pp. 245-246, testimony of Exxon controller, Archie L. Moore.

58. "Banana Bribes," *The Economist*, April 19, 1975, p. 32.

59. "The Great Banana Bribe," *Newsweek*, April 21, 1975, pp. 76, 81.

60. *The New York Times* (news service), April 10, 1975.

61. *The Wall Street Journal*, April 9, 1975.

62. An allegation was made that the payment was channeled through a former Honduran economic minister, but no proof was offered.

63. *The Wall Street Journal*, April 9, 1975.

64. *The Wall Street Journal*, January 12, 1976.

65. *The Wall Street Journal*, March 19, 1976.

66. *The Wall Street Journal*, August 5, 1976.

67. *The New York Times*, April 23, 1976.

68. *The Wall Street Journal*, March 10, 1976.

Appendix 4A
Companies Making Payment Disclosures, April 21, 1976

The following is a list of companies making payment disclosures (both domestic and foreign) to SEC as of April 21, 1976:

1. Abbott Laboratories
2. Allergan Pharmaceuticals
3. American Airlines
4. American Cynamid Co.
5. American Home Products

6. American Ship Building Co.*
7. American Standard, Inc.
8. AMF
9. American T&T Co.
10. Ashland Oil, Inc.*

11. Baxter Labs.
12. Boeing Co.
13. Braniff International
14. Bristol Myers Co.
15. Browning-Ferris Industries

16. Burroughs Corp.
17. Butler National
18. Carnation
19. Carrier Corp.
20. Castle & Cooke

21. Celanese Corp.
22. Cerro Corp.
23. Cities Services
24. Coastal States Gas
25. Coherent Radiation

26. Colgate-Palmolive Co.
27. Combanks
28. Cook Industries
29. Cook United, Inc.
30. Core Laboratories, Inc.

31. Del Monte
32. Diamond International
33. Diversified Industries
34. Dresser Industries
35. Electronic Associates

36. Exxon
37. Fairchild Industries
38. Gardner-Denver Co.
39. General T&E Corp.
40. General Tire & Rubber Co.

41. B.F. Goodrich
42. Goodyear Tire & Rubber Co.
43. Gulf Oil Corp.*
44. Harrah's
45. Honeywell

46. Hospital Corp. of America
47. Ingersoll-Rand Co.
48. Intercontinental Diversified
49. International T&T
50. Johnson and Johnson

51. Koppers Co., Inc.
52. Kraftco Corp.
53. Levi Strauss
54. McDonnell Douglas
55. Mercantile Bancorporation, Inc.

56. Merck & Co.
57. Minnesota M&M Co.*
58. Missouri Public Service Co.
59. NCR Corp.
60. Northrop Corporation*

*Listed in Exhibit B of the SEC report.

61. Northwest Industries, Inc.
62. Offshore Co.
63. Ogden Corp.
64. Otis Elevator
65. Pacific Vegetable Oil
66. Pfizer, Inc.
67. Phillips Petroleum Co.*
68. Public Service Co. of New Mexico
69. Pullman, Inc.
70. Republic Corp.
71. Richardson-Merrill, Inc.
72. Rockwell International
73. Rohm & Haas Co.
74. Rollins, Inc.
75. Sanders Associates
76. Sante Fe International
77. Schering-Plough Corp.
78. Searle & Co.

79. Security New York Corp.
80. Singer Co.
81. Smith International
82. Southern Bell T&T Co.
83. Standard Oil of Indiana
84. Stanley Home Products, Inc.
85. Sterling Drug
86. Sybron Corp.
87. Tenneco, Inc.
88. UOP, Inc.
89. United Brands
90. United Technologies
91. Upjohn Co.
92. Warner Lambert Co.
93. Westinghouse Elec. Corp.
94. White Consolidated Industries
95. Whitaker Corp.

Source: U.S. Congress, Senate, Committee on Banking, Housing and Urban Affairs, *Report of the Securities and Exchange Commission on Questionable and Illegal Corporate Payments and Practices*, Washington, D.C., May 1976, Exhibits A and B.

*Listed in Exhibit B of the SEC report.

Appendix 4B
Companies Making Payment Disclosures, April 21 to August 29, 1976

The following is a list of companies making payment disclosures (both domestic and foreign) to SEC between April 21 and August 29, 1976:

1. A-T-O, Inc.
2. Alcoa
3. Alcon Labs.
4. Allied Chemical Corp.
5. Ansul

6. Armour & Co.
7. Atlantic Richfield
8. Benguet Consolidated, Inc.
9. Burlington Industries
10. Burndy Co.

11. City Investing Co.
12. Cleveland Harris
13. Clark Equipment Co.
14. Curtiss Wright
15. Dart Industries

16. Dynaloctron
17. Emersons
18. Firestone
19. General Electric
20. General Foods

22. Hercules, Inc.
23. IBM
24. LTV Corp.
25. Loews Corp.

26. MGM
27. Mobil
28. Overseas National
29. Pacific Shipping Lines
30. Penney

31. Ralston Purina
32. Raytheon
33. Reeves Bros.
34. Reynolds Metals Co.
35. Scott Paper Co.

36. Signode Corp.
37. Sperry Rand Corp.
38. Squibb Corp.
39. Twentieth Century-Fox
40. Woolworth Co.

41. Xerox Corp.

Source: Compiled from *The Wall Street Journal*, April 21 to August 29, 1976.

5 Payoffs in the Context of Social Responsibility: Society, Business, and the Individual Executive

Practical life is occupied—to put it summarily—with two concerns, the adoption of ends, the selection of means. All the issues between wisdom and folly, or between right and wrong, can be put in these terms: what goods do you seek? what means do you use in obtaining them?

—William E. Hocking[1]

When we initially conceived the idea of writing this book on international payoffs, we had no intention of going beyond the factual surface, thereby letting each executive faced with decision making in this connection make up his own mind about the morality or immorality of his actions. However, as we delved deeper into the subject, it became clear that a dilemma exists and is caused by the intermingling of the roles of society, the business firm, and the individual executive. The emotion evoked by the debate on international payoffs results primarily from confusion relating to whose goals international payoffs serve. If international payoffs are immoral, who is immoral? Business, individuals who work for business, or the society that permits its citizens to act immorally?

Discussion of the propriety of international payoffs inevitably must turn to the larger question of business social responsibility and how business goals and societal goals interact. Is the individual executive caught in the middle? Does his success as a businessman clash with his responsibilities to society at large and with his conscience? It is becoming clear that the social environment of the business firm and the ethical standards of the individual executive who manages that firm are all bound up together.

There are two major schools of thought on crime and its control. One blames the criminals and advocates severe penalties for criminal acts. The other blames society for creating the conditions that "push" certain members of society to commit crimes. This latter school advocates, therefore, light penalties on the individual criminal and extensive efforts to improve society by eliminating conditions that generate crime.

Similarly, in relation to international payoffs, some blame both the payers and the payees and thus advocate strong measures against them. Others blame the competitive environment (arguments like "everybody does it," and "it is part of the business game") and therefore reject all legislation to control international payoffs.

The authors subscribe to neither extreme. Rather we believe that both society and the individual perpetrators of payoffs are to blame. Below we explore this belief by discussing the roles of society and business in international payoffs, and in Chapter 7 we propose measures to expose and control improper payments in view of such roles.

Society and International Payoffs

People, like other living organisms, are influenced by the environment in which they operate. The environment can either restrict or enhance the individual person's opportunity to act out self-interest. The government's role is to foster the creation of an environment that is conducive to optimal attainment of individual goals.

Government resorts to legislation that prohibits actions of others from infringing on the right to pursue individual goals. But government can also use moral suasion and leadership to influence individuals to promote and work for the common good. Both legal deterrence and individual voluntary compliance are necessary to insure adherence to and respect for the law of the land and to promote an environment conducive to the attainment of such goals.

How is it then that government officials elected to preserve the Constitution and protect individual rights have allowed international payoffs to go unchecked for so long? Why is the government's ability to control them even now, at best, questionable?[2]

Where Has Moral Leadership Gone?

The explanation for such apparent helplessness with regard to the control of international payoffs is that many government officials have abdicated their leadership function in the area of moral conduct. It is ironic that today leadership seems to be operating in reverse. It is coming from grass-roots movements like Common Cause and various public interest groups in an attempt to restore integrity in government at the very time when the citizens' trust in their leadership is at a low ebb.

For instance, it may be merely a matter of time before the public recognizes the hypocrisy of punishing business for illegally contributing (through its political slush funds) to politicians, while allowing the politicians, the beneficiaries of such illegal activities, to get off scott-free. The Senate ethics committee during its nine years of existence has a perfect record of never having carried out a formal investigation of any member of Congress, in spite of repeated complaints filed by Common Cause, a public affairs lobby. According to John W. Gardner, the chairman of Common Cause, "The committee is the worst kind of sham, giving the appearance of serving as policeman while extending a marvelous protective shield over members of Congress."[3] A recent survey of

American attitude on the most necessary attributes of today's leaders lists moral integrity, courage, and common sense as the three most important characteristics of leadership.[4]

The U.S. public, as political surveys of the 1976 primaries repeatedly show, values moral integrity. It is, relatively speaking, an informed public, although it takes time in a democracy for the people eventually to get the truth and to generate the necessary implications from it.

Legal Deterrence–Government's Social Responsibility

How then is society to make certain that its institutions serve societal goals? As we have seen, the elected government sets the tone and example for moral conduct within society. Government officials deemed unworthy of the people's trust ideally are replaced by others who can generate the conduct desired by society.

Also, the government effectively enforces compliance with majority rule by subjecting *individuals* (real people, *not institutions*, since the latter often take on characteristics of autonomy and nongovernability) who deviate from the rules to a range of punishments prescribed by society's legal code.

For now, we examine the law as a societal moral phenomenon; how these societal guidelines apply to international payoffs in a legal sense is discussed more fully in Chapter 7.

International payoffs are perceived by individual executives who carry them out as a means of accomplishing business goals. Success of the enterprise seems to hinge on whether or not such payments are made. Their knowledge of rights and responsibilities is so colored by self-interest (their own as well as that of the firm) that they become blind to the consequences of their actions. International payoffs become but another symptom of the breakdown of law and order. They symbolize economic license ultimately justifying the type of anarchy that has been characterized as "economic Darwinism."[5]

For the debate on international payoffs to be fruitful from a societal point of view, individuals (*not* institutions) must be held accountable to societal demands. The debate on international payoffs misses the point by concentrating on business morality and business responsibility to society. The reasoning behind this statement is three-fold:

1. Individuals *not* institutions violate the law.
2. By allowing individuals to violate society's laws in behalf of their institutions, government encourages the creation of multiple and often contradictory legal subsystems within society.
3. Within an individualistic society, individually oriented actions that significantly influence individual self-interest are more effective in generating compliance with society's majority rule.

Only individual persons can be moral or immoral; business firms are not real persons and hence cannot be moral or immoral. Actions attributed to business firms are performed by individuals. It is these individuals who must be considered personally liable for whatever business firms are accused of doing.

Business and International Payoffs

So far we seem to have absolved business from responsibility for wrongdoing by redirecting societal accusations of business to the individuals who work for business. But as our subsequent discussion of business goals shows, there is wide disagreement on this subject. Chapter 7 sets forth our view.

In order to form a judgment about business behavior, it is necessary to understand business goals since they shape the moral climate within which decision making takes place. How business goals are related to international payoffs can be demonstrated by examining the debate on social responsibility that surfaced in the 1960s in connection with environmental and discrimination issues.

The attitude of the business firm toward such social issues gives a clue as to what its attitude is on international payoffs, since the business firm that accepts what has been called its social responsibility deliberately creates the moral climate within which international payoffs cannot endure.

Since the 1960s a considerable body of literature has appeared that may be characterized as a "debate" concerning the social responsibility of business. On one side are those who uphold the classical tradition that profits are business' sole responsibility; on the other are those who stress commitment to public purpose as an important ingredient of business conduct.

Relying on Adam Smith's "invisible hand" and "self-interest" regulators,[6] Milton Friedman denounces social responsibility as a "fundamentally subversive doctrine"[7] and encourages businessmen to put high priority on profit making in the interest of preserving the free enterprise system.

Nowhere in the classic economic model is there room for social responsibility at the expense of the stockholder. Most economics texts apply the classical cost-benefit approach to public policy considerations whereby business is forced to obey its "public" interest only by somehow suffering a diminution of "self" interest.

In this atmosphere of challenge, the so-called social responsibility laws relating to environment and safety have been passed in the last decade to "force" business to do what most citizens feel should have been done without such prodding. Legislation ranging from nondiscriminatory hiring policies to environmental protection ushered in ever more intense pressures for business responsiveness to societal needs. Hostile business reactions have surfaced. The conclusion is inescapable: Either the American business community is incapable of accommodating social needs, given competitive pressures, or it does not wish to accommodate them for fear of transforming itself into a social rather than an economic institution. Resolution of this dilemma is not an easy task.

The literature of social responsibility has centered on the importance of commitment to public purpose as inherent in the goal of self-interest. Before reviewing selected spokesmen for both the classical notion of self-interest and the contemporary notion of business commitment to social needs, social responsibility must be defined and related to the specific topic of this book, namely, international payoffs.

Social Responsibility and International Payoffs

Dow Votaw defines *social responsibility* as follows:

The term is a brilliant one; it means something, but not always the same thing, to everybody. To some it conveys the idea of legal responsibility or liability; to others it means socially responsible *behavior* in an ethical sense; to still others the meaning transmitted is that of "responsible for," in a causal mode; many simply equate it with "charitable contributions," some take it to mean socially "conscious" or "aware"; many of those who embrace it most fervently see it as a mere synonym for "legitimacy," in the context of "longing," of being proper or valid; a few see it as a sort of fiduciary duty imposing higher standards of behavior on businessmen than on citizens at large. Even the antonyms, socially "irresponsible" and "nonresponsible," are subject to multiple interpretations.[8]

What is important in the above definition is that international payoffs (which relate to the question of ethical, legal, or legitimate business behavior) have now become part of the decade-long debate on social responsibility. Thus, drawing on the literature of social responsibility serves to clarify the relative merits of socially versus economically oriented business goals and generates insights into the problem of international payoffs.

To arrive at another definition of social responsibility, we can examine the types of social problems that occupy various activist groups since, as is shown below, they are concerned with business honesty and integrity. A recent survey of 200 social activists conducted by Opinion Research Corporation resulted in the following responses to the question about which problems large companies should work on especially hard:

58%, discrimination against minorities
54%, using up natural resources
45%, air pollution
43%, *dishonest business practices.*[9]

Other problems cited in descending order of importance are:

problems with cities
water pollution
having a satisfying job
inflation (cost of living)
litter and solid waste
corruption in government (12%)
problems of the poor
racial difficulties
slum and urban ghettos
quality of education
electric power shortage
invasion of privacy
respect of the U.S. in other countries (6%)
shortage of gasoline and oil
drug addiction
rising cost of food
problems of the elderly
welfare abuse
juvenile delinquency
crime and violence.[10]

From the above list, it is clear that payoffs—which may be perceived as dishonest business behavior—are an important part of this all-inclusive concept of social responsibility. The list provides agenda for action for the socially oriented corporations.

Our contention, which is developed in more detail in later chapters, is that social responsibility or international payoffs represent facets of the same basic question, namely, what ethical standards of conduct are expected of the business community and what is the basis for those standards? Social responsibility is one extreme of that broad spectrum of conduct; international payoffs are the other extreme. The business manager who puts the firm's self-interest or profit-maximization goals ahead of his own ethical standards is likely to reject social responsibility as being outside the framework of the legitimate activities of the firm and to embrace international payoffs as a legitimate method of promoting the profit goal. One of our correspondents in a speech on international payoffs stated: "The fact is that without ethics, there can be no social responsibility."[11]

Inherent in the problem of international payoffs are the same questions that have been raised in connection with business social responsibility in general. Should business be concerned with social problems (such as those cited by social activists) at the expense of profit maximization? Should the conduct of a corporation be ethical and moral while that of its competitors is barely legal? To put the debate in its proper perspective, arguments for and against business social responsibility are summarized below.

Business Goals (The Debate on Social Responsibility)

Rejection of Social Responsibility. Under a system of free enterprise, classical economists reject the notion of business social responsibility. According to Fredrick A. Hayek, for example, business managers should devote themselves "to the single task of employing the capital of their stockholders in the most profitable manner."[12] Hayek also contends that the extension of powers of corporate management over cultural, political, and moral issues increases the threat of government intervention.[13]

Similarly, Milton Friedman states:

There is one and only one social responsibility of business, to use its resources and engage in activities designed to increase its profits so long as it stays within the rules of the game, which is to say, engage in open and free competition without deception or fraud.[14]

It is interesting to note that Friedman's notion of self-interest includes "competition without deception or fraud." However, one of the problems that this book addresses is whether the self-interest doctrine is compatible with "competition without deception or fraud."

Another view against business social responsibility is advanced by Theodore Levitt. He states:

Indeed, as the profit motive becomes increasingly sublimated, capitalism will become only a shadow—the torpid remains of the creative dynamism which was and might have been.

Welfare and society are not the corporation's business. Its business is making money, not sweet music.[15]

Echoing Levitt's concern that business dedication to social responsibility may undermine the foundation of capitalism, Joseph McGuire highlights the incompatibility between the classicist's self-interest doctrine and the modern view of social responsibility. He argues vividly:

Do the actions that we intend to undertake improve the reality of competition? Do they strengthen the motive of self-interest? Do they make the system more just or more efficient? We cannot simultaneously demand that the system become ever more merciful, more egalitarian, more moral and more secure. Thus, we cannot continue to have legislation to price goods "fairly" out of sympathy for those producers who otherwise would fail (assuming, of course, that there is competition); or to have high tariffs to protect some industries from efficient foreign companies . . . or at least we cannot do all these and similar things and expect to remain capitalistic.[16]

It is important to note, however, that, although McGuire views "tinkering with the controls" as harmful to competition and economic efficiency, he does not specifically object to the doctrine of social responsibility. Rather, he points out that, *if* Americans wish to develop a more perfect system, they will have to create an alternative economic system "for which there is no model."[17]

Support for Social Responsibility. In connection with the limitations of laissez-faire capitalism, Adolf Berle, in a 1964 symposium for business executives, stated:

It is true . . . that maximizing profits for the shareholders is a major job of management; another of its jobs is maintaining institutions capable of making profits.[18]

George Steiner points out more specific limitations of the classical self-interest model:

1. It overstates the trend and ultimate magnitude of business' voluntary assumption of social responsibility;
2. It asks corporations to ignore society's demands, which is something they simply cannot do.[19]

Another view in support of business social responsibility is advanced by Dow Votaw, who states:

Growing both in size and persuasiveness is a body of evidence which compels the businessman seriously to consider the possibility that social responsibility is more than an expedient response to temporary conditions. . . . If it cannot adapt itself to its new less central, but nonetheless important role in society, it will find itself replaced by other institutions, and society may also be the loser.[20]

Similarly, the Committee for Economic Development, a private business-oriented research group, states:

. . . it is in the "enlightened self-interest" of corporations to promote the public welfare in a positive way.[21]

There is a growing body of literature in the field of business behavior that challenges the traditional profit-oriented economic model of the business firm and warns of the dire consequences of failure to adapt to public demands.[22]

Assessment of the Debate on Social Responsibility

What are then the goals of business? This question must be settled before the discussion on business means to achieve its goals is undertaken. As is usually the case with squared-off sides in an economic dispute, the hen-egg argument of which comes first—business profits or social responsibility—seems a fruitless exercise in semantics. Yet, for our purposes, the discussion highlights drawbacks and benefits that warrant the following conclusions:

Limitations of the Debate. 1. Business pays lip service to social responsibility. It often considers more important what people *think* business is doing for society than what business is *actually* doing for society. Thus, the public-relations aspect of social responsibility is emphasized often at the expense of real efforts of business in behalf of society. Joseph McGuire puts it succinctly when he states: "Businessmen continue to profit as hungrily as ever, but now they have better table manners."[23]

2. Competitive constraints are the real determinants of business orientation toward its social role, not the public relations department. In other words, whether business *can* in the short run contribute resources toward society's needs depends on whether it can *afford* to invest these resources in anticipation of long-run benefits.

3. Business has been warned by social activists that ignoring society's needs may result in government regulation of business and the demise of the free enterprise system. Although many business firms did not heed this advice, they did *not* face the penalties projected by the critics. In fact, during the last decade business remained as strong and powerful as ever. Furthermore, some business firms even opted to break the law in the realization that the projected profits from such action exceed the projected costs of penalties.

The debate on social responsibility has had little effect on business behavior because it assumes ideological rather than competitive differences in business response to society's needs. The discussion has been, by and large, misfocused and sterile since it deals with business morality rather than individual morality and suggests penalties for business institutions that break the law rather than for individuals who in fact break the law.

Yet the discussion on social responsibility has some benefits.

Benefits of the Debate. 1. It improves communication between business and society by identifying areas for business-harmonizing policies.[24] An example of such policy is pollution control wherein business invests *both* to meet society's needs *and* to increase its own profits in the long run.

2. It allows individuals who work for business to compare their own goals with societal and business goals.

3. It allows business to reevaluate its goals and the means to achieve them vis-à-vis societal goals and means.

Our conclusion is that business, as an economic institution in society, has primarily an economic goal to achieve. Individuals working for business have moral goals as well. Furthermore, for business to carry out its economic function in society effectively, it cannot in the long run ignore society's needs, since meeting these needs and transforming them into a profitable investment is the prime function of business. In the long run such transformation is a prerequisite for business survival.

Business social responsibility, like that of any member of society, is to adhere to the letter of the law. This social responsibility must be enforced in the strictest possible way. To adhere to the spirit of the law and work for the common good is in the long-run interest of business itself. It is not business' social responsibility.

Business Moral Climate

Once business determines its degree of commitment to social responsibility, it is in a position to set the corresponding moral tone for its employees. Some business executives suggest that a good place to start improving business moral climate is to establish realistic sales and profit goals. (For more on this point, see Chapter 7.) Setting such goals, however, can itself present variations in business moral climate. In his analysis of ethics in business, Theodore V. Purcell, S.J., points out that there is no way to differentiate between the executive as a private individual and as a corporate manager. He proposes that the following levels of ethical principles be applied to business decisions in the same way as they are applied to every other human action:

1. General ethical principle: Do good and avoid evil.
2. Applied ethical principles: Power requires responsibility. The good effect must outweigh the bad effect. A good end does not justify a bad means.[25]

He concludes that general acceptance of such principles creates a climate that reduces decision making to a consideration of the facts in specific cases, a much easier moral task for a pragmatic business executive.

This pragmatic approach is illustrated by the analysis of H. Gordon Fitch, who divides business social responsibility into the following classifications:[26]

1. Humanitarian-sentimental, which seeks to prevent all human suffering and enhance the quality of life.
2. Utilitarian, which views decisions from the cost-benefit approach;
3. Dysfunctional, which seeks to avoid threats to survival.

Fitch chooses the utilitarian principle as the most advantageous to the corporation's long-run self-interest and insists that business behavior is and should be pragmatic.

Whatever choice top management makes, however, determines the moral climate within which the individual executive must function and make decisions. Top management can be assisted in this task of assessing the company's moral climate and determining the moral goals by two models of corporate value systems that have been devised by Robert Hay and Edmund R. Gray and by S. Prakash Sethi.

In their study on the social responsibilities of business managers, Hay and Gray separate value systems and styles into three phases, which they consider historical development, but which can be used to illustrate levels of business moral climate today:[27]

1. The profit maximizer;
2. The trustee manager;
3. The quality-of-life advocate.

Their analysis includes economic, technological, social, political, environmental, and aesthetic values. The relative power that top management gives to each of these roles can determine the level of moral climate within the company. Table 5-1 reproduces this comparison.

S. Prakash Sethi classifies social responsibility criteria into a somewhat similar three-pronged schema:[28]

1. Proscriptive, which reacts only to short-run obligations, primarily legal in nature;
2. Prescriptive, which reacts to long-run considerations and revises norms of conduct over time;
3. Anticipatory and preventive, which assumes moral leadership.

His table is also reproduced here for comparison purposes, as Table 5-2. Sethi's schema has aided us in developing our professional guidelines for the business-man in Table 6-1 in the next chapter, wherein we delineate the criteria for decision making in international payoffs.

The Individual and International Payoffs

Just as the business firm is influenced by the moral climate of society, the individual executive is influenced by the moral climate within the business. The company's moral climate is the result of attitudes of top management toward social responsibility. While individual executives carry out moral or immoral corporate activities, policies of top management set the moral tone for the operations of subordinates and hence affect their ethical decisions.

Thus, the individual executive decides whether to engage in international payoffs or not. This decision is based on his perception of a three-tiered value system that starts with society (its legal deterrents and moral leadership) and then moves to the business firm (its attitude toward social responsibility leading

Table 5-1

Comparison of Managerial Values

Phase I Profit Maximizing Management	Phase II Trusteeship Management	Phase III Quality-of-Life Management
	Economic Values	
Raw self-interest.	Self-interest. Contributors' interest.	Enlightened self-interest. Contributors' interests. Society's interests.
What's good for me is good for my country.	What's good for GM is good for our country.	What is good for society is good for our company.
Profit maximizer.	Profit satisfier.	Profit is necessary, but . . . .
Money and wealth are most important.	Money is important, but so are people.	People are more important than money.
Let the buyer beware (caveat emptor).	Let us not cheat the customer.	Let the seller beware (caveat venditor).
Labor is a commodity to be bought and sold.	Labor has certain rights which must be recognized.	Employee dignity has to be satisfied.
Accountability of management is to the owners.	Accountability of management is to the owners, customers, employees, suppliers, and other contributors.	Accountability of management is to the owners, contributors, and society.
	Technology Values	
Technology is very important.	Technology is important but so are people.	People are more important than technology.
	Social Values	
Employee personal problems must be left at home.	We recognize that employees have needs beyond their economic needs.	We hire the whole man.
I am a rugged individualist, and I will manage my business as I please.	I am an individualist, but I recognize the value of group participation.	Group participation is fundamental to our success.
Minority groups are inferior to whites. They must be treated accordingly.	Minority groups have their place in society, and their place is inferior to mine.	Minority group members are people as you and I are.
	Political Values	
That government is best which governs least.	Government is a necessary evil.	Business and government must cooperate to solve society's problems.
	Environmental Values	
The natural environment controls the destiny of man.	Man can control and manipulate the environment.	We must preserve the environment in order to lead a quality life.
	Aesthetic Values	
Aesthetic values? What are they?	Aesthetic values are okay but not for us.	We must preserve our aesthetic values, and we will do our part.

Source: Robert Hay and Edmund R. Gray, "Social Responsibilities of Business Managers," *Academy of Management Journal*, March 1974, p. 142. Reprinted with permission.

Table 5-2
A Three-State Schema for Classifying Corporate Behavior

Dimensions of Behavior	State One: Social Obligation Prospective	State Two: Social Responsibility Prescriptive	State Three: Social Responsiveness Anticipatory and Preventive
Search for legitimacy	Confines legitimacy to legal and economic criteria only; does not violate laws; equates profitable operations with fulfilling social expectations.	Accepts the reality of limited relevance of legal and market criteria of legitimacy in actual practice. Willing to consider and accept broader, extralegal and extramarket criteria for measuring corporate performance and social role.	Accepts its role as defined by the social system and therefore subject to change; recognizes importance of profitable operations but includes other criteria.
Ethical norms	Considers business value-neutral; managers expected to behave according to their own ethical standards.	Defines norms in community related terms, i.e., good corporate citizen. Avoids taking moral stand on issues which may harm its economic interests or go against prevailing social norms (majority views).	Takes definite stand on issues of public concern; advocates institutional ethical norms even though they may be detrimental to its immediate economic interest or prevailing social norms.
Social accountability for corporate actions	Construes narrowly as limited to stockholders; jealously guards its prerogatives against outsiders.	Construes narrowly for legal purposes, but broadened to include groups affected by its actions; management more outward looking.	Willing to account for its actions to other groups, even those not directly affected by its actions.
Operating strategy	Exploitative and defensive adaptation. Maximum externalization of costs.	Reactive adaptation. Where identifiable previously externalize external costs. Maintain current standards of physical and social environment. Compensate victims of pollution and other corporate related activities even in the absence of clearly established legal grounds. Develop industry-wide standards.	Proactive adaptation. Takes lead in developing and adapting new technology for environmental protectors. Evaluates side effects of corporate actions and eliminates them prior to the action's being taken. Anticipates future social changes and develops internal structures to cope with them.

Table 5-2 (cont.)

Dimensions of Behavior	State One: Social Obligation Proscriptive	State Two: Social Responsibility Prescriptive	State Three: Social Responsiveness Anticipatory and Preventive
Response to social pressures	Maintains low public profile but if attacked, uses PR methods to upgrade its public image; denies any deficiencies; blames public dissatisfaction on ignorance or failure to understand corporate functions; discloses information only where legally required.	Accepts responsibility for solving current problems; will admit deficiencies in former practices and attempt to persuade public that its current practices meet social norms; attitude toward critics conciliatory; freer information disclosures than state one.	Willingly discusses activities with outside groups; makes information freely available to public; accepts formal and informal inputs from outside groups in decision making. Is willing to be publicly evaluated for its various activities.
Activities pertaining to governmental actions	Strongly resists any regulation of its activities except when it needs help to protect its market position; avoids contact; resists any demands for information beyond that legally required.	Preserves management discretion in corporate decisions, but cooperates with government in research to improve industry-wide standards; participates in political processes and encourages employees to do likewise.	Openly communicates with government; assists in enforcing existing laws and developing evaluations of business practices; objects publicly to governmental activities that it feels are detrimental to the public good.
Legislative and political activities	Seeks to maintain status quo; actively opposes laws that would internalize any previously externalized costs; seeks to keep lobbying activities secret.	Willing to work with outside groups for good environmental laws; concedes need for change in some status quo laws; less secrecy in lobbying than state one.	Avoids meddling in politics and does not pursue special-interest laws; assists legislative bodies in developing better laws where relevant; promotes honesty and openness in government and in its own lobbying activities.
Philanthropy	Contributes only when direct benefit to it clearly shown; otherwise, views contributions as responsibility of individual employees.	Contributes to noncontroversial and established causes; matches employee contributions.	Activities of state two, *plus* support and contributions to new, controversial groups whose needs it sees as unfulfilled and increasingly important.

Source: S. Prakash Sethi, "Dimensions of Corporate Social Performance," *California Management Review*, Spring 1975, p. 63. Reprinted with permission.

to its moral climate) and finally to the individual himself (his own value system). With this understanding, we are now in a position to discuss guidelines for decision making in Chapter 6.

Notes

1. William E. Hocking, *Types of Philosophy* (New York: Charles Scribner's Sons, 1959), p. 200.

2. Compare the statements of Presidential Task Force Chairman Elliot Richardson and SEC Chairman Roderick Hills (*The Wall Street Journal*, June 23, 1976).

3. "Common Cause and 45 Representatives Petition the House to Investigate Sikes for Conflict of Interest," *The New York Times*, April 8, 1976, p. 13.

4. Cf. "Who Runs America—Annual Survey," *U.S. News & World Report*, April 19, 1976, p. 29.

5. Leo C. Brown, S.J., "Marxism," *New Catholic Encyclopedia* (New York: McGraw-Hill, 1967), v. IX, p. 335.

6. Adam Smith, *Wealth of Nations*, 1776 (Modern Library edition).

7. Miltion Friedman, *Capitalism and Freedom* (Chicago: University of Chicago Press, 1962), p. 133.

8. Dow Votaw and S. Prakash Sethi, *The Corporate Dilemma: Traditional Values versus Contemporary Problems* (Englewood Cliffs, N.J.: Prentice-Hall, 1973), pp. 11-12. Reprinted with permission.

9. Kenneth Schwartz, "How Social Activists See Business," *Business and Society Review*, Summer 1975, p. 71 (emphasis supplied). Reprinted with permission. In this survey social activists include the following: corporate social-responsibility activists, environmentalists, consumerists, civil rights leaders, church-affiliate activists, labor leaders, and others.

10. Ibid.

11. William Wendel, Carborundum Company, speech to the Chemical Buyers' Group of the Purchasing Management Association, October 16, 1975. Reprinted with permission.

12. Fredrick A. Hayek, "The Corporation in a Democratic Society," in Melvin Anshen and George Bach, eds., *Management and Corporations, 1985* (New York: McGraw-Hill, 1960), pp. 99-100.

13. Ibid., p. 116.

14. Friedman, *Capitalism and Freedom*, p. 133.

15. Theodore Levitt, "The Dangers of Social Responsibility," *Harvard Business Review*, September-October 1958, p. 46. Copyright © 1958 by the President and Fellows of Harvard College; all rights reserved. Reprinted with permission.

16. Joseph W. McGuire, "Perfecting Capitalism—An Economic Dilemma," *Business Horizons*, February 1976, p. 12. Copyright, 1976 by the Foundation for the School of Business at Indiana University. Reprinted with permission.

17. Ibid. McGuire implies that all recent measures to perfect capitalism are incompatible with capitalism. This attitude is often reinforced by Marxists, who applaud the inevitable decline of capitalism. See also remarks of economist Joan Robinson in *The New York Times* (news service), April 4, 1976. This book, on the other hand, in offering proposals to eliminate payoffs, attempts to present measures that are compatible with the capitalistic system.

18. Adolf A. Berle, "Company Social Responsibility—Too Much or Not Enough?" *Conference Board Record*, April 1964, p. 11.

19. George A. Steiner, "Institutionalizing Corporate Social Decisions," *Business Horizons*, December 1975, p. 15. Reprinted with permission.

20. Votaw and Sethi, *The Corporate Dilemma: Traditional Values versus Contemporary Problems*, p. 43. Reprinted with permission.

21. Committee for Economic Development, *Social Responsibilities of Business Corporations*, New York, June 1971, p. 27.

22. See Clarence C. Walton, *Corporate Social Responsibilities* (Belmont, California: Wadsworth Publishing Co., 1967); Malcolm D. Schlusberg, "Corporate Legitimacy and Social Responsibility: The Role of Law," *California Management Review*, Fall 1969, pp. 65-76; Dow Votaw and S. Prakash Sethi, "Do We Need a New Corporate Response to a Changing Social Environment?" Parts I and II, *California Management Review*, Fall 1969, pp. 3-31; and Kenneth J. Arrow, "Social Responsibility and Economic Efficiency," *Public Policy*, Summer 1973, pp. 303-17.

23. McGuire, "Perfecting Capitalism—An Economic Dilemma," p. 8. Copyright, 1976 by the Foundation for the School of Business at Indiana University. Reprinted with permission.

24. For more on harmonizing policies, see Yerachmiel Kugel, "How to Avoid Expropriation," *Academy of Management Proceedings*, August, 1972, pp. 353-56.

25. Theodore V. Purcell, S.J., "A Practical Guide to Ethics in Business," *Business and Society Review*, Spring 1975, pp. 43-50. Copyright 1975 by Warren, Gorham, and Lamont Inc., 210 South Street, Boston, Mass. All rights reserved. Reprinted with permission.

26. H. Gordon Fitch, "Achieving Corporate Social Responsibility," *Academy of Management Review*, January 1976, pp. 38-46.

27. Robert Hay and Edmund R. Gray, "Social Responsibilities of Business Managers," *Academy of Management Journal*, March 1974, pp. 135-43. Reprinted with permission.

28. S. Prakash Sethi, "Dimensions of Corporate Social Performance: An Analytical Framework," *California Management Review*, Spring 1975, pp. 58-64. Reprinted with permission.

6

Criteria and Guidelines for Decision Making

. . . There were no guidelines; after the fact, business is being told, "Oh, my, look what you have done!"

—David James, Arthur Young & Co.[1]

Now that we have explored the nature and mechanics of international payoffs, their rationale, and specific evidence depicting various shades of empirical behavior, it is time to come closer to the bottom line and provide criteria for the determination of the conditions under which the individual business executive should or should not engage in international payoffs.

As discussed in the previous chapter, international payoffs constitute a dilemma for business. The main focus of this dilemma is the conflict between what is proper (ethics) and what is profitable (economics). Furthermore, Chapter 5 emphasized the importance of *individual* rather than business accountability for the rewards or penalties derived from payoffs.

The criteria and guidelines for decision making provided in this chapter are, therefore, individually oriented. These guidelines are designed to allow each executive to tailor his decision on the payoff situation he is facing to his own company and personal environment and values. A series of questions are asked that the executive is forced to answer for himself before arriving at the answers to the final, crucial questions:

1. Shall I make the payoff, or not?
2. If the payoff is unavoidable, how best should it be carried out?

Decision-making Model for International Payoffs

There are four distinct steps to be taken by the executive before a final decision whether or not to make the payoff can be made. These steps are depicted in the decision-making tree in Figure 6-1. (The models shown in the figure are described in Table 6-1.)

Step 1. In the first step the executive determines whether the payment he is asked to make is legal. If, as discussed in Chapter 2, such payment clearly falls within the white area and presents no problem of legality, the executive has no dilemma on making the international payment. If, on the other hand, the

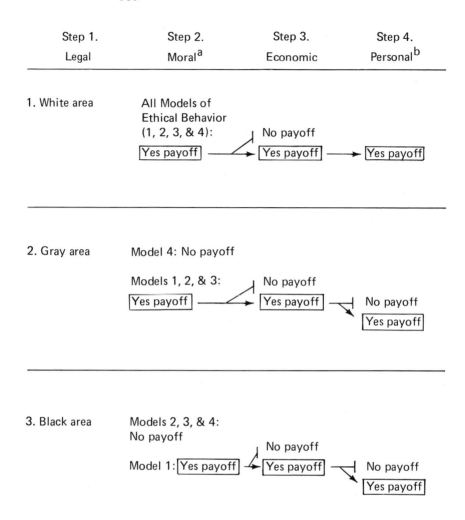

Note: For detailed description of models, see Table 6-1; for discussion of white, gray, and black areas, see Chapter 2.

[a]Business can be characterized by the following moral climate: *Model 1*—No moral consideration; *Model 2*—No moral consideration unless penalty; *Model 3*—Moral only for P-R purposes; and *Model 4*—Morality in toto. Selection of ethical models must be oriented toward future (short and long run) rather than past.

[b]Individuals, although influenced by institutional moral leadership or climate, determine institutional morality not vice versa. Before they decide whether to engage in payoffs, they must consider both personal economic and noneconomic factors that bear on such a decision. For comparison of ethical models for other professions, see Table 6-1.

Figure 6-1. Decision-making Model for International Payoffs.

executive has reservations about the legality of the payment (i.e., it is in the gray or black area), then he must move to the next step of the model.

Step 2. Once the conflict between economics and ethics has been joined, it behooves the executive to consider the matter in the context of the company's moral climate. Thus, the second step of the model deals with the moral climate of the company that constrains the individual executive. If that moral climate does not permit making a payoff classified in the gray or black area, the executive's decision must be to refuse the payoff, and no further consideration of the matter is required. If, on the other hand, the company moral climate is ambivalent enough to permit such payment, the executive should move to the next step of the model.

Step 3. The third step of the model deals with the economic considerations of international payoffs. These include costs of legal counsel, costs and benefits involving the company's public image, and expected direct and indirect costs and benefits to be derived from the proposed payoff. If the benefits of the payoff do not outweigh the costs, the payoff should be refused. If, on the other hand, the benefits outweigh the costs, then from the company's standpoint, the payoff should be made. However, there is still a final step.

Step 4. Individuals are responsible for company decisions; therefore, their own personal cost-benefit and moral calculations must be made before a decision on whether or not to make the payoff can be concluded. The final step of the model deals with the personal considerations involved in making the inter-national payoff.

Let us now take each step at a time, and discuss the types of considerations which the executive encounters as he gets involved in the decision-making process on international payoffs.

Legal Considerations

Most of the investigation concerning payoffs by multinational corporations has been done by two federal bodies: the Securities and Exchange Commission and the Senate Foreign Relations Subcommittee on Multinational Corporations.[2] While there is no law in the U.S. prohibiting payoffs in foreign countries, the SEC is concerned that U.S.-based multinationals are disguising or omitting significant payoffs from records available to stockholders. The Senate Foreign Relations subcommittee is concerned about the magnitude and scope of the payoffs in terms of foreign policy.

Despite the fact that bribery is absolutely prohibited in the United States, it is not a violation of U.S. law if paid to foreign officials. The SEC imposes the

Table 6-1
Models of Ethical Behavior

Classification	Illegal and/or Unethical Model 1	Model 2	Legal and/or Ethical Model 3	Model 4
General	Totally self-interest oriented.	Mainly self-oriented but legal.	Self-interest, P-R morality.	Self-sacrifice; total dedication to common good.
Specific: Moral	No moral consideration.	No moral consideration unless penalty.	Moral only for P-R purposes.	Morality in toto.
Legal	No legal consideration.	Will avoid obeying law unless severe penalty.	Obeys letter of law.	Obeys spirit of law. Initiates legal reform.
Economic	Money the only good—an end in itself.	Money most important goal.	Money important—some social considerations for P-R.	Social considerations paramount—money only means to end.
	Only short-run consideration (immediate gratification).	Mostly short-run considerations.	Some long-run considerations for P-R purposes.	Only long-run considerations (self-gratification postponed).
	Profession viewed only as monetary reward.	Minimum professionalism. Rewards paramount.	Professionalism for P-R purposes.	Total professionalism. Sense of mission.
Stereotyped professions	Prostitutes. Drug pushers.	Sexual surrogates. Gamblers.	Businessmen. Politicians.	Priests. Artists.
Specific professions	Specific models of professionalism			
Professor	Obtained degree by fraud. Dispenses false knowledge. Falsifies research.	Student involvement only when imposed. Lectures merely business. Quantity of research more important than quality.	Student involvement as P-R tool. Research only for personal reward.	Total student involvement. Sense of truth mission. Pure research.
Physician	Performs illegal operations for fee.	Limits practice to wealthy patients. Accepts kickbacks from suppliers.	Accepts poor patients for image purposes. Rejects kickbacks but condones practice.	Healing mission above reward. Rejects even referral fees.

Attorney	Mouthpiece for underworld. Client protection for fee.	Keeps silent. Uses confidentiality as screen. Law avoidance.	Resigns for P-R purposes. Emphasis on letter of law.	Initiates public disclosure. Implements spirit of law.
Journalist	On the take—paid to dispense false information.	Yellow journalism. Publication criterion—what will sell. Accepts all advertising.	Pays lip service to public service. May refuse some crass advertising for P-R purposes.	Sense of mission as public conscience. Truth determines coverage. Refuses advertising in poor taste.
Politician	Spy activities against public interest for foreign power.	Promotes legislation for personal interest.	Looks upon gratuities as good P-R.	Disowns all personal interest. Devotes self to public service.
Business Executive	Engages in secret bribes in violation of law.	Payoffs at all levels of activity if no severe penalty. No code of ethics.	Pays small sums to get things done but image important. Code of ethics for P-R purposes.	No gratuities of any kind. Code of ethics strictly enforced. Disclosure of all activities in public interest.
Accountant	Facilitates bribery.	Remains silent, uses confidentiality as screen.	Resigns for P-R purposes.	Public disclosure in public interest.
Director	Hides information on bribery. Gives false information under investigation.	Believes that business is business, incompatible with social norms.	Meets social norms under pressure.	Anticipates social norms.

Note: The authors acknowledge ideas obtained from Max Lerner, et al., *Saturday Review*, November 1975, and S. Prakash Sethi, *California Management Review*, Spring 1975, which were used in developing this table.

disclosure requirement on corporations to force them to reveal the name of the recipient and the amount involved if it is material. The definition of materiality is subject to question, and even if the company loses the argument, the penalty is usually a symbolic fine that may be minimal compared to the benefit received.

As specified in Regulation S-X of the Securities and Exchange Commission:

The information required with respect to any statement shall be furnished as a minimum requirement to which shall be added such further material information as is necessary to make the required statements . . . not misleading.[3]

Similarly, the Accounting Series Releases of the SEC under the Securities Act of 1933 require the disclosure of the financial statements of material transactions. Furthermore, the independent auditor is held liable for material misstatements or omissions existing in the certified statements accompanying a registration statement.

What shall be disclosed and in what form is closely regulated by accounting principles promulgated by the Financial Accounting Standards Board of the American Institute of Certified Public Accountants, the highest rule-making body within the accounting profession, whose standards are accepted as SEC guidelines.

Postulate C-5 of Accounting Research Study No. 1 specifies ". . . Accounting reports should disclose that which is necessary to make them not misleading."[4] Three concepts of disclosure generally proposed are adequate, fair, and full disclosure. There is no real difference among these concepts if they are used in the proper context. A positive objective is to provide the users of financial statements with significant and relevant information to aid them in making decisions in the best possible way. This implies that information that is not material or relevant be omitted to make the presentations meaningful and understandable. In regard to materiality, "an item should be regarded as material if there is reason to believe that knowledge of it would influence the decisions of an informed investor."[5]

Frequently, comments are made that certain types of information should not be disclosed, not because it is not material, but because it might be useful to the wrong party (i.e., sales volume of a specific product in a specific locale). However, large corporations have a responsibility to investors and the general public to disclose a proper amount of material information even though the reaction to the information may be unfavorable to the corporation.[6]

Applying these principles to international payoffs, John Burton, SEC chief accountant, offers the following common-sense guidelines:[7]

1. Was the payment within the normal corporate accountability system, or was it made in cash or disguised in some fashion?
2. Was the top management of the corporation involved, or was it something that happened unbeknownst to senior management?

3. What is the magnitude of the earnings generated by the line of business that was supported by these payments? How material were they to the total corporate picture?
4. What is the materiality of the assets that would be at risk if such payments came to be known?

The Internal Revenue Service gets involved in international payoffs through its tax-collection responsibility. For example, payments to employees or officials of a foreign country that would be illegal under U.S. laws if made to a federal officer or employee are not deductible for income tax purposes;[8] neither are kickbacks to employees or purchasing agents of customers in violation of the Federal Trade Commission regulations. Payments to agents for getting government orders are deductible, but payments for political influence are not.

The Internal Revenue Service may not recognize an international payoff as a deductible business expense, but there is room for argument. If the payoff amount is not too large, the tax effect may not be material.

On the other hand, the legal impact in the host country may deserve more attention from management. The law in a developing or totalitarian country may be subject to the interpretation of political figures in power. Thus, it may function differently from the parent country legal system. Other possible legal remedies should also be taken into account. Will the host government insist on the deserved legal penalty when that government is under outside economic and political pressure?

Finally, the good faith of management in acting for the welfare of all the stockholders, and in using due care in deciding the payoff, is expected without saying. Otherwise, the decisionmaker may be held personally liable by the stockholders.

The following questions are presented to determine the possible legal impact in general:

1. What are the legal consequences in the parent country?
2. How comprehensive is the law of the host country? What is the enforceability of its law?
3. Can the justice system in the host country be influenced?
4. Will the corporation be liable to its competitors for financial damages (such as unfair practice, restraint of trade)?
5. Will the decisionmaker be held liable by stockholders and/or the host or parent government?

Since this last question involves personal consequences for the individual executive, its implications are discussed more fully later. However, the company also has a problem relating to its obligation to defray the expenses of litigation for the executive involved since he may be acquitted or D & O insurance coverage may be made more difficult to obtain.

Application to Specific Cases. As Table 6-2 indicates, when we apply specific laws to the corporations that have been examined, we find that they have been derelict in compliance with statutory and legal guidelines.

Moral Considerations

While each individual executive sets his own ethical standards according to his conscience and value system, company policy and objectives are also involved in international payoffs. We have labelled this the moral business climate. Different cultures also have their own interpretation of what is right and wrong, and different values may be assigned to the same subject.

The following questions are presented to remind the executive of some of the factors which affect the company's moral image:

1. What is the company's policy regarding overseas payoffs? Will it cause any deviation from standard practice?
2. If the questionable payment is disclosed, will it damage the public image of the company in the parent country?
3. Will the payoff activity affect employee morale of the company at home or overseas?
4. What is the custom in the host country?
5. Does the public opinion of the host country carry the same weight as it does in the parent country?

Table 6-2
Compliance with Legal Guidelines

Industry and Firm	SEC[c]	IRS	Acct. Principles[c]
Aircraft			
Lockheed	No	n.a.[a]	No
Northrop	No	n.a.[a]	No
Oil			
Gulf	No	Yes[b]	No
Exxon	No	No	No
Food			
United Brands	No	No	No

[a]Not available. The question of compliance with IRS guidelines is still unanswered. Some of the payments may have been to bona fide agents. However, the subterfuge used to conceal the payments would lead one to believe that the payments and subsequent tax deductions were *probably* illegal.

[b]Payments made from after-tax profits and not deducted as expenses, for tax purposes, hence within IRS requirements.

[c]Failure to comply with disclosure requirements of SEC and Financial Accounting Standards Board.

Additional guidelines in the morality of goals desired by management are provided by the Sethi model in his three-tier schema for classifying corporate behavior reproduced as Table 5-2 in Chapter 5.

If top management desires to set high moral standards for its employees, company policy will prescribe through promotion, compensation, and other internal rewards (for more detail, see Chapter 7 on reform measures) to generate business behavior aimed at anticipating social norms. A lower moral goal implies a willingness to meet prevailing social norms. The lowest moral level is characterized by business behavior that confines legitimacy to legal and economic criteria only.

Economic Considerations

Questions of an economic nature are designed to determine the benefits and costs involved. All benefits are valued in the long-run view; a short-run profit may cost more in the end. Indirect complications should also be considered. Here are some of the questions to be answered by the executive considering international payoffs:

1. How does the expected gain compare with the company's total earnings?
2. What is the cost of payoff as a percentage of total revenue? Is it a one-time payment or a periodic contribution?
3. Is the company diversified in many countries?
4. Will the payoff trigger other host countries to make the same demand?
5. Will the payoff action cause retaliation from competitors?

The cost of a payoff varies from industry to industry. It also depends on geographical location of the market. For example, in aircraft sales companies have been known to pay Middle East consultants from 4 to 6 percent, but on less expensive equipment may end up paying agents more than 25 percent. A French firm paid $40 million on a contract valued at $200-$300 million.[9]

For question 3, the basic assumption is made that the more diversified the company is, the less damage it will suffer from any one host country if payoff activity is discovered. On the other hand, it can be assumed that the more diversified the company is, the less pressure it will bear to employ the payoff practice in one host country and hence can afford to reject it more easily. If the latter is the case, then the answers should be rearranged in the reverse order, as given in Table 6-4 below.

Foreign payoffs may put the company on the spot. Once it is regarded a soft touch for payoffs, it becomes a target for all kinds of demands. Moreover, when a company pays off a corrupt government, it may make itself a target for nationalization if an opposition party comes to power. In less developed nations, bribe-giving corporations contribute to an atmosphere of corruption that may add to the appeal of puritanical leftist movements.[10] Since different countries have responded in various ways to the revelation of the role that kickbacks and bribes have played in the awarding of contracts,[11] a complete analysis of the economic desirability of international payoffs for the multinational firm must consider the benefits and costs of all the major parties involved in the international transaction: the parent country, the host country, and in consequence its own. The following list of benefits and costs is not meant to be all-inclusive, but rather to provide a framework and methodology useful in assessing the economic desirability of international payoffs.[12]

Parent-Country (U.S.) Benefits

Political and Social Factors:

1. Defense policy—increased knowledge of potential enemies' strategic weapons and decision-making policies;
2. Foreign relations—increased trade influence may lead to increased political influence in host country;
3. Possible election of officials in host country who are sympathetic to multinational firm and therefore possibly sympathetic to parent country.

Economic Factors:

1. Multinational's exports—positively affect the balance of payments;
2. Increase in technology and competitive pricing in military sales;
3. Increase in GNP as well as increase in domestic employment;
4. Source of raw materials (oil) established;
5. Increased knowledge of "rules of the game" in foreign markets.

Parent-Country (U.S.) Costs

Political and Social Factors:

1. Possible political confrontation with host country over the morality of payoffs (self-reference criterion);
2. World image problems (is the U.S. contributing to corrupt regimes or escalating arms race?);
3. Problems with U.S. nationals who view bribes as immoral;
4. Potential of overseas payoff techniques applied domestically;
5. Blackmail potential;
6. Possible degradation of U.S. citizenship and employee morale;
7. Potential change in attitude towards trade (back to nationalism).

Economic Factors:

1. Potential loss of investment capital due to negative reaction of host country to payoffs (expropriation);
2. Price wars constantly increasing;
3. Dependence on influential foreign nationals as to size of exports;
4. Potential change of attitude in investors to overseas trade.

Host-Country Benefits

Political and Social Factors:

1. Increased leverage of host country in multinational dealings;
2. Increased political stability through cooperation with multinationals;
3. Recognition of cultural norms by outsiders;
4. Attitude change (for better) toward foreigners.

Economic Factors:

1. Ability to underpay government officials;
2. Contributions by multinational firms to charities, education, and so forth;
3. Increased knowledge of working of multinational firms;
4. Possible balance-of-payments improvement;
5. Higher standard of living (for those receiving payoffs).

Host-Country Costs

Political and Social Factors:

1. Corruption of government officials;
2. Decrease of faith of people in the government;
3. Possible increase in instability of government as multinational firms attempt to control elections;
4. Possible confrontation with parent country.

Economic Factors:

1. Possible change in attitude of multinational firms of attractiveness of country;
2. Increased costs of government purchases;
3. Possible deterioration in balance of payments.

MNC Benefits

Political and Social Factors:

1. Increased leverage in host country's government;
2. Increased knowledge of the culture of host country.

Economic Factors:

1. Increased sales;
2. Competitive edge over those firms that do not engage in payoffs;
3. Establishment of source of inside information concerning future host-country actions;
4. Ability to possibly avoid expropriation or nationalization;
5. Tax concessions;
6. Access to scarce raw materials.

MNC Costs

Political and Social Factors:

1. Possible deterioration of relationship between firm and parent country;
2. Possible public image damage in parent country;
3. Effect of payoffs on other customers as well as employees;
4. Risk of discovery by other foreign nationals and from expropriation or imprisonment.

Economic Factors:

1. Risk of blackmail;
2. Increased costs of doing business;
3. Extra planning and transportation costs;
4. Inability of conventional accounting system to work as control instrument;
5. Difficulty in measuring return on investment;
6. Potential of viewing only short-run benefits, rather than long-run benefits.

It must be remembered that bribes (the black area) are a form of treacherous tax or cost of doing business in countries where it is demanded. Once paid, the cost of the subsequent installment increases substantially. To minimize cost, the rational business executive will try to avoid paying bribes and taking the unnecessary legal risks involved in such action. Bribes should be considered only as a last resort when every other reasonable means has been tried and has failed.

For example, Gulf Oil, after investing $250 million in oil, fertilizer, and petrochemical products in South Korea, gave in to the payoff demand and contributed $3 million to President Park Chung Hee's political party. Since the South Korean government's existence depended on the presence of 42,000 U.S. troops and the U.S. government had already insured Gulf for $62 million against any loss from expropriation, why didn't Gulf turn to the U.S. embassy to protest Park's outrageous demand? "It never occurred to me," Gulf's chief executive Dorsey testified at the Senate hearings.[13]

In another case Del Monte hired a local influential businessman as a consultant only after eighteen months of frustrating attempts to obtain the government's approval for acquisition of a banana plantation in Guatemala. Half a million dollars in consulting fees were paid. Now Del Monte owns a profitable 55,000 acre banana plantation worth $20.5 million. Del Monte's choice is easy to understand in economic terms.

Personal Considerations

Thus far, we have emphasized the legal, moral and economic considerations of international payoffs as they apply to the business firm. In the final analysis, however, it is the individual executive who acts for the company and is personally rewarded or penalized based on the merit of such action. Although it is difficult to document instances in which executives have been rewarded for acting unethically in behalf of their corporations, it is becoming easier (and it may be much easier in the future) to document personal penalties or consequences for an executive who acts unethically or illegally in behalf of his corporation.

Below are some of the questions to be answered by the individual executive in assessing his personal cost-benefit calculation:

1. Will the top management find out about the payoff? If so, am I subject to censure?
2. Am I likely to be held personally liable for such action?
3. Does the company carry insurance to pay my legal fees if I am charged with violating a law?
4. Will disclosure of payoff harm my reputation and make it more difficult to obtain or retain a management position in the future?
5. How would my family and friends react to disclosure of such activity?

In the current investigation personal penalties or consequences have included the following examples:

Thomas V. Jones, fined $200,000, was permitted to resign as chairman of the board of Northrop Corporation,[14] and Northrop refunded $370,900 to the USAF as a reimbursement for illegal political contributions in the United States charged as expenses.[15] His subsequent return to the board does not remove the stigma.

William Gingery, former Civil Aeronautics Board (CAB) enforcement chief, killed himself in the belief that he was grossly derelict in his duties for not discovering illegal airline expenditures.[16]

Eli M. Black, chief executive of United Brands, took his own life as a result of his participation in approving payments to European officials and Honduran government representatives.

Yuri S. Sosrousky, director of a Russian government furniture manufacturing organization, was sentenced to death for kickback arrangements with a Swiss businessman.

Gulf Oil officers were asked to resign.

Thus, the impact of individual actions within business goes beyond the individual's economic role in society. It affects the individual's perception of his role in the community, family, profession, and church as well as his own moral consciousness and worthiness. A healthy perception of such roles is a prerequisite for an effective and efficient execution of the individual's economic role.

Since there are few absolute ethical standards to assist individuals in determining their moral disposition toward international payoffs, the authors have developed four distinct models of ethical behavior and four specific models of professionalism that may help each executive in choosing his own moral and professional role. The comparison between different professions with which executives interact within and outside the corporation is designed to provide a broader perspective for individual moral and professional choice. For a full description of the four models of ethical behavior and professionalism refer to Table 6-1 presented earlier in this chapter along with the decision-making model in Figure 6-1.

The individual apart from the corporation decision-making process may be viewed from another perspective. Depending on the executive's choice of ethical behavior, he will act toward international payoffs in accordance with Table 6-3.

The importance of Table 6-3 lies in its emphasis on individual veto power over any company decision for which he is responsible. It is the individual executive with given standards and moral convictions who finally determines whether international payoffs will or will not be made.

To insure that all the necessary factors have been taken into consideration in arriving at the decision on international payoffs, we set forth in Table 6-4 a final checklist for decision making that takes all four factors—legal, moral, economic and personal—and arrives at a final indicator. For those who need some quantitative result, this table should provide the answer.

Further Considerations in Strategy Planning

If management decides that a payoff is unavoidable and is willing to carry it out, the following additional questions must be answered to arrive at a decision about how best to accomplish the task:

Table 6-3

Decision-making Model for the Individual Executive

	Payoff Classification		
Model[a]	White	Gray	Black
Model 4	Accept company's desired payoff.	Reject company's desired payoff on the basis of personal morality.	
Models 2 or 3	Accept company's desired payoff.	Consider own personal benefits and costs including both economic and noneconomic considerations; include reputation and professional future.	Reject company's desired payoff.
Model 1	Accept company's desired payoff.	Accept company's desired payoff.	Accept company's desired payoff if economic benefits personally outweigh the costs.

Note: In this table we assume that the company has decided to make the payoff, i.e., that an affirmative decision has resulted from steps taken in Figure 6-1.

aModel numbers refer to explanations contained in Table 6-1.

1. To whom should the bribe be paid?
2. How much should the bribe amount be?
3. How should payments be made to please all parties? Should a middleman be employed?
4. Is there a legal means to charge off the bribe?
5. What type of fund should be set up?

Other considerations include the following:

1. *Effective internal control.* If a company uses complicated methods to transfer its funds back and forth and allocate them to various accounts so payment can be arranged, it may find maintenance of effective internal control very difficult. For example, Esso Italiana kept more than 40 secret bank accounts for payoff purposes that were kept secret even from internal auditors. Various rebates and kickbacks were funnelled into these accounts, which the company had no record of on its books. Only general manager Vincenzo Cassaniga had knowledge of them. As a result of such lack of internal control, Exxon lost $19 million in unauthorized political contributions.[17] The potential danger to internal control that payoff activities may cause should be closely monitored.

2. *Properly expensing the payment.* It is unwise to set up a slush fund. This violates present U.S. statutes. A careful study may find it possible to classify the payment as a consulting charge, market development cost, selling expense, or retainer fee. By proper planning, the company can also satisfy the disclosure requirements of the Securities and Exchange Commission.

Table 6-4
Final Checklist for Payoff Decision Making

No. and Type	Questions to be Answered	*1* For Payoff	*2* Uncertain	*3* Against Payoff
Legal				
	1. What are the legal consequences in the parent country?	Light	Fair	Severe
	2. How comprehensive is the law of the host country? What is the enforceability of its law?	Limited	Somewhat extensive	Very extensive
	3. Can the justice system in the host country be influenced?	Yes	Maybe	No
	4. Will the corporation be liable to its competitors for financial damages (such as unfair practice, restraint of trade)?	Very unlikely	Possible	Probable
	5. Will the company be held liable by stockholders in the host or parent country?	Very unlikely	Possible	Probable
Moral				
	1. What is the company's policy regarding overseas payoffs? (Will it cause any deviation from standard practice?)	Acceptable	If necessary	Unacceptable
	2. If the questionable payment is disclosed, will it damage the public image of the company in the parent country?	Slightly	Somewhat	Seriously
	3. Will the payoff activity affect employee morale of the company at home or overseas?	No	Maybe	Yes
	4. What is the custom in the host country?	Acceptable practice	Illegal, but everyone does it	Absolutely prohibited
	5. Does the public opinion of the host country carry the same weight as it does in the parent country?	If less, No	Depends	If more, Yes
Economic				
	1. How does the expected gain compare with the company's total earnings?	High	Medium	Low
	2. What is the cost of payoff as a percentage of total revenue? Is it a one-time payment or a periodic contribution?	High	Fair	Low
	3. Is the company diversified in many countries?[a]	Yes	A few	No

Table 6-4 (cont.)

No. and Type	Questions to be Answered	1 For Payoff	2 Uncertain	3 Against Payoff
4.	Will the payoff trigger other host countries to make the same demand?	Very un-likely	Maybe	Very likely
5.	Will the payoff action cause retaliation from competitors?	They started it	Possible	Yes
Personal				
1.	Will top management find out about the payoff? If so, am I subject to censure?	Very un-likely	Maybe	Very likely
2.	Am I likely to be held personally liable for such action?	Very un-likely	Possible	Probable
3.	Does the company carry insurance to pay my legal fees if I am found guilty of violating a law?	Yes	Uncertain	No
4.	Will disclosure of payoff harm my reputation and make it difficult to obtain or retain a management position in the future?	Very un-likely	Maybe	Very likely
5.	How would my family and friends react to disclosure of such activity?	Approve	Indif-ferent	Disapprove

Total Number of Items Checked (per column):

The Final Indicator (see instructions below):

Instructions for Use of Checklist

1. Add the total number of items checked per column.
2. Assume all the answers carry equal weight:
   Use 1 x (no. in column 1) + 0 x (no. in column 2) + (−1) x (no. in column 3) = final indicator.
3. Assign a different weight to each question as desired:
   Use 1 x (total weight of column 1) + 0 x (total weight of column 2) + (−1) x (total weight of column 3) = final indicator.

Interpretation of the final indicator:

1. Positive: At least the gain is greater than the risk. The higher the total, the less important risks become.
2. Zero: The gain and risk are fifty-fifty.
3. Negative: The gain is outweighed by the risks.

aSee text for a fuller discussion of this question that can lead to a reversal of the answers.

3. *Avoiding direct involvement.* A trustworthy third party is essential to handle the details of the payoff, whenever this is feasible. It is hazardous for a company to get involved in a different environment if it does not fully understand local business practice and the political situation. For example, Lockheed paid a painful price in the Indonesian operation. In May 1967, after General Suharto came to power, Lockheed decided to handle the payoff by itself and discharged the local agent who had no influence with the new government. It made a connection with an air force general, only to find out that the general was to be replaced within a few months. Later the Lockheed representative met another air force general, and an agreement was made. This time payment was rejected because the general could not afford the risk of cashing the check; so a cash payment had to be arranged. Unfortunately, Lockheed's latest report indicated it might have been paying the wrong general.[18]

The lesson is to let an experienced local consultant do the work. It may save the company a lot of trouble.

4. *Insuring the intended receives the payoff.* In most instances, the payment is made secretly with no record; therefore, it is difficult to confirm with the recipient. It may even cause more problems if the recipient refuses to admit accepting the payment. A dependable messenger trusted by both sides, however, solves the problem.

5. *Benefiting the general public rather than ruling elite.* Whenever a payoff can be broadened to benefit the general public, all efforts should be made to insure this result. Broadening the base of the beneficiary gains more public support and understanding for the company. Contributions to political parties is accepted by the people of South Korea and Italy, for example.

When there is only the choice of benefiting some key persons, the fewer who know, the better the payoff can be kept confidential. This consideration tends to minimize the risk.

Conclusion

Our purpose in this chapter has been to take the company executive step-by-step through the decision-making process in determining, first, whether international payments should be made and, second, if so, how they will be carried out. It must be emphasized that the company rather than outsiders must make this analysis. Except for application of the legal considerations to specific cases, which we have attempted in this chapter, no application of the other factors can be made by an outsider because only an insider can ascertain a company's moral climate, the true economic costs, and the benefits involved in specific payments. And no one but himself is privy to the personal considerations of each executive.

Whatever action the executive finally arrives at must be his own decision. However, in Chapter 7 we also have some guidelines for policymakers and top management so that the risks of international payoffs of the gray and black types hopefully will become so high as to make them an irrational business decision. This will take planning, time, and a vast amount of good will and commitment on the part of all concerned.

Notes

1. *Forbes*, February 1, 1976, p. 41.

2. U.S. Congress, Senate, Foreign Relations Committee, Subcommittee on Multinational Corporations, *Hearings*, Washington, D.C., May-September, 1975, (hereafter referred to as Senate Hearings); and U.S. Congress, Senate, Committee on Banking, Housing and Urban Affairs, *Report of the Securities and Exchange Commission on Questionable and Illegal Corporate Payments and Practices*, Washington, D.C., May 1976.

3. Securities and Exchange Commission, *Regulation S-X*, page 50.

4. Maurice Moonitz, "The Basic Postulates of Accounting," *Accounting Research Study No. 1* (New York: American Institute of Certified Public Accountants, 1961), p. 50.

5. Eldon S. Hendrickson, *Accounting Theory* (Homewood, Ill.: Richard D. Irwin, 1965), pp. 452-53.

6. Ibid., pp. 455-56.

7. *Forbes*, February 1, 1976, p. 43. Reprinted with permission.

8. U.S. Department of the Treasury, *Internal Revenue Code*, Sec. 162(c); *Federal Tax Regulations*, Sec. 1, 162-18.

9. "Payoff Is Not Acceptable Practice," *Fortune*, August 1975, p. 205.

10. "Lifting the Lid on Some Mysterious Money," *Time*, June 23, 1975, p. 54.

11. For examples of the variety of reactions by host countries, see "Heat Grows on U.S. Business for Dubious Dealings Abroad," *U.S. News and World Report*, August 4, 1975, p. 72. Additional discussion of host-country considerations appears in Chapter 7.

12. Much of the following methodology is adapted from Yerachmiel Kugel, "How to Avoid Expropriation," *Academy of Management Proceedings*, August 1972, pp. 353-56. Reprinted with permission.

13. Senate Hearings, p. 17.

14. "The Corporation on the Carpet," *Fortune*, July 1975, p. 19.

15. "SEC to Re-examine Forms Filed by 25 Top Defense Contractors," *Aviation Week and Space Technology*, June 23, 1975, p. 19.

16. "The Multinational Corporation," *The Nation*, May 24, 1975, p. 619.

17. *The Wall Street Journal*, November 14, 1975.

18. *The Wall Street Journal*, November 17, 1975.

'Well, There Goes The Image'

Fri., September 17, 1976　　　　ST. LOUIS POST-DISPATCH

7 Policy Considerations: Measures for Reform

To be good is noble; but to show others how to be good is nobler and no trouble.

—Mark Twain, "Following The Equator,"
prefatory note to *Pudd'nhead Wilson's Maxims* (1897)

Before analyzing antipayoff[1] measures, let us review the basic rationale for international payoffs and the criteria for their use. In discussing the history of bribery in Chapter 2, we quote Lord Macaulay to the effect that bribes "were common, as every crime will be common when the gain to which it leads is great, and the chance of disgrace and punishment is small." This statement is as true today as it was in the nineteenth century. Thus, for an executive to decide rationally in favor of international payoffs, he must obtain a pro-payoff response on a majority of the business and personal questions listed in Table 6-4.

The task of policymakers, then, is to change an environment that generates a pro-payoff response to one which generates an antipayoff response. This is easier said than done.

The risk of making recommendations for legislation in this connection is very great in view of the fact that there are many disadvantages as well as advantages to any proposal. That old cliche of "the rock and the hard place" reminds us that no decision making is easy. To advocate more regulation of business is to invite a barrage of invective and the charge that a new bureaucracy not only does not solve any problems but is likely to create more. Economists Milton Friedman and Murray Weidenbaum are two members of the academic community who argue that more regulation is counterproductive.[2] There is also some doubt that a majority of U.S. lawmakers favor antipayoff legislation,[3] since many fear that its disadvantages outweigh advantages in world competition.

To dispel this uncertainty and arrive at a consensus that an antipayoff environment is desirable, policymakers must conduct a cost-benefit analysis similar to the model presented in Chapter 6, all the while keeping in mind that idealism is long-range realism. The benefits from international payoffs are largely of a short-run nature. In the long run there is no viable alternative to the promotion of a dynamic and competitive[4] economic system to support a democratic political system throughout the world.

Once legislation is deemed desirable, sanctions against international payoffs must be severe enough to enable society, business, and individual executives to perceive the disadvantages of such payoffs so that they are encouraged to comply with reform measures in spite of the risk involved. In other words, noncompliance must be made even riskier.

Fortunately, policymakers throughout the world are already pursuing ways of controlling international payoffs. If this trend continues, they may soon be blamed for overreaction rather than inaction. To illustrate, we set forth below some of the existing proposals and measures against international payoffs at the transnational, national, business, and individual levels that will enable policymakers to assess the current status of the war against payoffs and the role they can play in such a campaign. For individuals this list demonstrates the ever increasing cost of personal involvement in payoffs so that they can reassess their disposition toward such involvement.

Transnational Measures for Reform

Proposals for an international code of conduct for multinational firms have been under consideration for some time. In the 1970s efforts grew to deal with specific questions of illegal or unethical payments. These efforts were implemented by the following organizations:

Organization for Economic Cooperation and Development (OECD)

On June 21, 1976, the twenty-four members of the Organization for Economic Cooperation and Development adopted a code of conduct for multinational firms heralded as a breakthrough in international cooperation. OECD emphasized that MNCs were acting contrary to everybody's interests by anticompetitive behavior in host countries designed to improperly influence governmental officials.

Disclosure of improper activities is the main enforcer of the new code. Multinational companies are expected to provide yearly information on all financial transactions, capital sources, and operations. For their part, host countries are urged to treat MNCs the same as their own domestic business firms.

The OECD code was criticized as "the least common denominator,"[5] but one businessman who supports the idea, stated:

It includes an excellent statement of general principles that not only says that multinational corporations should not bribe public officials, but that they should not be solicited or expected to render any bribe or improper payment.[6]

He adds, however, that it goes too far "in areas of financial disclosures, intracompany management, and employee relations." As a result, its enforceability is in doubt.

United Nations (UN) Commission on Transnational Corporations

The Commission on Transnational Corporations was formed by the UN Economic and Social Council (ECOSOC) to promote research on the effect of multinationals in the area of economic development and international relations. The resolution grew out of Chile's charge that International Telephone and Telegraph Corporation interfered in the internal political affairs of that country.

ECOSOC's study appeared in 1974 and its recommendations led to the establishment of the Commission on Transnational Corporations, which is composed of representatives of forty-eight nations and had its first meeting in March 1975. Along with the Commission was formed a new research center, which began work shortly thereafter.

The Commission was given the following charge:

1. Formulate a code of conduct for multinational corporations;
2. Set up a method for obtaining MNC information, including all financial data (contracts, regulations, and national policies designed to control MNC activities are also to be collected);
3. Begin studies designed to evaluate the social, political, and economic implications of multinational corporations and their activities;
4. Coordinate the various programs involving multinational corporations, especially in the area of technical cooperation.

On December 15, 1975, the UN adopted a resolution condemning corrupt practices and calling on member governments to cooperate in eliminating them. The Commission's efforts to draft a code of conduct for multinational corporations met with obstacles partially created by developing countries who were accused of using the Commission as a vehicle for extracting more concessions from MNCs.

United Nations Conference on Trade and Development (UNCTAD)

The Transfer of Technology Committee of UNCTAD, formed in 1974, met in Geneva from November 24 to December 5, 1975. International payoffs were indirectly involved in these discussions since again developing countries see the committee as a way of focusing international codes for sharing MNC technology.

In addition to these international deliberations, various groups in the United States indicate interest in promoting greater control over activities of multinational firms through self-policing action.

U.S. Chamber of Commerce

The U.S. Chamber of Commerce has suggested that MNCs stay neutral in host-country political activities and continue plans to maintain investment on a long-range basis. To carry out responsibilities to the host country, the Chamber urges that MNCs give nationals permission to invest in the host-country affiliate while the MNC at the same time uses a portion of its worldwide earnings to expand such affiliate facilities. Foreign nationals should be promoted by the MNC, the Chamber contends, and no part of the MNC's investment should be phased out without long prior notice and efforts to lessen the adverse impact on the host-country employment situation.

U.S. Senate

The U.S. Senate passed Resolution No. 265 in November 1975, by unanimous vote, to the effect that U.S. representatives under the General Agreement on Tariffs and Trade (GATT) exert great effort to bring about an international code for elimination of "bribery, indirect payments, kickbacks, unethical political contributions and other such similar disreputable activities."[7]

Securities and Exchange Commission (SEC)

The SEC added its voice to those calling for a cessation of questionable payments and, in addition, proposed the requirement that firms stopping the practice be protected from competitive disadvantage vis-à-vis those that continue it. This suggestion was made on the theory that the 1930 Tariff Act permits retaliation against unfair acts and that a case can be made for the fact that payoffs constitute unfairness in international trade.[8] This proposal appears to be an excellent device for encouraging compliance with antipayoff legislation by U.S. MNCs without their losing ground to foreign competitors. Moreover, retaliation against such "unfair" action by other countries would enhance worldwide compliance with business antipayoff behavior.

Presidential Task Force

When President Gerald Ford established the Task Force on Questionable Corporate Payments Abroad, he called for a sweeping review for the purpose of developing a new policy. At the same time, he summarized other "initiatives" that had been approved by the United States in this connection and referred to the UN resolution of December 15, 1975, condemning corrupt corporate practices and a similar resolution passed by the Organization of American States (OAS) in July 1975.

From the above agreements and proposals to combat questionable payments, it is clear that a significant number of countries have already realized the necessity of curbing international payoffs and other forms of anticompetitive economic behavior in the world economy. However, only nation-states can mold this transnational initiative into effective antipayoff legislation. Some of these national measures are discussed below.

National Measures for Reform: Parent Country (the United States)

Because of its leading role in world trade, the United States assumed the leadership in the drive to curb international payoffs. Among its activities are the following:

Senate Foreign Relations Subcommittee on
Multinational Corporations

The Senate Foreign Relations Subcommittee on Multinational Corporations, chaired by Senator Frank Church, charges that government agencies in the U.S. Departments of Defense, State, and Treasury have been lax in their policing of arms contracts and have permitted payoffs to escape normal auditing control to promote their own self-interest. For example, the U.S. Treasury Department has been accused of encouraging Mideast arms sales to improve U.S. balance of payments, which was adversely affected by Organization of Petroleum Exporting Countries (OPEC) actions. In the eyes of the U.S. State Department, U.S. arms sales are said to be viewed as a way of coordinating balance in the Mideast. The subcommittee feels that the U.S. Defense Department uses arms sales as a method of on-the-job training for military maintenance crews. Even congressmen are convinced that arms trade alleviates the unemployment problem at home.

The Senate Foreign Relations subcommittee would solve the problem of international payoffs through control, either by the U.S. government or the OECD, or both. In connection with arms sales, Senator Church was quoted to the effect that a vicious cycle is created:

Bribery leads to insurgency and the need for U.S. weapons . . . and the sale of those weapons leads to bribery.[9]

Senate Banking Committee

The Senate Banking Committee, headed by Senator William Proxmire, had three bills before it when Congress adjourned in October 1976,[10] but none was passed. In summing up the need for congressional action, Senator Proxmire criticized the executive branch for not acting to curb international payoffs.[11]

Presidential Task Force

The Presidential Task Force on Questionable Payments Abroad gave an immediate response to Senator Proxmire's charge of executive inaction in the form of a report in June 1976, under the chairmanship of Secretary of Commerce Elliot Richardson. The Task Force was charged by the President with coordinating various international and domestic actions being taken to deal with the payoff problem and with responsibility for exploring "additional avenues [to] be undertaken in the interest of ethical conduct in the international marketplace and the continued vitality of our free enterprise system."[12]

The Task Force recommendations for legislation include the following:

1. Disclosure of the amount of all payments in excess of some minimum, including purpose and name of recipient;
2. Communication of the information to the foreign government involved;
3. Imposition of civil and/or criminal penalties for failure to report and, of course, for deliberate misrepresentation;
4. Requirement that corporate internal auditing controls be improved to properly reflect all transactions.

The Task Force specifically recommended against what it called "criminalization" of payoff activity on the ground that disclosure accomplishes the objective of prevention. Creation of a new executive agency is recommended to police these matters.

Securities and Exchange Commission (SEC)

The SEC objected to the Task Force recommendations on the ground that SEC is already playing an active role in exposing corporate international payoffs and is getting compliance through its voluntary disclosure policy. Serious payoff cases and some complaints of perjury were referred to the U.S. Justice Department for criminal indictments early in 1976. This action, in turn, encouraged individual stockholders to bring class-action civil suits against the companies involved in overseas payoffs to force a more accurate disclosure.

The SEC made several proposals for legislation and transnational cooperation, among which is establishment of controls limiting the scope and size of payoffs. According to SEC Commissioner Irving Pollack, disclosure has an advantage for the firm in that it permits open discussion of the fact that a U.S. firm lost an account to some other country because the purchaser wanted a bribe.[13]

The SEC disclosure program resulted in reports by over 130 firms as of August 1976,[14] which came in periodically on form 8-K as changes occur or on the firm's annual 10-K report for stockholders. According to SEC, adequate record keeping permits executives and stockholders to make more informed decisions about these payments.

The SEC also requested auditors to come forward with opinions on suspicious corporate payments to foreign officials. A partner of one large CPA firm agrees with the idea but states that, as a practical matter, "it's going to be difficult to uncover all illegal activities if a U.S. corporation wants to conceal them."[15]

Internal Revenue Service (IRS)

The IRS is cooperating with the SEC to find possible tax violations in falsification of records by labelling payoffs as legitimate business expenses. Payoffs are not deductible for tax purposes in the United States, even though the payment itself may not violate any U.S. or foreign law. These matters are discussed in detail in Chapter 6 under Legal Considerations. Since current U.S. federal law does not prohibit overseas payments, legal penalties result mainly from false statements filed with a government agency. Similar to SEC potential penalties, any false statements to IRS constitute criminal fraud under 18 U.S.C. Sec. 1001. In summary, IRS considerations include the following:[16]

1. When payoffs are deducted from taxes as a business expense, the claiming of such deductions may constitute a criminal tax violation.
2. When payoffs are not disclosed to SEC and the amounts involved are "material," such violation may constitute criminal fraud.

Thus, in summary, proposals in the parent country are concentrating on the passage of laws outlawing international payoffs but no steps are being taken in the direction we propose, namely, to focus on legislation against individuals and to remove corporate protection from those who engage in payoffs. This position is discussed more fully in our proposal for reform.

National Measures for Reform: Host Country

The host country has less incentive to stop payoffs since it can rely on the parent country to stop MNC corruption through legislation. It has been said that in many of the countries in which multinational firms operate, payoffs have been a part of the culture for decades. Host countries like Iran and Japan have been quick to deny such allegations, however, and have taken action to counter them. Nevertheless, there is some evidence that in some countries payoffs are considered payment for services, the same as any other remuneration that the multinational firm owes for benefits derived in the host country.[17]

Congressional hearings disclose that Saudi Arabia and other Mideast countries require a national agent in connection with sales to their governments. Northrop's Economic and Development Corporation (EDC) and Adnan Khashoggi's Triad were developed for this purpose.[18] Most foreign governments, however, fear larger and more numerous payoffs due to increased competition in the arms market with OPEC funds. Scarcity of oil gives host countries in oil-producing regions more leverage in obtaining a larger share of the economic pie. The success of cartels such as OPEC also leads to the combination of other commodity-producing countries to exert pressure for greater concessions from MNCs operating in their territories.

Larger and larger payoffs create greater potential for abuse of political as well as economic power. Retaliatory actions against individuals with political overtones include the following.

1. The President of Honduras was ousted after disclosure of the United Brands' $1.25 million bribe to reduce the banana export tax.

2. Bolivia jailed a Gulf Oil official, ordering his prosecution for "compromising the integrity" of a Brazilian official. It has also asked the OAS to censure Gulf for its "sordid activities" in developing countries.[19]

3. Russia reported execution of an official for accepting a bribe in connection with a government purchase.

4. Japan conducted a year-long investigation of governmental officials involved in the Lockheed payoff. A former prime minister and several lesser officials were indicted. Corporate officials of the Marubeni Trading Company, which was to the Far East what Triad is to the Mideast, are also in trouble under Japan's strict foreign exchange control laws. They are accused of failing to report the large sums involved in the Lockheed disclosures.

5. In The Netherlands the Prince Consort was stripped of all his public authority on August 29, 1976, and retired from the Queen's inner council of advisors due to his Lockheed connections.

All these host-country penalties are squarely in agreement with our proposal for reform in that they concentrate on the individuals who paid or received the payoffs. This is not to deny that political considerations have played a role in such sanctions, but the evidence is that the zero hour for international payoffs is in sight in these countries, particularly since MNC executives can now anticipate such retaliation. Also, the favorable public relations that the host country seeks among other multinational corporations to induce their investment is giving off good vibes to prevent repetition of payoffs in the future.

Not all countries responded against individuals engaged in payoffs as severely as those mentioned above. In fact, some limited their retaliation to the business firm (which is contrary to our reform proposal for reasons explained later). The following are examples.

1. The Costa Rican government demanded an investigation by the SEC and threatened to nationalize the holdings of U.S. fruit companies, although there were no disclosures of improprieties there.

2. The Honduran government is continuing its investigation of banana payoffs with a view toward nationalizing all United Brands' holdings.

3. Foreign companies operating in Iran are henceforth required to submit written affidavits that payoffs will not be used to obtain government contracts.

4. In Italy new legislation was enacted after the Esso Italiana disclosure, to provide for government financing of political campaigns as well as to require disclosure of all contributions in excess of $1,600.

5. Peru nationalized a chain of filling stations owned by Gulf Oil in the wake of Korean disclosures, even though no similar improprieties were uncovered in Peru.

On the other hand, South Korea stands as a shining example of a complete do-nothing attitude on the part of government despite the reports of multi-million-dollar political contributions by Gulf Oil Company. No individuals were censured, and Gulf's contracts were renewed.

The point is that most host countries are reacting unfavorably to payoff disclosures regardless of their previous attitude. MNCs therefore are on notice to reassess their position and to cooperate with parent and host countries by complying with antipayoff measures. Below is discussed the role business can take in combating payoffs by using its economic deterrence to influence individual members of the business community.

Business Measures for Reform

In line with limited objectives for reform, it is important at the outset to distinguish between the business firm as an initiator of action and the business firm as a reactor to happenings over which it has little control. The latter we shall designate as external factors, while the former are of an internal nature.

External Factors

Market Discipline. Some economists and businessmen argue that no reform is necessary to control international payoffs since competition in the market is the best discipline.[20] Business executives are well aware of the fact that the market is an important external factor determining whether international payoffs, from an economic point of view, are good or bad for the firm.

For instance, if key corporate personnel get caught for engaging in international payoffs, it may lead to their prosecution and the loss of personnel who otherwise could have contributed much to the company. This situation has important repercussions on the morale of subordinates. Poor image of the company and deterioration of confidence in its leaders causes further disadvantages in recruiting efforts, control of operations, loss of contracts, and the like. (For more on the costs of international payoffs, see Chapter 6.)

Trade Associations. Adoption by an industrywide trade association of certain standards of conduct for all firms who are its members can be an additional pressure for control of misconduct. The "everybody's doing it" argument can be somewhat diluted by adoption of codes of conduct on an industrywide basis. While some may argue that antitrust problems can result from such trade association activity, it appears that setting minimum international standards is no more violative of antitrust statutes than similar action in connection with professional standards and International Labor Organization (ILO) conventions. Any activity that is contrary to public policy can be outlawed on an industry-wide basis, and minimum standards of conduct can be enforced through industrywide action. Whether such policing can be effective without the kind of power that really would constitute an antitrust violation is open to question. However, strong public statements condemning international payoffs and declarations of policy in opposition to them serve to alert firms in the industry that no support of payoff activities is likely, and every effort will be made to cooperate with disclosure if this becomes necessary.

Setting such a moral climate is the heart of most of the proposals that have been made for curtailing business overseas payoffs at the industry level. Other suggestions include selection for a Hall of Fame of respected and highly ethical but also extremely successful businessmen to serve as the good image for the business profession in general.[21] The other side of the coin is reflected in the choice of bad examples as well to show what not to do in promoting a better moral climate within the business community.[22]

Influential Representation. Related to external factors, although initiated by the corporation, is the attempt of some MNCs to control external impact on their image by employing the professional services of respected individuals to represent them in the payoff investigations. This practice is based on the theory that as a client of a respected public figure, the firm can benefit from his counsel and take advantage of his influence with international and national governments in both host and parent countries. Whether or not this belief represents a true evaluation of the situation, it is one way to go. In this connection the following are examples:

1. Former Defense Secretary, representing Phillips Petroleum Company.
2. Former SEC chairman, representing Northrop Corporation.
3. Former State Department advisor, representing Gulf Oil Corporation.
4. Former Attorney General and Secretary of State, representing Lockheed Corporation.

Internal Factors

The best area for business measures for reform is that over which the firm has control and can take economic sanctions against individuals who fail to comply with its standards.

Moral Leadership. No matter how much top corporate officers try to place the responsibility for management decisions on lower eschelon executives, there is no substitute for strong declarations of policy and exemplary conduct at the top levels. Fred T. Allen of Pitney Bowes calls upon top corporate officers to realize the importance of their leadership:

In the final analysis, any corporation's adherence to a code of ethics must be scrupulously maintained at the top and published through the company, if morality is to be practiced at all levels. Employees must know exactly what is expected of them and how to respond when tempted by others to pursue illegal or unethical practices.[23]

Increased Corporate Control. Although much of the international payoff activity is done in behalf of the corporation, the benefit to the individual executive cannot be ignored completely. Expense accounts and easy cash flows without accountability encourage a laxity that leads to increasing temptation to engage in international payoffs. Enhancement of the corporate profit position goes hand in hand with improved career opportunities. Corporate executives move up the success ladder on the basis of previous performance inevitably measured by the bottom line.

To eliminate the incentives for self-enriching payoff schemes, one remedy that has been recommended is better control of financial transactions. The McCloy report in the Gulf Oil case stresses this point:

In any corporation the front line control over the use of corporate funds is at the disbursing level. The person making the disbursement is accountable to his superior, as is the latter to his superior, and so on up the line. In the normal case, all expenditures are evidenced by appropriate documentation such as invoices, receipts, checks, vouchers and the like. . . . The system did not work in this case because the Comptrollers did not exercise that control.[24]

In addition to such day-to-day control, outside auditing practices play an important part in uncovering suspicious activities and reporting them to appropriate corporate authority. But the outside audit is no substitute for internal control, as the Gulf report further elucidates:

> In view of the elaborate measures taken by Gulf officials to conceal the facts, it is doubtful that any outside auditor, performing normal audit procedures, would have detected the facts.[25]

The Securities and Exchange Commission and the accounting profession continue to have a running battle over how much control the auditing firm should exercise over its corporate client's activities and how much whistle-blowing it should be charged with. The American Institute of Certified Public Accountants supports SEC's Accounting Series Release 165, by calling for full disclosure of any disputes existing between the outside auditor and the firm. This presumably enhances the reliability of financial statements and discourages shopping by companies for favorable accounting treatment of controversial matters.[26]

Other recommendations for increasing internal control include appointment of outside experts to the board of directors and employment of a top-ranking corporate officer to police ethical standards and to act as an ombudsman for whistle-blowing. Complete restructuring of the company's organizational chart may be necessary to insure proper communication that facilitates detection and control of payoffs.

Realistic Goals. Under competitive pressure to improve the profit position of the corporation and at the same time insure his own job security and career objectives, the individual executive may be faced with unrealistic goals. These high goals, while advantageous for productivity purposes, may be an incentive for improper business behavior.

A lesson in the negative aspects of unrealistic goals can be learned from the Russian experience. Output quotas delegated from the central government to business firms are often too high when compared to the input provided for attainment and the time allotted for accomplishment. Although fear of failure in the free world may not be as severe as in the sphere of Soviet domination, the results are the same, namely, that there is individual incentive for corruption. One top corporate officer sums up the warning as follows:

> Under the pressure of unrealistic goals, otherwise responsible subordinates will often take the attitude that "anything goes." Deals may be made under the table simply because they are seen by the subordinate as the only way he can comply with the chief executive's targets.[27]

Adequate Salary Levels. While the level of salary schedules for top corporate executives is normally well above the poverty level, it has been suggested that insufficient income at the lower management eschelon may create the necessity to engage in international payoffs for personal gain. Thus, increased pay scales have been proposed to remedy this problem. The theory behind this proposal, of course, is that underpaid personnel have more incentive to risk exposure to wrong doing than their well paid colleagues. They have less to lose and hence their cost-benefit analysis is weighted on the benefit side of payoffs.[28]

While pay increases add to business costs at the same time that they decrease the payoff incentive for individuals, the long-run interest of the corporation is enhanced through avoiding payoff involvement.

Codes of Conduct. Of all the measures proposed for payoff reform, codes of conduct represent the one most often mentioned by businessmen as the step they took or are contemplating for avoiding international payoffs. It has been suggested that much of this activity has a public relations purpose. Thus, firms that pay only lip service to code enforcement are likely to fail in influencing individual conduct. In addition, many codes are too general to provide meaningful guidelines for employee behavior and to allow their effective enforceability.

Many companies, on the other hand, are serious about the intent to curb corruption. Their codes are therefore specific and subject to greater potential enforceability. One company that has distinguished itself by its efforts in this field is Caterpillar Tractor Company. Its code of conduct has been adopted by many firms.

Another company that has made headway in its efforts in this area is The Norton Company. Its code spells out that, at minimum, laws and standards considered ethical in the United States should be obeyed as the worldwide rules by Norton employees, except that "in countries where there are stricter laws, we must respect them." The Norton code further suggests that one guideline for action on payoffs is whether the amount is meaningful to stockholders of the company. If it is too small to be of significance (such as a $25 tip for cutting the time for getting a visa), then the employee should not hesitate to pay the "grease." Norton's Nine Commandments are as follows:

1. Place the interests of the company ahead of your own personal interests, and those of society ahead of the company.
2. When in doubt, talk to the superior about specific use of funds or assets for questionable purposes.
3. No funds are to be used for political contributions even if lawful in some countries.
4. There are to be no unrecorded or undisclosed assets or funds.

5. There are to be no false or artificial entries in the books or records.
6. Payment shall be only for the purpose described in such documents and no other.
7. When information contrary to the guidelines is known, blow the whistle.
8. There will be no bribes of public officials to advance company interests to induce dishonest action; e.g., where there is great discrepancy between value paid and value received.
9. Acquire business solely on the quality of our product and service, not because of entertainment or gifts in improper amounts.[29]

Finally, for companies interested in developing their own codes of conduct, the list below summarizes the subjects covered in most business codes, according to a survey of one hundred major U.S. corporations conducted by Business Roundtable in December 1975:[30]

1. Conflict of interest situations;
2. Dealings with suppliers;
3. Obey laws (antitrust, commercial bribery, etc.);
4. Corporate political contributions;
5. Product quality and marketing;
6. Confidential and proprietary information;
7. Company property.

Other areas include:

1. International operations;
2. Relationship with employees;
3. Press relations;
4. Electric power conservation;
5. Truthful, candid reports;
6. Employees who run for public office;
7. Credit data organizations.

The report concludes with guidelines for incorporating the code of conduct into the management system:[31]

1. Cover all areas mentioned above;
2. Write in clear and concise style and give examples;
3. Publish both policy letters for management and an employee booklet;
4. Plan periodic evaluation and a certification procedure;
5. Call management meetings for awareness sessions;
6. Top management moral leadership should be demonstrated by good example.

Individual Measures for Reform

Nowhere is there more diversity of opinion than in the area of how incentives and disincentives are created for the individual executive to encourage avoidance of international payoffs. Clearly, once legal and economic measures have been taken, little seemingly remains to be done except to observe how the employee reacts to these stimuli. As a reactor, the individual executive, as is explained in Chapter 5, is the product of his previous environment including family background, education, peer influences, and finally the corporate moral climate within which he performs his function.

The measures discussed above form both positive and negative reinforcement of individual moral codes. The result is a wide range of reactions in their application to business decisions. According to Albert W. Levi, these alternatives may be summarized as follows:[32]

1. Ethics and business are by nature incompatible.
2. In competitive activity the morally lowest necessarily sets the standard.
3. Morality is a matter of "knowledge," and with plural answers, there is no way to choose between them.
4. Immorality is a defect of personal character. It will always exist.
5. Morality means following the rule of religion.

The first reaction reflects the legal attitude, namely, "I will do anything which the law cannot punish me for." This guide becomes a negative fear, not a positive conception of duty. Levi concludes: Legality is not enough, and religious requirements are too vague and inaccessible; therefore, the only solution is to make business a profession.[33] Our reform model (Table 7-2) emphasizes the importance of all influences (legal, economic, and moral) to induce moral behavior, and it calls for the "responsible professional behavior," which Levi endorses.

Others have toyed with the idea of professionalizing businessmen. The M.B.A. degree is a step in this direction. However, due to the diversity of business activities, the most important element of a profession, a uniform set of standards, is difficult to arrive at. Standards are already operative in specific business endeavors, such as insurance, real estate, auditing, and lately personnel administration, but the general practitioner in business is still considered on the outer fringes of what may be called a true profession, as can be seen from his position among the various occupations depicted in Table 6-1.

This table on professionalism allows each executive to determine his own professional standards and the ethical level at which he wishes to function. In making such a decision, the executive considers the legal and economic incentives discussed in this book that may bear on his decision. As an additional guide on the negative side, Table 7-1 lists the various laws and penalties that an executive faces as an individual in his everyday activities.

In addition, a list of "gray" areas in which the business executive finds his severest test in upholding professional ethical standards is reprinted below:[34]

Gray Area	Recommendation
1. The incomplete disclosure.	Disclose more rather than less.
2. The corrupt boss.	If things can't be set straight, get out.
3. The corrupt subordinate.	Get rid of him.
4. The inadvertent remark.	Zipper your lip.
5. The purified idea.	No shopping around for an agreeable lawyer or accountant.
6. The passive director.	Rubber-stamps are out.
7. The expense-account vacation.	One or the other, not both.
8. The stock option trap.	No personal gain from inside information.

Table 7-1
Individual Risks Executives Face under Federal Law

Agency	Maximum Individual Penalty
Internal Revenue Service	$5,000, 3 years, or both
Antitrust Div., Justice Dept.	$100,000, 3 years or both
Food & Drug Administration	$1,000, 1 year, or both[a] $10,000, 3 years, or both[b]
Federal Trade Commission	Restitution, injunction
Securities and Exchange Com.	$10,000, 2 years, or both
Environmental Protection Agency	$25,000 per day, 1 year, or both[a] $50,000 per day, 2 years, or both[b]
Consumer Product Safety Commission	$50,000, 1 year, or both
Office of Employee Benefits Security (ERISA) Labor Dept.	$10,000, 1 year, or both, reimbursement

Source: Compiled from *Business Week*, May 10, 1976, p. 113.
[a]First offense.
[b]Thereafter.

The business executive is not alone in facing these pressures. For all the professions, insistence on high ethical standards is increasing daily,[35] and the role of the professional is slowly changing to respond to these new pressures. Under such conditions, positive and self-initiated action of professionals to meet society's higher standards is preferable to government regulation or expulsion from the profession.

U.S. Supreme Court Chief Justice Warren Burger insists that "a profession lay claim to at least placing public duty ahead of private gain,"[36] and in a Law Day speech Senator Sam Ervin quoted Alexander Hamilton's *Federalist* remark with approval when he said:

It has been frequently remarked with great propriety that a voluminous code of laws is one of the inconveniences necessarily connected with advantages of a free government.[37]

Proposal for Reform

What, then, is the result of the various measures that have been proposed? As the above account indicates, far from being passive toward the problem, there is growing consensus on the transnational level about the importance of curbing international payoffs.

It is at the national level, however, where most current reform activity is being concentrated. Our proposal, therefore, focuses on this level. It discusses the desired scope and goals of national measures to combat international payoffs and evaluates some of the current proposed measures in the light of the philosophy advanced in our proposal for reform.

At the business level, our proposal is limited to actions that can be taken by the business community to self-regulate and control itself. Why the business community should not be regulated from without is analyzed in our national-level proposal.

Finally, at the individual level, our proposal concentrates on urging the individual to acquaint himself with the legal, economic, and moral influences that bear on the kind of moral behavior that suits each executive's own circumstances. In Table 7-2 we present a model of the transnational, national, business, and individual measures that we propose to combat international payoffs.

Reform at the Transnational Level

Although it could be worthwhile to create incentives for moral action and disincentives for immoral action through simple worldwide legislation aimed at

Table 7-2
Model for Institutional Antipayoff Measures Aimed at Individual Executive

| | Level and Type of Reform Measures | | |
Type of Influence on Individual	Transnational	National	Business
		Consensus Stage	
Legal	1. Support agreements. a. Payoffs are undesirable. b. Legislation is desirable. 2. No support for individual violators. 3. Promote discussion at conferences.	1. Support legislation. a. Outlaw payoffs. b. Heavy penalties against individual violators. 2. Research support.	1. Promote consensus. a. Intrafirm. b. Interfirm. c. Interindustry. d. Trade associations. 2. Lobby for legislation.
		Action Stage	
	1. Conclude pacts and agreements. a. Policy statements condemning payoffs. b. Cooperation on disclosure. c. Exchange of information. d. Emphasis on individual responsibility and penalty. 2. Follow-up reports and continuing discussion.	1. Enact legislation. a. Clear definition of payoff violation. b. Penalties against personal disclosures. c. Penalties against all individuals involved. d. Increased vigilance in SEC and IRS controls. e. Congressional oversight. f. Promotion of state laws controlling indemnity and insurance coverage. 2. Enforcement drive. a. Emphasis on severe penalties. b. Hitting recidivists.	1. Compliance in the firm. a. Clear policy statement on compliance b. Careful auditing procedures and controls. c. Constant self-policing and follow-up. d. Outside directors. e. Cooperation in complete disclosure. f. No support for individual violators. g. Cooperation in promoting enforcement. h. No insurance for wrongdoers. 2. Promotion of compliance among competitors.

Primary Influence	Moral[a]	Legal[b]	Economic[c]
Economic	(Consider long-run boycott alternatives in case of serious recidivism by multinational and inaction by national government.)	(Consider economic sanctions only in case of corporate recidivism.) 1. Positive protection of individuals who suffer reprisals for proper disclosure. a. Legal service. b. Reinstatement requirement. c. Antiblacklist. 2. Aid in job search. 3. Temporary public employment and/or subsidy, if necessary.	1. Sanctions and penalties. a. Discharge and discipline. b. Refusal to hire. c. Refusal to promote. d. Removal from Boards. e. Public censure. 2. Incentives. a. Bonus and benefits based on good conduct. b. Promotion. c. Public recognition. 3. No retaliation for proper disclosure.
Moral	1. Active moral leadership by heads of state. a. Policy declaration. b. Immediate reaction to unethical conduct. 2. Personal integrity and openness. 3. Pressure for removal from official position.	1. Moral leadership at all government levels. 2. Personal integrity. 3. Public disclosure of personal activities. 4. Censure of unethical conduct. 5. Removal from official position for wrong doing.	1. Moral climate and leadership. a. Management and directors chosen for integrity. b. Community involvement. c. Emphasis on professional behavior. 2. Code of ethics. 3. Openness in dealings.

Totality of Influences Lead to Support of Individual Personal Moral Code and Sense of Professionalism.[d]

[a] National sovereignty presently precludes effective legal measures at the transnational level. Economic sanctions at this level may be considered, but their enforcement must rely on nation-states. Moral leadership is therefore the only viable alternative.

[b] At the national level both enactment and enforcement of legislation can be effectively implemented. Such action, of course, has economic consequences but the origin of these consequences is primarily legal. National group refers to both parent and host countries.

[c] Because of long-run economic calculations, business abides by law and creates economic deterrence against individuals whose immoral actions may cause their business an economic loss.

[d] The above institutional (legal, economic, and moral) sanctions lead the individual increasingly to refrain from international payoffs.

all levels of activity from top policymaker on down to the individual citizen, this goal is not feasible at this time or in the foreseeable future. The concept of national sovereignty prevents imposition of any one legal standard on nations not choosing to adhere to such a standard. Should that be possible, the machinery for enforcement of such international legislation is too cumbersome and therefore ineffective and counterproductive. The only hope for cooperation at the transnational level lies in the slow realization of various developing countries, especially those not currently on the morality bandwagon, that a corrupt economic environment is not as inviting to foreign investors as is a corruption-free economy.

In the long run market constraint is the ultimate code enforcer for all developing countries. Multinational companies are forced by economic pressure to take their investment elsewhere if the cost of maintaining local standards gets too high. Thus, the market eventually pressures even rich developing countries to realize that compliance with international standards to control payoffs is preferable to loss of investment potential. In other words, since there is no current enforceable international law against payoffs, market discipline must be relied on to bring heads of state closer to consensus on the need for international antipayoff legislation.[38]

Fortunately, as the analysis of initiatives at the transnational level shows, there seems to be a movement toward greater consensus on the need for action to curb corruption in world trade. Such consensus is a prerequisite for world policymakers to demonstrate the moral leadership needed for the implementation of an effective world antipayoff campaign.

Reform at the National Level

Consensus at the transnational level and moral leadership among heads of state cannot alone assure success of an antipayoff campaign. The teeth for such campaign must come from national leaders who support, enact, and enforce legislation against international payoffs. Legal deterrence, supplemented by moral leadership, is the primary influence of national policymakers. This legal deterrence must be directed at individuals[39] (not corporations) who engage in international payoffs.

At the national level, there is an increasing demand for national policymakers to provide moral leadership to their constituencies and to sponsor effective legal deterrence against individuals who corrupt society. The 1976 U.S. presidential campaign affirms this. Morality was one of the hottest campaign issues. The above account of national measures for reform is a vivid confirmation of this trend.

Under these conditions in a democracy, the requirements of moral leadership at the national level are quite clear. Like any other individual in society, if a head of state is caught in an immoral act or even in failing to discharge his duties relating to morality, the discipline of the "political market" removes him from office. The newly elected successor is likely to learn the lesson and to provide the required moral leadership.

But this political pressure on national policymakers may result in overreaction to the problem of international payoffs. Indeed, judging from current national efforts to combat payoffs, policymakers seem to have charged too many agencies, working at too many proposals, aimed in too many directions. This uncoordinated activity, although massive and expensive, can hardly be effective.

To prevent overreaction our proposal deals next with the desired scope and goals of the antipayoff campaign.

Scope of Antipayoff Campaign. To assure an optimum allocation of resources in the antipayoff campaign, it is important to clarify its goal. Initially we must refrain from setting standards that are too high for immediate success, considering the various institutions that must undertake reform. It takes time for heads of state to realize that their political and economic systems cannot survive under continuous charges of abuse, deceit, and corruption.

More specifically, then, how high should we set the goals for an antipayoff campaign? For total elimination of all business corruption, there must be complete information on all business transactions. To achieve that goal, there is the risk of moving from "the watergate of the executive to the witchhunt of the legislative,"[40] or in this case, a witchhunt of the business community. In other words, the right to know may conflict, at a certain level, with the right to privacy.

Blanket legislation against payoffs may be counterproductive by punishing the do-gooders as much as the evil-doers. For example, in industries where the market mechanism makes it possible to avoid a "bribe tax," because of success in offering better products and services, imposition of strict and costly disclosure requirements on all firms may well inhibit free trade. This fact is also true for operations mostly of a retail nature where largely monetary outlays are not involved in single transactions. Costly disclosure requirements may also hurt business firms that cannot afford the accounting and legal services necessary to justify complicated financial information. This situation may result in mergers and further diminution of competition in the market.

The process of limiting the scope and cost of an antipayoff campaign can be guided by considerations that have already surfaced in the rationale for international payoffs. In Chapter 2 payoffs are classified according to who receives them, their purpose, and their legality. Understanding the various shades of international payments leads to concentration on those that are unquestionably improper. Chapter 3 shows that improper payments are more likely to occur in certain industries and markets and are paid by firms having certain economic relationships with the host country. Consequently, measures may be directed primarily at individuals employed by firms in those industries that are more prone to payoffs.

Chapter 4 sorted out the bottom line of all the headlines on payoff disclosures to date, namely, that two firms (Lockheed and Gulf) have been accused of gross misconduct in connection with overseas payoffs.[41] In the absence of laws against international payoffs as such, it is only the amount of such payoffs that can make their nondisclosure a serious infraction. Also, the nondisclosure of such materially important data makes their deduction as a business expense a serious violation of IRS laws. Thus, concentration on large payoffs (certainly larger than the $1,000 proposed in S. 3133[42]) may be another way of limiting the scope of the antipayoff campaign.

From the discussion on the ethical conceptual framework in Chapter 5, it is clear that a national antipayoff campaign may be further restricted by being directed at individuals rather than corporations. Concentrating on the individual executive allows emphasis on society's moral leadership not just legal deterrence. Also, casting antipayoff activity in the long-run self-interest of business firms (not as their social responsibility) encourages executives to provide moral leadership and "economic deterrence" through dismissal of employees who violate the law.

Finally, if society and business carry out their responsibilities by creating an environment conducive to moral action, the individual executive is more likely to rely on his own moral values to deter him from immoral conduct. Thus, the need for large-scale legislation and an extensive government bureaucracy for its administration diminishes.

Evaluation of Measures for Reform. To explain more fully our own reform proposal and at the same time to critique measures that have been proposed at the national level, we have concentrated on three major topics:

1. Disclosure;
2. Penalties;
3. Indemnification.

Disclosure. Most current legislation is misdirected at institutions rather than at individuals. For instance, disclosure should be aimed at individuals who make payoffs, not at corporations who do not. Imposing strict and costly disclosure requirements on small firms and on large companies not engaging in overseas payoffs hinders free trade and allows the real culprits to continue in their corrupt ways since they find ways to hide their activities. The need to defend themselves against unjustified complaints interferes with many companies' capability to comply with the law and reduces their ability to cooperate in enforcement. Related to personal disclosure, permitting executives to plead nolo contendere prevents discovery of the true story of individual corruption. This is worse for disclosure purposes than "taking the Fifth" since no immunity can be offered in exchange for information. In our individualistic society personal rewards and personal penalties that flow from personal disclosure requirements are likely to generate higher ethical standards than hard-to-enforce business disclosure laws.

Thus, what is needed is cessation of all the great debates on the pros and cons of antipayoff legislation against business and concentration of national energy on antipayoff measures against individual violators.

Penalties. In addition, as our proposal suggests, penalties for individual violators should be severe enough to discourage violation of the antipayoff laws.

Lack of severe penalties for white-collar crimes and laxity in bringing violators to justice are common complaints today. As Table 7-3 indicates, there appears to be a double standard when comparing executive-suite crimes with street crimes. A study of all sentences imposed in the Southern District of New York in 1972 shows that bank robbery and narcotics created a high likelihood of imprisonment (83 and 77 percent, respectively), whereas tax fraud was punished in 35 percent and bribery in only 25 percent of the cases. There is also great disparity in the length of prison sentences, ranging on average from 70 months for bank robbery to 11 months for bribery and only 6 months for tax fraud.

Table 7-3
Comparison of White-Collar and Street Crimes

Type of Crime	Likelihood of Imprisonment (percent)	Average Length of Prison Sentence (months)
White Collar		
Bank embezzlement	23.2	18.0
Bribery	25.0	11.0
IRS (tax fraud)	35.4	5.9
Street		
Bank robbery	82.8	69.6
Guns	50,0	28.2
Narcotics	77.0	62.4

Source: Compiled from The Bureau of National Affairs, Inc., *Special Report on White-Collar Crime*, SRLR No. 348, Part II, Washington, D.C., April 14, 1976.
Note: Data are for the Southern District of New York Federal Court from May to October 1972.

Indemnification. The practice of permitting business to indemnify individuals for legal fees and fines in connection with civil and criminal suits is also in need of reexamination.

Obviously, there is something to be said for protecting individual executives who act as directors and officers (D & O) for the corporation that employs them. Limitation of the liability of such executives finds its justification in the basic structure of the corporation itself, which is deeply rooted in Western industrial society.

As every student of economic history knows, corporate charters originated in special acts of kings and legislatures to get specific economic functions performed. For example, the Hudson Bay Company, which was instrumental in early American colonization and trade, was such a monopoly grant. Franchises for service awarded to utilities in various communities today, and ICC and FAA route designations for railroads and airlines are the modern version of such grants. It soon became conventional business practice to use the corporate structure as a method of amassing needed capital for industrial expansion without jeopardizing the individual fortunes of the collaborators. It is safe to say that this institution played a major role in economic growth.

The law recognizes that a corporate stockholder has limited liability in that his possible loss as a partial owner of the corporation is confined to the value of his shares. This concept of limited liability, however, has serious disadvantages for control of international payoffs since an aura of unaccountability arises that the use of the "fictitious person" legalism cannot dispel. It has become the fashion to cloak individual responsibility in the mantle of corporate impersonality, and the combination seems to justify the conclusion that "nobody" is minding the store.[43]

This problem is especially acute in the international payoff investigation since some multinational companies refuse to divulge information about where, by whom, and to whom payoffs were made in order to protect the individuals involved from being penalized for carrying out their corporate duties. Such duties heretofore have been defined solely in the light of corporate responsibilities. Business ethics has emphasized refraining from any "conflict of interest" entanglement that may jeopardize the individual executive's total loyalty and accountability to the corporation that employs him. However, in order to enforce even the laws regulating business activities that have already been passed, it is imperative that government and the public know who is responsible for corporate conduct so that responsibility for corporate action can be placed squarely on the shoulders of live, flesh-and-blood persons (rather than on the "artificial" corporate person) who can be charged with crimes, fined, and put in jail. Penalties must act as a deterrent to recidivism if they are to be effective in crime prevention. Penalizing the corporation not only fails to accomplish this objective, it actually punishes innocent persons in that it detracts from the profitability or image of all the stockholders, most of whom have no responsibility for corporate activities except in the very general and nebulous sense of providing an infinitesimal part of the operating capital. The fact that they can withdraw their investment funds is no solution in the short run.

For these reasons present corporation law must be reexamined to change those provisions that encourage individual irresponsibility. Foremost among them are two sections of the Model Business Corporation Act, which relates, first, to indemnification of corporate directors, officers, employees, and agents and, second, to the corporation's right to purchase insurance to reimburse those individuals for whatever expenses, including attorney's fees, they may incur in defending themselves from litigation arising from their corporate responsibilities.[44]

Of the fifty states only Illinois has no indemnification provision in its corporation law. The other forty-nine not only permit indemnification but require that it be paid in certain circumstances. The Model Business Corporation Act, promulgated by the American Bar Association, Section on Corporations, Banking, and Business Law, Committee on Corporate Laws, which has been adopted by twenty-nine states, includes the following provisions for indemnification of corporate directors and officers:

1. Indemnification against outsider suits (e.g., government and consumers);
2. Indemnification against insider suits (e.g., stockholders);
3. Reimbursement of all expenses in case of successful defense;
4. Permission to advance payment for legal fees and expenses;
5. Broader indemnification terms permitted if approved by Board of Directors or stockholders;
6. Broader terms if permitted by corporate bylaws;
7. Indemnification insurance may be purchased;
8. Duty survives present corporate structure and passes on both to survivor company and individual's heirs.

In the light of an unknown risk, rational business conduct demands that corporations insure themselves against a potentially heavy liability. The escalation of attorney's fees in these cases makes purchase of D & O insurance a prudent act, as long as it is permitted by law.

However, strict limitations are needed on this type of insurance so that the individual executive is not provided with so extensive a security blanket that he engages in misconduct because he judges it to be in the best interests of the corporation and is not likely to bear personally the economic loss entailed in defending such actions.

While it is true that present insurance and indemnification provisions do not protect the individual if he violates a law, the gray areas in international payoffs are such that there is some justification for leaning in favor of them when legal defense is guaranteed. Also, when the indemnification law permits broadening the coverage in these areas by corporate bylaw or resolution, likelihood of economic sanctions for the individual is diminished through the nolo contendere device.

Only six states prohibit corporate relaxation of the strict controls over indemnification that the state law sets forth. This is the reform that we propose. We believe that no company should be permitted to enlarge the area of indemnification through passage of bylaws or resolutions by the board of directors or stockholders. This support should be declared against public policy since it encourages misconduct and permits private corporate law to supersede state law.

Reform at the Business Level

Given the increasing consensus on the need for enforcement of antipayoff legislation at both the transnational and national levels, it behooves the business community to consider the preferable alternative of self-policing while it is still available. This alternative is preferable not because of social responsibility but because it is now an acceptable way to promote self-interest.

The promotion of both the corporate and the individual self-interest consistent with societal goals is what this book seeks. Thus, along with our suggestions, at the national level, to tighten constraints on executives who engage in international payoffs and to loosen constraints on those who oppose them at the business level, our proposal urges executives to be aware of the increasing economic and personal costs of international payoffs.

To that end we devote a whole chapter. In that chapter each executive is provided with a list of important questions that bear on the legal, economic, and moral consequences of business involvement in international payoffs (see the tables in Chapter 6). The executive is presented with the benefits and costs for the MNC derived from engaging in payoffs in the host country as well as the parent country.

The result of analysis of the self-interest of the corporation and of the executive must be a greater commitment of the business community to put its own house in order. Some of the measures that have been taken by business are mentioned earlier in this chapter. As the external pressure for business self-discipline grows, business is encouraged to increase the economic deterrence against international payoffs and general corruption.

But, to encourage business to put its house in order, legislation (as discussed in our proposed national measures for reform to be implemented by business firms) should include the individual sanctions coupled with personal disclosure requirements to apply not only to the "hit man" but also to the top corporate officer who "puts out the contract" or at least shuts his eyes to the transaction.

As a further disincentive, the corporation, realizing the increasing self-interest it derives from objection to international payoffs, should cancel all liability insurance for directors and officers (D & O) who are caught in corruption.

Thus, by removing company protection from executive corruption, and insisting on personal disclosure, promoting openness within the organization to facilitate the detection of wrongdoing, and rearranging the company reward and penalty system to reflect the company's interest in executive moral behavior, the company promotes its self-interest.

Just as the "watergate mentality," which allowed corruption in government, is no longer tolerated so is the business "organization man" mentality now rejected. Business has no alternative but to create a "free man" mentality to encourage adherence to the law of the land rather to the law of the corporation if they are incompatible.

Only free men and women, capable of independently judging their actions without undue constraints, can change the role of business in our society from that of "accused privileged minority"[45] to that of revered and appreciated leaders in our society. This is important not only for the status and personal feeling of present business leaders but, more so, for the future of the business community and with it our free society.

Reform at the Individual Level

The bottom line of our proposal for reform is the individual. He is a reactor to whatever measures we have proposed at the transnational, national, and business levels. As Table 7-2 shows, the individual, subject to the moral, legal, and economic influences generated by transnational, national, and business measures, uses his own personal moral code and sense of professionalism to arrive at his decision of whether or not to engage in international payoffs.

More specifically, the long-run goal of reform activity, regardless of whether the individual involved is head of state, top corporate officer, or lower-level manager, is to increase the risk of acting immorally and to decrease the risk of acting morally. Just as any serious criminal act by an individual is investigated regardless of the institutional association of the criminal (as evidenced by the Nixon debacle), legislation against international payoffs can be similarly enforced. Given the increasing personal exposure and lack of institutional protection that we advocate, it becomes increasingly risky to engage in improper payments and to use business exigency for winking at questionable actions. It is this dichotomy between personal codes of conduct and business codes of conduct that must be removed so that individual responsibility is seen as the most important element in every business decision.

Since, in the final analysis, it is only the individual who does or does not make international payoffs, the major focus of this book is the individual. If we contribute to a more informed business executive who is able to consider not merely the short-run but also the long-run impact of international payoffs on both the corporation and his own life, we have achieved our purpose in writing this book.

Conclusion

Review of the elements of our proposal for reform in the model in Table 7-2 points up our multilevel approach to combat improper behavior in the field of international payments. It focuses on the individual executive to produce the incentives and disincentives that enable him to resolve the dilemma created by a conflict between his personal code of conduct (ethics) and business exigency (economics). To support his personal moral values, we propose tangible legal and economic incentives and sanctions.

We leave the various decisionmakers with their own consciences since we promised not to do any moralizing. We have presented the pros and cons of international payoffs. We have delineated the gray areas relating to various questionable payments. We have proposed measures for reform at four levels of decision making—transnational, national, business, and personal. We have given guidelines and the steps to be taken by each decisionmaker—international leader, national head of state, corporate director, and individual manager—to draw up his own cost-benefit analysis based on how he evaluates his responsibilities in the light of this new phenomenon of international payoff disclosures.

We wish him luck and, if he opts for payoff, we leave him with this final warning: *Don't get caught!*

Notes

1. It is important to differentiate between *payoff* and *payment* when considering measures for reform. Payment refers to all international transfers of whatever nature, including even those designated as the white area in Chapter 2. Payoff, on the other hand, has a distinct connotation of wrong doing. Measures for reform discussed in this chapter are limited in application to payoffs—that is, the black area and questionable payments in the gray area, as defined in Chapter 2.

2. Cf. Milton Friedman, "The Uses of Corruption," *Newsweek*, March 28, 1976; p. 73; Murray Weidenbaum, *The Wall Street Journal*, April 6, 1976; see also editorial, *The Wall Street Journal*, May 12, 1976.

3. The 94th Congress adjourned without enacting any antipayoff legislation as such, although riders on two tax and trade bills impose certain sanctions for Internal Revenue Service enforcement.

4. Competition among MNCs obviously is not the competition of economic theory. Although most MNC market structures are closer to the oligopoly model, they nevertheless represent a firm foundation for the market system, for which we believe there is as yet no better alternative in the free world.

5. *St. Louis Post-Dispatch*, editorial, July 19, 1976.

6. Cf. *U.S. News & World Report*, April 12, 1976, p. 36.

7. *The Wall Street Journal*, November 14, 1975. See also statement released by White House Press Secretary, March 31, 1976, establishing the President's Task Force on Questionable Corporate Payments Abroad.

8. *The Wall Street Journal*, September 10, 1976.

9. *The New York Times*, May 5, 1975.

10. S. 3133, to amend the Securities Exchange Act of 1934 to require issuers of securities registered pursuant to Section 12 of such act to maintain accurate records and to furnish reports relating to certain foreign payments; S. 3379, to require reporting and analysis of contributions, payments, and gifts made in the conduct of international business; and S. 3418, to amend the Securities Exchange Act of 1934 to prohibit certain issuers of securities from falsifying their books and records.

11. U.S. Senate, Committee on Banking, Housing and Urban Affairs, "Prohibiting Bribes to Foreign Officials," *Hearing*, May 18, 1976, p. 2.

12. Ibid., p. 58.

13. *The New York Times*, May 5, 1975.

14. By October 1976 this number had increased to 235 with new reports coming every day. Cf. *The New York Times*, October 14, 1976.

15. *The New York Times*, May 16, 1975.

16. White House, *Press Release*, March 31, 1976.

17. *The New York Times*, May 5, 1975.

18. U.S. Congress, Senate, Foreign Relations Committee, Subcommittee on Multinational Corporations, *Hearings*, Washington, D.C., May-September, 1975 (Part 12), pp. 351-53.

19. *The Wall Street Journal*, May 21, 1975.

20. These are generally the same laissez-faire proponents mentioned in connection with the discussion of social responsibility in Chapter 5.

21. Cf. "The Hall of Fame For Business Leadership—1976," *Fortune*, January 1976, pp. 118-25.

22. Cf. Milton Moskowitz, "Profiles in Corporate Responsibility," *Business and Society Review*, Spring 1975, pp. 28-42.

23. Fred T. Allen, "The Case for Corporate Morality," speech before Swiss-American Chamber of Commerce, October 16, 1975, p. 5. Reprinted with permission. (Mr. Allen is chairman of the board and president of Pitney Bowes.)

24. Securities and Exchange Commission, *Report of the Special Review Committee of the Board of Directors of Gulf Oil Corporation*, Washington, D.C., December 30, 1975, p. 202.

25. Ibid., p. 208. For additional methods of stopping individual crime, see "How a Memphis Bank Stopped Its Crime Wave," *Business Week*, October 27, 1975, p. 63.

26. Cf. American Institute of Certified Public Accountants, *Proposed Statement on Auditing Standards: Illegal Acts by Clients*, May 12, 1976, SRLR No. 352, F-1-3. On June 15, 1976 a suit was filed by Arthur Andersen & Company, one of the largest accounting firms, to prevent SEC from enforcing this provision and standards promulgated by AICPA's Financial Accounting Standards Board. *SEC Docket*, August 18, 1975.

27. Fred T. Allen, "The Case for Corporate Morality," p. 6. Reprinted with permission.

28. Cf. *Business Week*, October 27, 1975, p. 63, wherein a Memphis banker cites lack of control and low pay scales as the causes for employee crime and explains the success his organization had in stopping it.

29. Robert Cushman, "The Norton Company Faces the Payoffs Problem," *Harvard Business Review*, September-October 1976, pp. 6-7. Reprinted with permission.

30. Business Roundtable, *A Survey of Business Roundtable Members on Business Conduct Guidelines*, New York, December 1975, pp. 2-5. Reprinted with permission.

31. Ibid., p. 8.

32. Albert W. Levi, "Ethical Confusion and the Business Community," in Joseph W. Towle, ed., *Ethics and Standards in American Business* (Boston: Houghton Mifflin, 1964), pp. 20-29.

33. Ibid.

34. *Business Week*, March 30, 1974, p. 88. Reprinted with permission.

35. "The Troubled Professions," *Business Week*, August 16, 1976, pp. 126-38; and "Closing in on the Professions," *Business Week*, October 27, 1975, pp. 106-08. See also "Professional Responsibility Symposium," *Dickinson Law Review*, Summer 1975; Duke N. Stern and David R. Klock, "Public Policy and the Professionalization of Life Underwriters," *American Business Law Journal*, Fall 1975, pp. 225-38; and Norman Redlich, "Lawyers, The Temple and the Market Place," *Record of New York City Bar Association*, March 1975, pp. 200-06.

36. Warren Burger, "A Sick Profession," *Tulsa Law Journal*, 1968, pp. 10-12.

37. Sam J. Ervin, Jr., "The Role of the Lawyer in America," *New England Law Review*, Fall 1975, pp. 1-6. (Senator Ervin chaired the Senate Watergate Committee.)

38. Another example of the working of the market mechanism is the case of expropriation. If one country frequently expropriates foreign companies, the parent country of these firms can do very little to reverse such decision or otherwise protect the foreign property of its citizens. But the market may discipline the expropriating country since it thus becomes a riskier investment location, and astute businessmen throughout the world increasingly favor a less risky environment for investment.

39. At a later stage, to supplement efforts against individual corruption, attention may turn to institutions that "seed" a high frequency of such individual corruption. Recidivist corporations may be penalized in accordance with their size and financial strength to force their compliance with the law of the land. We would be naive to ignore the problems that the U.S. Defense Department may face in losing the only source of a particular good or service. Therefore some kind of phasing-in process of viable alternatives must accompany any such legislation where competitive capability is absent.

40. *The New York Times*, November 3, 1975.

41. Payoff indictments and penalties in the United States have been confined to domestic political contributions by corporations. Notoriety for most firms has come from voluntary disclosure of all payments, both foreign and domestic, in SEC reports to avoid the sanctions of the SEC laws described in Chapter 6. Foreign international payoffs have not resulted in legal penalties for individual executives in the United States, except for perjury. In Japan, however, individuals have not fared so well.

42. S. 3133 is the bill proposed by Senator William Proxmire, chairman of the Senate Banking Committee. This provision is not in S. 3664.

43. The *Forbes* advertisement (e.g., *The Wall Street Journal*, June 18, 1976) depicting BD members as the three "no see, no hear, no speak evil" monkeys is humorous precisely because of the half-truth it represents.

44. The text of these two sections of the model law and a sample D & O insurance contract appear in Appendix 7A. In the original, the Brook article, which is partially reproduced there, also contains a table listing the states that have indemnification provisions or have adopted the Model Corporation Law. Ralph Nader proposes federal licensing for all multinational corporations. We do not believe that this of itself would bring about reform.

45. Cf. Leonard Silk and David Vogel, *Ethics and Profits* (New York: Simon & Schuster, 1976).

Appendix 7A
Directors' Indemnification
and Liability Insurance

Herbert C. Brook[a]

The increased protection afforded directors by indemnification statutes and directors' and officers' indemnity insurance is reviewed in this article. Particular emphasis is placed upon the evolution of the indemnification statues of New York, Delaware, California and the Model Act, and the impact of these laws on status and non-status claims. Litigation in the above states involving indemnification is reviewed, concerning indemnification of expenses in compromise settlements, status claims against directors, availability pendente lite, availability upon partial success, availability in an indemnity action, and judicial attitudes when bylaws are broader than statutes. General judicial attitudes indicate a restrictive view when the director's conduct is faulty. A discussion ensues which may assist in deciding whether a corporation should purchase indemnity insurance. . . .

Conclusion

The protective measures now available in the form of indemnification statutes, many of which are comprehensive in nature, together with directors' and officers' liability insurance, provide substantial security to directors from the risks of litigation against them. For their own long-range best interests, directors, in overseeing the utilization of these protective measures, should make sure that their administration is characterized by good faith and an awareness of the admonition of Ray Garrett, Jr., Chairman of the Securities Exchange Commission, that "[a] corporation director's job is to protect stockholders, not management."*

Model Business Corporation Act,
approved by American Bar Association

The 1959 Model act provided that each corporation shall have power:

To indemnify any director or officer or former director or officer of the corporation, or any person who may have served at its request as a director or officer of another corporation in which it owns shares of capital stock or of which it is a creditor, against expenses actually and reasonably incurred by him

---

Forbes, March 1, 1975, p. 11.

[a]Reprinted from an article by Herbert C. Brook, entitled "Directors' Indemnification and Liability Insurance," appearing in *New York Law Forum*, Summer 1975, pp. 1-39. Copyright 1975 by New York Law School. Reprinted in *Corporate Counsel's Annual* (New York: Matthew Bender & Co., Inc., 1976), pp. 58-89.

in connection with the defense of any action, suit or proceeding, civil or *criminal*, in which he is made a party by reason of being or having been such director or officer, except in relation to matters as to which he shall be adjudged in such action, suit or proceeding to be liable for negligence or misconduct in the performance of duty *to the corporation*; and to make any other indemnification that shall be authorized by the articles of incorporation or by any by-law or resolution adopted by the shareholders after notice.

The 1967 *Act* provided:

(a) A corporation shall have power to indemnify any person who was or is a party or is threatened to be made a party to any threatened, pending or completed action, suit or proceeding, whether civil, criminal, administrative or investigative (other than an action by or in the right of the corporation) by reason of the fact that he is or was a director, officer, employee or agent of the corporation, or is or was serving at the request of the corporation as a director, officer, employee or agent of another corporation, partnership, joint venture, trust or other enterprise, against expenses (including attorneys' fees), judgments, fines and amounts paid in settlement actually and reasonably incurred by him in connection with such action, suit or proceeding if he acted in good faith and in a manner he reasonably believed to be in or not opposed to the best interests of the corporation, and, with respect to any criminal action or proceeding, had no reasonable cause to believe his conduct was unlawful. The termination of any action, suit or proceeding by judgment, order, settlement, conviction, or upon a plea of *nolo contendere* or its equivalent, shall not, of itself, create a presumption that the person did not act in good faith and in a manner which he reasonably believed to be in or not opposed to the best interests of the corporation, and, with respect to any criminal action or proceeding, had reasonable cause to believe that his conduct was unlawful.

(b) A corporation shall have power to indemnify any person who was or is a party or is threatened to be made a party to any threatened, pending or completed action or suit by or in the right of the corporation to procure a judgment in its favor by reason of the fact that he is or was a director, officer, employee or agent of the corporation, or is or was serving at the request of the corporation as a director, officer, employee or agent of another corporation, partnership, joint venture, trust or other enterprise against expenses (including attorneys' fees) actually and reasonably incurred by him in connection with the defense or settlement of such action or suit if he acted in good faith and in a manner he reasonably believed to be in or not opposed to the best interests of the corporation and except that no indemnification shall be made in respect of any claim, issue or matter as to which such person shall have been adjudged to be liable for negligence or misconduct in the performance of his duty to the corporation unless and only to the extent that the Court of Chancery or the court in which such action or suit was brought shall determine upon application that, despite the adjudication of liability but in view of all circumstances of the case, such person is fairly and reasonably entitled to indemnity for such expenses which the Court of Chancery or such other court shall deem proper.

(c) To the extent that a director, officer, employee or agent of a corporation has been successful on the merits or otherwise in defense of any action, suit, or proceeding referred to in subsections (a) and (b), or in defense of any claim, issue or matter therein, he shall be indemnified against expenses (including attorneys' fees) actually and reasonably incurred by him in connection therewith.

(d) Any indemnification under subsections (a) and (b)(unless ordered by a court) shall be made by the corporation only as authorized in the specific case upon a determination that indemnification of the director, officer, employee or agent is proper in the circumstances because he has met the applicable standard of conduct set forth in subsections (a) and (b). Such determination shall be made (1) by the board of directors by a majority vote of a quorum consisting of directors who were not parties to such action, suit or proceeding, or (2) if such a quorum is not obtainable, or, even if obtainable a quorum of disinterested directors so directs, by independent legal counsel in a written opinion, or (3) by the stockholders.

(e) Expenses incurred in defending a civil or criminal action, suit or proceeding may be paid by the corporation in advance of the final disposition of such action, suit or proceeding as authorized in the manner provided in subsection (d) upon receipt of an undertaking by or on behalf of the director, officer, employee or agent to repay such amount unless it shall ultimately be determined that he is entitled to be indemnified by the corporation as authorized in this section.

(f) The indemnification provided by this section shall not be deemed exclusive of any other rights to which those indemnified may be entitled under any by-law, agreement, vote of stockholders or disinterested directors or otherwise, both as to action in his official capacity and as to action in another capacity while holding such office, and shall continue as to a person who has ceased to be a director, officer, employee or agent and shall inure to the benefit of the heirs, executors and administrators of such a person.

(g) A corporation shall have power to purchase and maintain insurance on behalf of any person who is or was a director, officer, employee or agent of the corporation, or is or was serving at the request of the corporation as a director, officer, employee or agent of another corporation, partnership, joint venture, trust or other enterprise against any liability asserted against him and incurred by him in any such capacity or arising out of his status as such, whether or not the corporation would have the power to indemnify him against such liability under the provisions of this section.

Sample D & O Insurance Contract

Directors' and Officers' Liability Including
Company Reimbursement

I. INSURING CLAUSE

In consideration of the payment of the premium and subject to all of the terms, conditions, and exclusions of this policy, Underwriters agree:

(a) with the Directors and Officers of the Company that, if during the policy period any claim or claims are made against any of the Directors and Officers for a Wrongful Act, the Underwriters shall pay on behalf of such Directors and Officers all loss which such Directors and Officers shall become legally obligated to pay, except for such loss which the Company shall indemnify such Directors and Officers;

(b) with the Company that, if during the policy period any claim or claims are made against any of the Directors and Officers of the Company for a Wrongful Act, the Underwriters shall pay on behalf of the Company, all loss for which the Company may be required or permitted by law to indemnify such Directors and Officers.

II. EXTENSION

If the Underwriters shall cancel or refuse to renew this policy, the Company or the Directors and Officers shall have the right, upon payment of an additional premium of 10% of the three year premium hereunder, to an extension of the cover granted by this policy in respect of any claim or claims which may be made against any of the Directors and Officers during the period of ninety (90) days after the date of such cancellation or non-renewal, but only in respect of any Wrongful Act committed before the date of cancellation or non-renewal of the policy. This right of extension shall terminate unless written notice is given to Underwriters within ten (10) days after the effective date of cancellation or non-renewal.

III. DEFINITIONS

(a) "Company" shall mean:
   (1) the Company named in Item A of the Declarations;
   (2) any subsidiary of the Company which existed prior to or at the inception of this policy;
   (3) any subsidiary of the Company which is acquired or created subsequent to the inception date of this policy, subject to the provisions of Paragraph VIII (b).

(b) "Directors and Officers" shall mean:
   (1) any persons who were, now are, or shall be Directors and/or Officers of the Company;
   (2) the estates, heirs, legal representatives or assigns of deceased persons who were Directors and/or Officers of the Company;
   (3) the legal representatives or assigns of Directors and/or Officers of the Company in the event of their incompetency, insolvency or bankruptcy.

(c) "Wrongful Act" shall mean any actual or alleged error or misstatement or misleading statement or act or omission or neglect or breach of duty by the Directors or Officers in the discharge of their duties, individually or collectively, or any other matter not excluded by the terms and conditions of this policy, claimed against them solely by reason of their being Directors or Officers of the Company.

(d) "Loss" shall mean any amount which the Directors and Officers are legally obligated to pay for which they are not indemnified by the Company, or for which the Company may be required or permitted by law to pay as indemnity to the Directors and Officers, for a claim or claims made against them for Wrongful Acts, and shall include, but not be limited to, damages, judgments, settlements and costs, cost of investigation (excluding from such cost of investigation and defense, salaries of officers or employees of the Company), and amounts incurred in the defense of legal actions, claims or proceedings and appeals therefrom, cost of attachment or similar bonds; providing always, however, such subject of loss shall not include fines or penalties imposed by law, or matters which may be deemed uninsurable under the law pursuant to which this policy shall be construed.

IV. EXCLUSIONS

(a) Underwriters shall not be liable to make any payment for loss in connection with any claim made against the Directors or Officers:

(1) which, at the time of such claim, is insured by any other existing valid policy or policies under which payment of the loss is actually made, except in respect of any excess beyond the amount or amounts of payments under such other policy or policies;

(2) for which the Directors and Officers are entitled to indemnity and/or payment by reason of having given notice of any circumstance which might give rise to a claim under any policy or policies, the term of which has expired prior to the inception date of this policy;

(3) for bodily injury, sickness, disease, or death of any person, or for damage to or destruction of any tangible property including loss of use thereof;

(4) arising from charges of seepage, pollution or contamination and based upon or attributed to violation or alleged violation of any federal, state, municipal or other governmental statute, regulation or ordinance prohibiting or providing for the control or regulation of emissions or effluents of any kind into the atmosphere or any body of land, water, waterway or watercourse or arising from any action or proceeding brought for enforcement purposes by any public official, agency, commission, board of pollution control, or administration pursuant to any such statutes, regulations or ordinances or arising from any suits alleging seepage, pollution or contamination based upon Common Law nuisance or trespass.

(b) Except insofar as the Company may be required or permitted by law to pay as indemnity to the Directors or Officers, the Underwriters shall not be liable to make any payment for loss in connection with any claim made against the Directors or Officers:

(1) for libel or slander;

(2) based upon or attributable to their gaining in fact any personal profit or advantage to which they were not legally entitled;

(3) for the return by the Directors or Officers of any remuneration paid in fact to them without the previous approval of the stockholders of the Company, if payment of such remuneration shall be held by the Courts to be in violation of law;

(4) for an accounting of profits in fact made from the purchase or sale by the Directors or Officers of securities of the Company within the meaning of Section 16(b) of the Securities Exchange Act of 1934 and amendments thereto or similar provisions of any State statutory law or common law;

(5) brought about or contributed to by the dishonesty of the Directors or Officers; however, notwithstanding the foregoing, the Directors or Officers shall be protected under the terms of this policy as to any claims upon which suit may be brought against them by reason of any alleged dishonesty on the part of the Directors or Officers, unless a judgment or other final adjudication thereof adverse to the Directors or Officers shall establish that acts of active and deliberate dishonesty committed by the Directors or Officers with actual dishonest purpose and intent were material to the cause of action so adjudicated.

It is agreed that any fact pertaining to any one Director or Officer shall not be imputed to any other Director or Officer for the purpose of determining the application of Exclusions IV (b) above.

V. LIMITS OF LIABILITY

(a) Underwriters shall be liable to pay 95% of loss excess of the amount of retention as determined under Clause V (b) up to the limit of liability shown under Item C of the Declarations, it being warranted that the remaining 5% of each loss shall be uninsured.

(b) In the event a single loss is covered in part under both Insuring Clause I (a) and I (b) the retentions set forth in Item D shall be applied separately to that part of the loss covered by each Insuring Clause and the sum of the retentions so applied shall constitute the retention for each single loss provided, however, the total retention as finally determined shall in no event exceed the retention applicable to Company Reimbursement—Insuring Clause I (b).

(c) Claims based on or arising out of the same act or interrelated acts of one or more of the Directors or Officers shall be considered a single loss and only one retention shall be deducted from each single loss.

(d) Subject to the foregoing, Underwriters' Liability for all loss shall be the amount shown in Item C of the Declarations, and shall be the maximum liability of Underwriters in each policy year (regardless of the time of payment by the Underwriters).

VI. COSTS, CHARGES AND EXPENSES

No costs, charges or expenses shall be incurred, or settlements made, without Underwriters' consent, such consent not to be unreasonably withheld; however, in the event of such consent being given, Underwriters will pay, subject to the provisions of Clause V, such costs, settlements, charges or expenses.

VII. NOTIFICATION

(a) If during the policy period or extended discovery period any claim is made against any Director or Officer, the Company or the Directors and Officers shall, as a condition precedent to their right to be indemnified under this policy, give to the Underwriters notice in writing as soon as practicable of any such claim.

(b) If during the policy period or extended discovery period:

    (1) the Company or the Directors and Officers shall receive written or oral notice from any party that it is the intention of such party to hold the Directors and Officers, or any of them, responsible for a Wrongful Act; or

    (2) the Company or the Directors and Officers shall become aware of any fact, circumstance or situation which may subsequently give rise to a claim being made against the Directors and Officers, or any of them, for a Wrongful Act;

and shall in either case during such period give written notice as soon as practicable to the Underwriters of the receipt of such written or oral notice under Clause (1) or of such fact, circumstance or situation under Clause (2), then any claim, which may subsequently be made against the Directors and Officers, arising out of such Wrongful Act shall for the purpose of this policy be treated as a claim made during the policy year in which such notice was given, or, if given during the extended discovery period, as a claim made during the last policy year.

(c) Notice to Underwriters provided for in this Paragraph VII shall be given to the person or firm(s) shown under Item F of the Declarations.

VIII. GENERAL CONDITIONS

(a) Warranty Clause:

It is warranted that the particulars and statements contained in the written proposal, copy of which is attached hereto, and the Declarations are the basis of this policy and are to be considered as incorporated in constituting part of this policy.

(b) Adjustment Clause:

This policy is issued and the premium computed on the basis of the information submitted to Underwriters as part of the proposal referred to in the Declarations. Premium adjustment and coverage revision may be required by Underwriters in the event (1) the Company acquires any other entity or (2) the Company creates or acquires a subsidiary subsequent to the inception date of the policy. The Company agrees to give notice to Underwriters in writing as soon as practicable of the happening of either of the foregoing and furnish such information in connection therewith as Underwriters may require.

(c) Cancellation Clause:

This policy may be cancelled by the Company at any time by written notice to the Underwriters or by surrender of this policy. This policy may also be cancelled by, or on behalf of, the Underwriters by delivering to the Company or by mailing to the Company by registered, certified or other first class mail, at the Company's address shown in this policy, written notice stating when, not less than thirty (30) days thereafter, the cancellation shall become effective. The mailing of such notice as aforesaid shall be sufficient proof of notice, and this policy shall terminate at the date and hour specified in such notice. If this policy shall be cancelled by the Company, the Underwriters shall retain the customary short rate proportion of the premium hereon. If this policy shall be cancelled by or on behalf of the Underwriters, the Underwriters shall retain the pro rate proportion of the premium hereon. Payment or tender of any unearned premium by the Underwriters shall not be a condition precedent to the effectiveness of cancellation, but such payment shall be made as soon as practicable.

If the period of limitation relating to the giving of notice is prohibited or made void by any law controlling the construction thereof, such period shall be deemed to be amended so as to be equal to the minimum period of limitation permitted by law.

(d) Subrogation Clause:

In the event of any payment under this policy, Underwriters shall be subrogated to the extent of such payment to all rights of recovery therefore, and the Directors and Officers or the Company shall execute all papers required and shall do everything that may be necessary to secure such rights including the execution of such documents necessary to enable the Underwriters effectively to bring suit in the name of the Directors or Officers or the Company.

(e) Company Authorization Clause:

Except as respects the giving of notice to exercise extended discovery under Clause II, by acceptance of this policy, the Company named in Item A of the Declarations agrees to act on behalf of all Directors and Officers with respect to the giving of all notice to Underwriters as required herein, the receiving of notice of claim or cancellation, the payment of premiums, and the receiving of any return premiums that may become due under this policy; and the Directors and Officers agree that the Company shall act on their behalf.

(f) The Company and the Directors and Officers shall give the Underwriters such information and co-operation as they may reasonably require.

(g) Loss shall be paid in United States currency.

8

Chronology and Bibliography

Introduction

Rather than proliferate the number of daily and weekly news releases having reference to international payoffs during the 1975-76 investigations, we have chosen to compile a sample chronology of events beginning and ending with dramatic personal tragedies: the suicide of United Brands' Eli Black on February 3, 1975, and the retirement of Netherlands Prince Bernhard on August 29, 1976. This inquiry, which extended some nineteen months, represents a most extensive news coverage of one facet of business operations at the multinational level and is the direct result of and comparable in effect to the Watergate investigation on the political scene. Table 8-1 shows the crescendo buildup.

An extensive bibliography of books and periodicals, covering general ethical themes as well as specific references to international payoffs, is included for the reader's further guidance. The authors have also compiled a book of readings to complement the international payoffs text.

The story of international payoffs erupts almost daily in the newspapers and is not likely to die until conclusion of the many trials and investigations currently in progress to uncover additional payments and to bring retribution to those who have violated existing laws. In addition, legislatures all over the world, as well as the United Nations, are developing a common body of ethical conduct to expose and hopefully to prevent similar happenings in the future. The final chapter of this book thus remains to be written as an epilogue sometime in the future.

Table 8-1
Newspaper Accounts, International Payoffs, February 3, 1975, to August 29, 1976, by Month and Number

Year and Month	Number
1975	
February	4
March	0
April	7
May	1
June	12
July	3
August	1
September	3

Table 8-1 (cont.)

Year and Month	Number
October	3
November	12
December	13
Total for 1975 (11 months)	(59)
1976	
January	15
February	38
March	72
April	29
May	64
June	87
July	59
August	62
Total for 1976 (8 months)	(426)
Total February 3, 1975 to August 29, 1976	485

Note: Based on a sample survey by the authors that relied primarily on *The Wall Street Journal*. Daily and weekly newspapers and magazines in authors' data bank were also used to compile the chronology. In addition to *The Wall Street Journal*, these include *Barron's, Forbes, The New York Times, Business Week, Newsweek, U.S. News & World Report, London Daily Telegraph, International Herald Tribune, London Times, San Francisco Chronicle, St. Louis Post-Dispatch*, and *Washington Post*.

Chronology: International Payoffs and Business Ethics

1972

April: Deadline effective date for law requiring public disclosure of political contributions of more than $100.

1973

August: Gulf directors retain Eckert firm to conduct investigation after release of list showing $100,000 donation from Gulf's corporate funds to Nixon campaign.

November: Claude C. Wild, Jr., of Gulf pleads guilty to charges.

1974

March: SEC files suit against Gulf and Wild alleging $10.3 million in illegal payments between 1960 and 1973, of which $5.4 million was paid in the United States and $4 million in South Korea.

October: *Fortune* article on bribery in Iran appears.

December: McCloy committee report is due on Gulf Oil payments. Testimony taken in suit by shareholders against Gulf.

1975

February 3: Eli M. Black of United Brands commits suicide.

February 15: Senators assail Arabs' blacklist as contrary to U.S. policy in letter to Treasury Secretary William E. Simon: "Arab oil money should not be permitted to enter our country on a basis contrary to our morality and Constitution."

February 24: SEC Commissioner Irving M. Pollack issues statement that action would be taken against companies who participate in Arab boycott against Jews and would encourage National Association of Securities Dealers to enforce principles of trade and open markets through their rules of ethical standards for their members.

February 26: *The New York Times* lists companies on Arab blacklist (74 listed).

April 9: First report of SEC on investigation of bribery overseas in connection with United Brands inquiry appears. SEC suspends U.B. stock trading.

April 10: First reaction of businessmen is to decry government overregulation.

April 17: Editors draft new ethics code for American Society of Newspaper Editors (first revision since 1923).

April 18: Common Cause calls for tighter lobbying laws. Gulf Oil accused of "stonewalling" political slush fund by *The Wall Street Journal.*

April 21: *Newsweek* highlights "great banana bribe."

April 28: *Newsweek* highlights other bribery cases: Northrop, Ashland Oil, and airlines; announcement of Internal Revenue Service audit and congressional investigation by Senate subcommittee on multinational corporations.

May 16: Federal grand jury weighs criminal charges against United Brands. Exxon discloses political contributions in Canada and Italy. SEC requires disclosure even if not illegal.

June 6: Northrop discloses payments to Senate subcommittee on multinational corporations through Swiss-based Economic and Development Corporation.

June 7: Revelations about Northrop payments and connection with CIA continue.

June 9: Summary of bribery stories in *The Wall Street Journal.*

June 11: Follow-up story appears in *The New York Times* on revelations on international bribery to Senate subcommittee on multinationals.

June 12: *The New York Times* continues coverage of Senate subcommittee hearings on Northrop and Swiss EDC.

June 19: *The Wall Street Journal* discloses bribery and extortion of union officials in connection with trade shows in Chicago.

June 22: Senate subcommittee seeks disclosure of report by Department of Defense listing twenty American arms contractors and agents' fees.

June 26: Northrop agents disclosed in *The New York Times.*

June 30: Ashland Oil admits questionable payments following report by special investigating committee. Special report appears in *Barron's* on Italian "Watergate" scandal involving major oil company. Arab boycott problem erupts again in university contract negotiations. *The New York Times* summary of Arab boycott impact cites contributions by U.S. oil companies to Arab cause.

July 1: *The Wall Street Journal* summary of Supreme Court decisions on business regulation implies that SEC will lose its bid to expand its area of regulation.

July 11: Oil companies accused of charging more than FEA permits by using imports.

July 15: *The New York Times* reports payment by Exxon through Italian affiliate, Esso Italiana.

August 15: United Brands' stockholder meeting introduces new officers—board chairman, vice chairman, general counsel and five directors—and announces suits by stockholders.

September 3: Lockheed chairman reported expecting legislation outlawing overseas payments, in interview with *The New York Times.*

September 9: Middle East deals reported pointless in *The New York Times* interviews with overseas agents. SEC chairman implies that documents filed by some multinationals are falsified.

October 1: *The Wall Street Journal* reports that Pentagon has not changed its practices in awarding overseas contracts for arms sales.

October 6: *The Wall Street Journal* reports on foreign stock market manipulation and maintenance of secrecy, especially in connection with takeover operations.

October 18: American Home Products Corporation discloses foreign payments after internal investigation.

November 3: *Business Week* features story on Nigeria's reneging on letters of credit in connection with cement purchases and reports movement of capital overseas.

November 5-7: Three-part series appears in *Christian Science Monitor* on multinational corporations and payments abroad as a "tough ethics question," summary of investigation to date, and business response.

November 10: Report on Practicing Law Institute Seminar on securities regulation and disclosure of questionable payments appears. *The Wall Street Journal* reports on grain inspection scandal and hearings before House Agriculture Committee.

November 11: Gulf Oil official reports illegal campaign contributions, naming members of Congress who received them.

November 14: *The Wall Street Journal* reports on Exxon Italiana political fund, as disclosed in Senate subcommittee on multinationals hearings.

November 15: *The New York Times* reports that U.S. firms may lose orders as result of questionable payments.

November 17: *The Wall Street Journal* summarizes Lockheed disclosures of payoffs. *The Wall Street Journal* summarizes SEC testimony on Gulf Oil political payments in United States.

November 18: *The Wall Street Journal* features interview with Bendix chairman on businessmen's code.

November 26: *The New York Times* summarizes Gulf Oil case.

November 29: McDonnell-Douglas reports $2.5 million foreign payments, 1970-75.

December 3: *The Wall Street Journal* features "multinational firms at crossroads."

December 4: *The Wall Street Journal* features Lockheed payoff story on Netherlands and West Germany.

December 5: *The New York Times* reports Association of Manufacturers seminar on business morality, with high level officials from business and SEC on panel.

December 6: *The New York Times* reports conflict of interest in job exchanges between business and government, investigated by House subcommittee on energy and environment.

December 12: Occidental Petroleum Corp. cited by SEC for payoffs. Gulf Oil's Bahamas Exploration Company activities detailed in investigation against former lobbyist, with controller granted immunity. *The Wall Street Journal* has feature on Gillette's quality and safety specialist for social responsibility. *The New York Times* reports compliance with Arab boycott; Commerce Department and companies refuse to disclose operations, in hearings before House commerce subcommittee on oversight and investigations.

December 13: Monsanto Co. cited for contributions to political funds, under new Justice Department ruling on administration. Occidental Petroleum Corp. chairman ordered to stand trial for political contributions after entering guilty plea.

December 16: Lockheed data ordered to SEC after ruling on subpoena.

December 22: Gulf Oil investigative committee requests delay in deadline for filing report based on new testimony by former lobbyist. Japan approves application from six major Japanese steel mills for permission to form export cartel, for shipments to EEC.

December 30: Multinationals discussed at annual meeting of American Economic Association, reported in *The New York Times*.

1976

January 1: Rockwell files report with SEC on international payoffs.

January 2: *The Wall Street Journal* features payment by Rockwell. *The Wall Street Journal* reports on Gulf Oil's special committee submission to SEC.

January 6: *The Wall Street Journal* features article on history of dirty tricks.

January 12: *Newsweek* reports on Gulf SEC disclosures. Drug companies disclose international payoffs.

January 13: *The Wall Street Journal* reports that Gulf disclosures will result in management shake-up.

January 15: SEC reports that 30 companies are under investigation for improper payments, in testimony before Senate subcommittee of the Congressional Joint Economic Committee. Gulf reports resignation of its chairman in *The Wall Street Journal* summary of board meeting.

January 16: Civil Service Commission director discloses trip paid for by Rockwell. *The Wall Street Journal* discloses pattern of favors by subcontractors to U.S. prime contractors in report of General Accounting Office.

January 17: Report on Rockwell's business with Civil Service Commission appears.

January 24: Complete list of Pentagon officials who accepted Northrop hunting lodge entertainment published in *The New York Times* as result of testimony before Congressional Joint Committee on Defense Production.

January 26: *The New York Times* has feature on multinationals and Brazil's economic growth rate.

January 28: United Brands consent order signed, ending SEC suit for alleged payoffs and setting up special investigating committee for review.

February 1: *Forbes* features interview with Arthur Young partner on disclosure guidelines.

February 4: Lockheed is investigated in Japan. Senate subcommittee on multinationals features disclosures on Lockheed, as result of auditor records.

February 5: *The Wall Street Journal* summarizes subcommittee testimony on Japanese activities of Lockheed.

February 6: Subcommittee hearings continue on Lockheed's Dutch bribes.

February 7: Lockheed disclosures result in congressional demands for legislation and international code of business ethics. Amendment to military aid bill to require disclosure of gifts, fees, and commissions on weapons sales abroad.

February 11: Japan cancels Lockheed order due to bribes. President Ford calls for investigation and punishment and sets up cabinet-level committee. Treasury and Justice Departments begin investigations. Political slush funds disclosed by 39 firms, 19 of which made overseas payments.

February 12: Dutch open inquiry into Lockheed payment. *The New York Times* reviews Lockheed case. Top officials agree to resign. Chairman Burns calls for legislation to make bribes criminal offenses.

February 13: *The Wall Street Journal* features report on Boeing Co. investigation by SEC on payoffs; SEC negotiating over documents since August. *The Wall Street Journal* publishes feature on crisis at Lockheed; Senate

Banking Committee starts investigation on Lockheed loans. Lockheed gets award for "good citizenship" from Los Angeles Chamber of Commerce and KHJ-TV. Conference Board study published, indicating 50-50 split on propriety of payoffs among U.S. businessmen. Dutch agent acquitted of payoffs.

February 14: Lockheed officers resign in payoffs scandal.

February 15: Tenneco, Inc. discloses overseas payments of $12 million from 1970-75. Netherlands Prince Bernhard implicated in Lockheed payoffs. Results in review of whole background of cases. Lockheed officials suggest new code of international business. Phillips Petroleum Co. consents to decree on political slush fund; Justice Department threatens criminal proceedings.

February 17: Lockheed threatened with loss of Canadian order.

February 19: Northrop officers reelected after resignations in bribery case; case is reviewed. Japan calls for names in bribe cases involving Lockheed.

February 21: Senate subcommittee on multinationals studying Boeing financial records in spite of denials of wrong-doing. Suit filed against Lockheed by public research group in connection with federally subsidized projects.

February 23: *U.S. News & World Report* features Lockheed payoffs. *Newsweek* features Netherlands payoff story and lists ten "biggest spenders" among forty corporations accused of bribes. *Business Week* features story on SEC confessions; cites shock over Lockheed disclosures. Additional disclosures on Lockheed and Northrop payoffs.

February 25: Iranian Navy head convicted on bribe in anticorruption move by Shah government; Grumman Corp. cited for payoffs. Lockheed sued by stockholder to bar bribes; suit filed by Center for Law in Public Interest, seeking appointment of special master to investigate secret payments and full accounting. Richardson-Merrill, Inc. is fifth major American pharmaceutical company to disclose payments, but refuses to specify amounts or countries involved, claiming that nothing illegal has been done. Lockheed Tokyo office searched and documents seized in connection with investigation of bribery charges.

February 26: Danish shipowner cites "inevitability" of bribes in Far East and Africa.

February 27: Report of convictions in payola record case—first case on record under legislation resulting from 1950 congressional investigation. *The Wall Street Journal* reports on decline of U.S. arms sales abroad and Pentagon denial that bribery investigation is responsible.

February 27: Gulf Oil payments in Japan termed *normal business* in McCloy report (system of rebates to avoid Japanese foreign exchange restrictions). Mobil's Italian subsidiary official fined and disbarred for life from holding public office.

February 28: Business International Corporation research study favors multinationals in exports and employment but not investment in the United States, according to *The New York Times* report. Honeywell, Inc. reports foreign payments but no illegal activity (all recorded and most for services rendered).

March 1: Lockheed sales to Canada will continue, exceeding $1 billion. *The New York Times* features Lockheed's relationship with Japanese officials.

March 2: *The New York Times* publishes feature on government-business relationship in historical context. National Cash Register Corp. discloses foreign payments in voluntary report to SEC and adopts code of conduct. Reports continue on Japanese investigation of Lockheed activities. SEC gives its information on Lockheed to Japanese investigators. Canada delays Lockheed deal, citing cash shortage. Japan still refuses purchase.

March 3: *The New York Times* runs two-part series on Lockheed case in Japan. Lockheed consent decree worked out, similar to United Brands' case. SEC reports continuing negotiations. Rollins, Inc. announces its policy to continue payments in Mexico, but Translinear, Inc. refuses them in Haiti, in testimony before Congressional Joint Economic subcommittee. Complaint to State Department to no avail.

March 4: Goodyear Tire and Rubber Company discloses payments to SEC after internal investigation. SEC refuses to divulge names and countries where payments were made in testimony before Senate Banking Committee; SEC investigating 84 companies, of which 55 in *Fortune*'s 500 are making voluntary disclosures. Iranian ambassador rebukes U.S. companies for international payoffs at conference of financial executives. *The Wall Street Journal* reports Lockheed's financing troubles. Smith International, Inc. discloses payment in SEC report. Lockheed planes sold to Egypt. Japanese refuse to deal with Lockheed; key officials resign.

March 5: Boeing discloses international payments as normal, *The Wall Street Journal* reports in feature article. Gulf Oil requests return of illegal political contributions from politicians to recover shareholder money. Lockheed refuses to allow General Accounting Office to inspect its records in oversight on government loans. Japanese investigation continues. Occidental Petroleum executive Hammer enters guilty plea in Watergate political contribution case; previous denial of illegal payoffs proves false. SEC 10-K report discloses use of internal auditing committee to investigate Venezuelan payments of $3 million from 1967-71.

March 6: State Department officials agree to give Japan evidence on bribes. News Services review history and report disclosures of General Telephone and Electronics Corp., American Cyanamid Corp., and Honeywell, without identifying countries or recipients. Boeing reports legal payments to sales agents and subcontractors after court orders compliance with SEC subpoena. American Cyanamid disclosures brings to 6 drug companies involved in payoffs; no tax liability involved. Political figures agree to return contributions to Gulf Oil in response to request. Japanese investigation continues, disclosing two main channels as trading company and sales agent Kodama, who was kept secret to avoid his tax liability.

March 7: *Parade* magazine lists top ten defense contractors, of which eight are aircraft companies, and five involved in payoffs.

March 8: Justice Department agrees to give foreign governments payoff data; State Department reports multilateral agreement on corrupt practices proposal before U.N. Commission on Transnational Corporations meeting in Peru. *Newsweek* features article entitled "The Big Lockheed Raid." SEC issues guidelines for proxy report disclosures of payoffs if top company officials have been involved, for benefit of public investors and insurance requirements. Pentagon surveys 43 defense contractors on entertainment of Defense Department officials and discloses 8 or 10 involved that warrant further investigation. Lockheed payoff denied by Turkish official; NATO awards Litton Industries, Inc. $40 million contract. Netherlands cancels annual business conference due to payoffs.

March 9: Goodyear Tire and Rubber Co. continuing SEC investigation—discloses slush funds in three foreign subsidiaries. Internal Revenue Service investigating for tax fraud in payoffs, intensifies audits; review of cases appears in *The Wall Street Journal*. Italian investigation of Genesco begins. Gulf Oil issues statement of business principles.

March 10: Johnson & Johnson and Sterling Drug file SEC reports on payoffs; *The Wall Street Journal* reviews drug company investigation, including eight companies, with Merck having highest amount. Carnation Co. disclosed overseas payments in 8-K report to SEC. Lockheed refinancing is featured in *The Wall Street Journal*. Report of Lockheed officials' resignation from other boards appears.

March 11: Gulf Oil McCloy report is selling in paperback as "Great Oil Spill." Northrop gets Saudi Air Force contract for $1.5 billion. Khashoggi claims commission but is refused payment.

March 12: *The New York Times* publishes editorial on Arab boycott "backsliding." Signal's UOP unit discloses payments abroad from 1971-75. *The Wall Street Journal* features Nader and Green article on "What to Do About Corporate Corruption."

March 13: General Tire and Rubber Co., International Telephone & Telegraph Corp., and Westinghouse Electric Corp. report questionable payments to SEC, which brings number of reports in a week to 9.

March 15: *Business Week* publishes feature on the global costs of bribery, accountant's liability for failure to spot fraud, and relaxation of Arab boycott. *U.S. News & World Report* reports use of foreign partner firms for overseas payments.

March 16: *The Wall Street Journal* reprints article from *Foreign Service Journal* as editorial feature on multinationals revealing cancellation of White House conference, and urges more government help for multinationals instead of attack. SEC reports 80 companies have voluntarily made disclosures with more than 100 scheduled to do so; Fairchild Industries and Coastal States Gas make negative reports with Ingersol Rand conducting internal inquiry. Phillips Petroleum recommends bylaw prohibiting illegal political contributions at suggestion of Episcopal Church's Domestic and Foreign Missionary Society, reversing stand taken at 1974 and 1975 meetings. Assets of Japanese officials involved in Lockheed payoffs seized by government; West Germany Chancellor forms special panel to investigate possible Lockheed payoffs in ten-year-old sale. Merck auditor implicated in SEC disclosures by special company committee; officials ignore warning signals of payoffs. New policy statement on political contributions; IRS checking for tax fraud. IRS checks firms suspected of bribes. Japanese official involved in Lockheed payoff plans appeal. Officials of IRS and Japan meet on exchange of bribe data.

March 17: Pentagon censured for Rockwell entertainment. Hercules, Inc. discloses special commissions paid by foreign subsidiaries at annual meeting.

March 18: *The Wall Street Journal* feature on payoff scandals in Holland and Japan assesses effect on multinational image.

March 19: International accounting federation proposed at twelve-nation meeting (began discussion in 1967; International Accounting Standards Committee set up in 1973). General Telephone and Electronics Corp. reports in proxy statement on payments of $2.6 million as a result of internal audit; plans to prevent recurrence. Warner-Lambert Co. discloses $2.2 million in overseas payoffs in report to SEC—mostly sales commissions, incorrectly listed in books and requiring payment of additional income tax for 1970-73.

March 22: Disclosures made to SEC by General Refractories Co., Pfizer, Inc., Kraftco. Gulf withholds incentive pay from executives involved in payoffs. SEC wins in court test for subpoena of ITT documents in payoff inquiry. TransUnion Corp. reports subsidiary's questionable payments at stockholders meeting, contravening company policy. CPC International, Inc.

at annual meeting announces that auditing staff has been "alerted all over the world" to look for violations of a strict antipayoff policy.

March 23: Lockheed payoff results in arrest of Italian general and lawyer. Jack Anderson features column on multinational tie-in with CIA.

March 24: *The Wall Street Journal* has entire page on payoffs, domestic and overseas; report on bill for lobby disclosures (new Lockheed problems with SEC); Occidental Petroleum's Hammer and sentencing; Clay and travel expenses; Braniff's slush fund and CAB penalties.

March 25: Offshore Co. discloses overseas payments by subsidiaries in 1971-72 of $100,000, and $15,000 a year from 1971-75 to "low-level" officials for expediting purposes. Indiana Standard Oil Co. discloses payments and amends tax returns, in proxy report, of $386,000 for five years to one consultant, and $218,000 to another, listed as travel and hotel expenses.

March 29: *Business Week* features articles on personal penalties for French plant managers for failure to enforce safety regulations; lawyers and bankers withdrawn from boards of directors because of threat of liability.

April 5: *Business Week* features article on multinational codes of conduct as result of OECD meeting in Paris to force disclosures. *Post-Dispatch* publishes article on "Good Ethics Are In." Kepone disclosures reported resulting in indictments. *The Wall Street Journal* letter to editor criticizes Nader and Green article.

April 6: *The New York Times* features article on Joan V. Robinson, economist, as "enemy of capitalism." *The Wall Street Journal* features article by Murray Weidenbaum on "over-regulation" of business as cause of slush funds.

April 8: *The New York Times* features Common Cause petition for investigation of Sikes for conflict of interest. *The Wall Street Journal* features article on Pentagon disclosures of wining and dining by contractors as "end of free lunch."

April 12: Treasury Asst. Secretary advocates international ethics code. *Business Week* features article on Japan aftershock of Lockheed affair.

April 13: Northrop reaches accord on U.S. claim of improper billings for some payments after report of Defense Contract Audit Agency. Koppers Co. discloses payoffs of $1.5 million since 1971 in SEC 8-K report (internal audit being made; has foreign sales of $19.3 million representing 2 percent of total sales).

April 14: Internal Revenue Service questionnaire on illegal payments criticized. General Dynamics Corp. Chairman Lewis makes statement on refusal to bribe to gain profits. Royal Dutch Shell Oil admits Italian payments of $5 million 1969 to 1973 for favorable price adjustments, as part of oil industry plan worked out by Italian association; similar admission made by British Petroleum. *The Wall Street Journal* features article on avoiding payment of bribes entitled "Innocents Abroad," covering Ingersoll-Rand and tips from U.S. Treasury.

April 15: Ogden Corp. admits $1.3 million kickback in Western Europe in 1971, together with Northrop and Rorer-Amchem. Defense Department repaid; 96 corporations file with SEC disclosures ranging from $6,672 (Cook United) to $25 million (Lockheed), lists all corporations.

April 19: *Business Week* features article on deceptive ads.

April 23: Bristol-Myers investigation discloses questionable payments 1971-75.

April 26: *The Wall Street Journal* features article on "virtues of disclosure." *Business Week* highlights article on financial statements with more disclosures to stockholders in SEC 10-K reports. Special article appears on advice for congressional appearances. Report on SEC guidelines for foreign payoffs termed "vague."

April 27: McDonnell-Douglas Chairman J.S. McDonnell tells shareholders that bribes are a "way of life" in foreign business. IBM discloses payments of $53,000 in seven years, which results in discharge and demotion for officials involved, with sales of $1.29 billion per quarter.

April 28: General Tire discloses payoffs in FTC inquiry, called unfair method of competition, in keeping out Goodyear. Other U.S. companies must make charge of unfair competition. Phillips Petroleum reports peaceful stockholders meeting. Board members named in settlement of stockholders suit approved, with discipline proposed for employees who violate law relating to illegal contributions.

April 29: General Electric discloses overseas payments in accordance with voluntary disclosure program of SEC.

April 30: Court upholds SEC subpoena for ITT records in bribe case of $3.8 million. SEC seeking data on all payments over $1,000 since 1968. Company denies materiality with sales of $14 billion annually, from 250 subsidiaries in 80 countries.

May 1: *Fortune* features article on Chief Executive Profile for 500 top companies and discusses ethics.

May 2: U.S. companies begin cutting back operations in Europe due to risk and cost.

May 3: *U.S. News & World Report* features article on offshore tax havens and secret bank accounts.

May 7: House begins inquiry into Sikes conflict-of-interest case brought by Common Cause. *The Wall Street Journal* features article on Boeing and foreign bribery.

May 11: Correction appears of *The Wall Street Journal* editorial comment on Nader and Green corruption article. Japanese official involved in Lockheed payoffs faces foreign exchange and tax-evasion violations charges; Socialist Party chief accuses CIA of helping Lockheed in payoffs in Morocco and Mexico, and Arab boycott. General Tire agrees to consent decree in settlement of 25-page SEC complaint, involving payoffs in Morocco and Mexico, and Arab boycott.

May 12: Northrop annual meeting (previously delayed) causes no excitement this year; company cites "painful" process of disclosure and approves new outside directors; investigation is continuing. LTV Corp. cites no illegal payments at annual meeting. Similar statements reported for many companies, including Reliance Group, Inc. Pan American World Airways announces creation of new public relations division. Minnesota Mining and Mfg. Co. annual meeting reports resignation of chairman in 1976 as result of political contributions scandal and fines for misdemeanor. Two other officers are under indictment for tax violations growing out of scandal. Thailand to purchase 16 Northrop fighters at value of $50 million. Emersons, Ltd. charged by SEC on in payoffs by beer suppliers, part of same management fraud as overseas payoffs; two company officers suspended and ordered to repay the money used for personal benefit, such as home improvements, maid, and luxury automobiles, shown on books as company costs; consent to court injunction; accounting firm withdraws audit report because of irregularities. Revised federal campaign finance law passed. *The Wall Street Journal* editorial "Commissars for Corporations" decries Senator Church's proposal for more controls.

May 13: SEC submits Senate report on 103 companies making questionable payments, together with legislative proposals aimed at restoring financial recordkeeping control and integrity enforcement action taken in 14 cases. Materiality test ambiguous; hence Senator Proxmire wants complete disclosure. International payoff problem serious and sufficiently widespread to cause deep concern; 95 corporations already cited with 30 more under investigation; drug and oil industries, largest number with 12 each. United Brands annual meeting highlighted by questions on illegal payments. Company has new policy for the United States, but foreign payments will be considered on case basis. ITT payments of $350,000 in Chile (to protect $153 million investment) disclosed at annual meeting called legal. Quarterly sales of $2.69 billion reported. SEC guidelines list payments not requiring disclosure in report to Senator Proxmire and recommend penalties for executives who misinform outside auditors, if case involves 5 percent to 10 percent of profit or sales. Insignificant payments need not be disclosed if properly recorded. Absolves all payments to commercial agents and consultants in foreign countries, as benign payments, or gratuities to low-level governmental officials to perform obligations. In draft bill SEC could seek civil injunction or recommend criminal prosecution by Justice Department. Present authority is shaky. Norwegian shipping company official held in Ogden unit payoff, on charge of "gross faithlessness." No bail is set until court decision to go to trial after 2 weeks.

May 14: *Post-Dispatch* features article on "corporate bribery." Lockheed financing plans disclosed. ITT given $2.3 million contract for French installation. Senate rejects House boost of taxes on U.S. income abroad.

May 18: Executive salaries are reported to be losing to inflation. Lockheed gets $16.7 million Air Force contract. Atlantic Richfield suspends talks with Venezuelan government on technology transfer after nationalization. Pacific Shipping Lines agrees to curb illegal rebates, so-called tea money, and set up neutral bodies to monitor compliance. Penney discloses improper payments of $98,100 from 1971-75 at annual meeting, since terminated, on sales of $1.73 billion annually. Sears engaged outside auditor but finds no illegal payments. Consolidated Edison Company stockholder meeting is peaceful after proposal to disclose 30 largest stockholders is defeated.

May 19: Senator Proxmire compromises on foreign bribes ban in requiring disclosure of all payments exceeding $1,000, with penalties for lying. SEC opposed to such burden and hopes to make outside auditors more effective, in accordance with Senator Church proposal. Support sought from New York Stock Exchange for similar requirements for listed companies. SEC Advisory Committee seeks comment on materiality definition among others by September 30. Canada purchase from Lockheed runs into financing trouble ($1 billion deal). Joint projects proposed with French firms by McDonnell to compete with Boeing; British also involved. Pentagon permits renegotiation of shipbuilding contract due to inflation for 1 percent profit on $8 billion orders. Material Service Corp. discloses bribes to Illinois legislators.

May 20: Canada cancels Lockheed order. *Post-Dispatch* features article on Gulf Oil nun director, who would reduce executive "princely" salaries.

May 21: *The Wall Street Journal* features article on whistle-blowing entitled "Spilling the Beans." Congressional study finds flaws in SEC bribe-disclosure program. Stockholders criticize Exxon for $59 million in payments in

Italy, but vote down proposal for disclosure of other countries involved. Xerox stockholders meeting reviews payments of $10,000 in four instances; CEO McColough warns against "witch hunt."

May 23: Lockheed ex-chairman Haughton denies wrong doing and cites "rules of game."

May 24: Exxon payments in Italy reviewed in *The Wall Street Journal.* Otis Elevator Co. payments of about $5 million from 1971-76 revealed by United Technologies merger data. Occidental Petroleum Corp. stockholders' meeting reviews payments as insignificant when compared with total dollar volume. Japanese political leaders threatened by Lockheed payments. *Business Week* features article on unions for executives in middle management who feel pressures for unethical conduct. *U.S. News & World Report* features article on state action to require politicians to report income; also on congressional financial-disclosure statements.

May 25: *The Wall Street Journal* reports on social responsibility resolutions in 1976 annual meetings, with 120 companies facing 170 resolutions by social activists. General Refractories seeks to sever ties with Swiss businessman involved in contested interests under SEC charges. Gulf Oil holds up options of ousted officials. SEC proposes overhaul of recordkeeping procedures to reduce paperwork. House Commerce subcommittee criticizes SEC leniency on payoff disclosures. SEC revises rules for foreign concerns in accordance with NY Stock Exchange recommendations.

May 26: Celanese Corp. explains $2.2 million in payments. Senate votes to deny tax breaks on business involving overseas bribes. *The Wall Street Journal* features article on stalling tactics of corporate lawyers, increasing costs and delaying court action. Tougher standards for real estate accounting proposed by American Institute of CPA's Financial Accounting Standards Board.

May 28: Lockheed sales to Japan rescued by Defense Department; Canadian order also threatened. *The Wall Street Journal* features article on "Code for Multinationals." Moynihan reports on UN bribery.

May 30: Lockheed executives subpoenaed in Japanese case. OECD members agree on strict code for multinationals. Secretary of Commerce Richardson defends U.S. business in Japanese visit.

May 31: *U.S. News & World Report* features article on "Ripoffs" and advises on how companies can finance politics.

June 1: *Fortune* publishes feature on Gulf disclosures. *The Wall Street Journal* features article on "Government, Business and Morality."

June 2: Seven oil firms indicted on price fixing charge from 1967-74. *The Wall Street Journal* editorializes about antitrust "follies." New charges reported in Japan over Lockheed case. *The Wall Street Journal* features article on takeovers and mergers and secrecy involved. Beatrice Foods' officer indicted over illegal refunds. *The Wall Street Journal* features article on "The Nixon Men."

June 3: Disclosure of gas-price lobbying by House Energy subcommittee results in suspension of FEA aide. Lease accounting plan reconsidered by Financial Accounting Standards Board of CPA's; proposal for new inflation accounting system shelved.

June 4: Cabinet task force on payoffs misses deadline date for report. *The Wall Street Journal* features article on two ousted officers of Sanitas after SEC probe. Lockheed wins $625 million job from Saudi Arabia. *The New York Times* features article on insurance effects of SEC investigations.

June 7: SEC rules on Arab boycott disclosures.

June 8: *The Wall Street Journal* feature on steel construction job in Indiana entitled "Bribery Buildup." Firestone admits $330,000 in political gifts; Butler National Corp. charged with failing to disclose payments to SEC, signs consent decree.

June 9: Reynolds Metals Co. discloses payments of $300,000 in 4 countries.

June 10: Beer bribery probes disclosed by SEC, featured as "Brewing Scandal?" Loews Corp. advises of questionable payments totalling $1.5 million in connection with sales of tobacco products from 1971 to 1973. Burndy Corp. discloses illegal payments of $155,000 for 5 years.

June 12: Gulf requests delay in SEC inquiry.

June 14: *The Wall Street Journal* features article on regulation of business, with guidelines. Venezuela denies Occidental Petroleum Co. indemnity for nationalizing holdings. A-T-O Inc. discloses payments by foreign subsidiary in 10-K report to SEC. Allied Chemical Corp. discloses improper payments of $335,750 in 4 years in 8-K filing with SEC.

June 15: President Ford proposes foreign payoffs bill. Lockheed gets Defense Department contract for sale to Egypt. Boeing reports Pakistan agent with family ties to Chief Operating Officer (COO) of airline. Senate votes curbs on arms export to foreign governments, with provision on bribes.

June 16: SEC sues Firestone for failure to disclose improper payments sooner. Mattel stockholders ask 30 questions on overseas payments in three-hour meeting. PIRG group seeks review of Gulf settlement to require individual penalties. *The New York Times* features article on consumer problems getting satisfaction revealed by Nader's Center for Study of Responsive Law and Call for Action.

June 17: SEC Hills and Department of Commerce Richardson disagree on curbing bribery. Congress seeks more control over arms exports. Feature on accounting firm executive denouncing regulation of business appears in *St. Louis Post-Dispatch*. Gulf shareholder suit on illegal political contributions filed by Project on Corporate Responsibility (PIRG group). AT&T employees are reported to have altered data in EEOC case. IBM report stresses "tough foreign competition." Venezuela nationalizes United Corp. properties. Senate Defense Appropriations subcommittee OK's $104.7 billion in defense spending for FY 1977.

June 18: Sperry Rand Corp. discloses $2 million in improper payments. Woolworth Co. discloses small questionable payment in five-year period at stockholders meeting. MGM discloses $246,000 in foreign payments since 1971 in 8-K report to SEC (recipients unknown). *Forbes* ad of "three monkeys" depicts BD's in bribe cases.

June 21: *Business Week* features article on West Point cheating and voter distrust of nation's leadership. Boeing gets Air Force and Army contracts totalling $29.4 million. *The Wall Street Journal* editorial applauds Richardson's questioning of SEC investigations. Tenneco discharges executive for conversion activities. J. Ray McDermott & Co. construction firm admits 1 percent payoff activities as "in line with the going rate." Lockheed case results in indictment of All Nippon Airways President for perjury. Test flight of Trident delayed by Lockheed in manpower reduction. Occidental Petroleum Co. sues Saudi Arabia for payment of $180 million.

June 22: SEC Chairman Hills claims that Ford proposal duplicates SEC activity; he urges higher pay for outside directors, in speech before American Enterprise Institute for Public Policy Research. New York Mercantile Exchange president warns Congress to keep out of potato inquiry until internal investigation is done. Arthur Andersen & Co., accounting firm, protests SEC policy (ASR 150) on accounting rules giving authority to Financial Accounting Standards Board of CPAs. Occidental Petroleum Co. contracts with Iran for 11 percent shares worth $125 million. Angola feature on Boeing and Gulf activities entitled "Playing Both Sides" appears in *The Wall Street Journal*. House acts in Hays scandal with task force proposal for reform. OECD adopts rules of conduct for multinationals.

June 23: Boeing required by court order to disclose payments to SEC, including accountant's work papers. Japanese executives arrested over

Lockheed bribes. Senate Banking Committee approves antibribe legislation, incorporating SEC proposals; review of whole payoff inquiry appears in *The Wall Street Journal* report.

June 24: Accounting firms criticize Andersen's challenge of FASB rule-making powers. SEC seeks to cut back 8-K monthly interim reports to reduce paperwork.

June 25: Iran reports on joint ventures with Occidental Petroleum Corp. Lockheed continues to repay U.S.-backed debt, reducing amount from $245 to $160 million. Boeing negotiates with Canada to supply fleet of patrol planes worth $1 billion in competition with Lockheed. McDonnell gets $510 million F-15 contract; Northrop, $135 million on F5.

June 28: *The Wall Street Journal* features article on potato futures defaults. Bribery in Illinois reported over truck weights; six found guilty after trial. *Business Week* features article on Lockheed upturn. Malagasy nationalizes all foreign oil firms. American Bar Association defends its rule banning ads by lawyers; contests antitrust action. Another Japanese businessman of Marubeni corporation accused of perjury in Lockheed payoffs.

June 29: Burlington Industries, Inc. reports questionable payments of "less than $100,000" in five years. SEC Chairman Hills requests more tools from House Government Operations subcommittee to catch foreign violators. U.S. managers discouraged from employment in foreign subsidiaries due to taxes on bonuses. Individual penalty assessed against former president of Bestlin Products, Inc. of $1 million for violating Trade Commission order.

June 30: Internal Revenue Service withdraws tax exemption from Teamsters pension fund to initiate lawsuits for disclosure purposes. Shakedown of Teamster's official by forcing contractors to put him on payroll in Chicago is reported. Milwaukee Road and four officers involved in SEC suit for diversion of funds. Boeing gets $25.1 million in Army and Air Force contracts. SEC Chairman Hills cites foreign bank secrecy as factor in bribery. Ex-officers of corporations act as consultants is featured in *The Wall Street Journal* article entitled "Sweet Deal."

July 1: *The Wall Street Journal* features article on Texas Grain Elevator export fraud entitled "Spreading Scandal?" *The Wall Street Journal* features article on antibusiness bicentennial group. Atlantic Richfield gets $118.5 million for fuel Defense contract. American Management Associations' poll of company presidents discloses that 67 percent fear for life of present corporations. Lockheed gets Australia job for 12 aircraft totalling $115 million. Two top Freuhauf Corp. officers sentenced to jail and fined in corporate tax case. Japanese critics silenced at annual stockholders meetings. Another Lockheed figure arrested in Japan for concealing income.

July 2: Marubeni Corp. official in Japan indicted over Lockheed scandal for perjury. House Ethics Committee finds Representative Sikes guilty of charges brought by Common Cause that he used his office for personal gain and recommends reprimand.

July 5: *The New York Times* features article on "What is Happiness?" including discussion of moral virtues. *The New York Times* features article on Washington, D.C. lawyers' ethics committee dispute with American Bar Association.

July 6: SEC investigating Raytheon sales fees of $23 million to Arabian businessman Adnan Khashoggi, focussing on accounting methods. Bodin Apparel Inc. discloses accounting errors in pricing inventory. SEC Chairman Hills' management of investigation criticized by Chairman Senator Williams of Senate Banking subcommittee. Occidental Petroleum planning defense of bribe charges by shareholders in class action suit. Indonesia plans change in production-sharing contracts with foreign oil companies, increasing its share to 95 percent on new contracts. Exxon receives $124.5 million in defense jobs; Lockheed subsidiaries get $7.1 million for Navy's Trident program. Two more Japanese executives arrested in Lockheed payoffs, bringing total to seven.

July 7: State Department presses UN Commission on Transnational Corporations for international treaty on bribes, covering members of International Chamber of Commerce, supported by Chamber's Unethical Practices Commission and OECD advisory bodies.

July 9: *The Wall Street Journal* features article on congressional ethics. SEC studying questionable payments by Benguet Consolidated Inc. in Philippines. Mobil Corp. container subsidiary made over $570,000 in foreign payments in five years, according to Marcor Inc., bringing to 130 number of companies making such disclosures to SEC. General Tire & Rubber Co. is sued for payoffs to win construction job at Sonatrach's expense. Canada postpones buying 18 Lockheed planes. All Nippon Airways president arrested in Lockheed payoffs, bringing number to nine in Japan. *The Wall Street Journal* features article entitled "Bribery (cont.)," alleging that investigation is beginning "to sputter."

July 14: Marubeni Corp. chairman arrested in Japan over Lockheed payoffs. Reeves Brothers Inc. reports $23,600 payments by foreign subsidiary over four years.

July 15: Alcon Laboratories, Inc. and Scott Paper Co. disclose improper payments. *The Wall Street Journal* features article on accounting firms and dispute with SEC over 100 filings on auditing methods.

July 16: Alcoa reveals request to make payment to Jamaica political party by U.S. ambassador in 1971. SEC investigates Raytheon sales fees of $23 million to Arabian businessman Khashoggi. Democratic candidate Carter promises moral uplift and new leadership.

July 21: House eases curbs on soft-drink firms regarding exclusive territorial arrangements under antitrust law. Carton makers enter no contest pleas in price-fixing case. Seatrain Lines Inc. of Tenna Corp. cited for questionable transactions, causing American Stock Exchange to delay trading shares.

July 22: General Foods admits improper payments. Lockheed signs $1.03 billion contract with Canada. Greyhound Corp. discloses payments by Armour & Co. unit. Pentagon changes ordering methods to cut costs, reducing specifications.

July 23: Lockheed payoff person in Japan, Kodama, denies charges under questioning by upper house special committee. Banking firms warn against change in accounting procedures. Carter pledges role for business leaders.

July 24: B.F. Goodrich Co. discloses illegal payments. Goodyear Tire & Rubber Company files suit to prevent SEC from disclosing details concerning company's business abroad to foreign governments.

July 26: B.F. Goodrich Co. reveals additional foreign payments; audit committee directs management to seek reimbursement from employees involved.

July 27: Tanaka, former prime minister of Japan, arrested in Lockheed payoffs. Justice Department sues American Ship Building Co. for charging illegal contributions to government contracts, requesting forfeit of $5,400,000 under False Claims Act plus $500,000 in damages. Senate approves antiboycott plan and payoffs penalty. Lockheed gets $30 million contract for F104 maintenance. House Ethics Committee recommends censure for Representative Sikes. Senate denies tax benefits on income resulting from bribe payments.

July 28: *The Wall Street Journal* features article on Tanaka's arrest and effect on government and economy; charged with violation of foreign exchange law.

July 29: Sunshine law approved by House for all federal agencies. Two Japanese businessmen accused of bribery by Russia. Arthur Andersen & Co. plea rejected by SEC to revise ASR 150. Japan indicts two more in Lockheed payoff, bringing to 16 number arrested so far. House reprimands Representative Sikes 381 to 3. Civil engineers society accused of violating antitrust decree by enforcing code of ethics prohibiting price quotation when another member has started negotiations with client.

August 2: Arthur Andersen & Co. sues SEC to enjoin enforcing ASR 150 and ASR 177.

August 3: Squibb Corp. and City Investing Co. disclose questionable payments overseas. Drug industry sales practices to be studied by FTC. Lockheed gets $9.7 million contract from Navy; McDonnell Douglas Corp. gets $3.3 million Navy contract. Inquiry into grain scandal spreads to fifteen states.

August 4: President Ford seeks bribe law as result of task force report. Lockheed gets $17.2 million Navy contract. Lockheed profits down 24 percent in second quarter. FTC investigation of U.S. auto industry for antitrust violations.

August 5: Meat inspectors indicted in New York. Corporate spending for public TV increased, as reported by The Conference Board. Ex-Gulf aide gets jail sentence in payoffs case for perjury. Upjohn Co. reports questionable foreign payments of $4.1 million in 5 years.

August 6: Lockheed, McDonnell Douglas, and Boeing bid for $537 million U.S. order. Lockheed stops ex-aides' consultant fees.

August 9: Ansul Co., Del Monte Corp., and Dart Industries, Inc. disclose payments; H.J. Heinz Co. questions accounting procedures in 8-K SEC report. *The Wall Street Journal* features article on regulation and competition.

August 10: Fees for directors rise in wake of more demanding responsibilities. Tanaka aide indicted in Lockheed payoff case, for violating foreign currency regulations by receiving $1.7 million. Carter criticizes Ford's bribery proposals as too "lenient." Cleveland Harris Corp. reports payments over six years of $1.8 million; Dynalactron reports $125,000 (both on form 8-K to SEC).

August 11: Grumman Corp. terminates Ataka & Co. contract as sales representative. *The Wall Street Journal* features article on D.C. bar ethics committee proposal for regulating hiring of former government lawyers to practice before agencies they worked for.

August 12: Overseas payoffs reported by Twentieth Century-Fox Film Corp., Xerox Corp., and Overseas National Airways. Schering-Plough Corp. and H.J. Heinz continue investigation, as reported in 8-K SEC filing.

August 13: Oil firms agree to Indonesia's new production-sharing contract to stretch out cost recovery. Commodity futures trading regulation agency (CFTC) criticized for inaction in potato scandal in *The Wall Street Journal* feature article. Goodyear withdraws suit against SEC over disclosure of payments data to foreign governments; SEC agrees to seek order first.

August 15: *San Francisco Chronicle* features story on "Japanese Watergate." First Dutch payoff inquiry report on Prince Bernhard's involvement with Lockheed.

August 16: FTC urged to inquire into Gulf Oil's Texas transactions under antitrust laws. LTV Corp., Curtiss-Wright Corp, Atlantic Richfield, and Signode Corp. report overseas payments, supplementing SEC May 12 report to Senate Banking Committee. Boeing gets contracts for $25 million from private companies. Beef packers in Iowa named in price-fixing suit.

August 17: Japan's Tanaka indicted in Lockheed payoffs case. Emerson's Ltd. restaurant chain names three outside directors and special counsel in consent decree settling SEC case.

August 18: Clark Equipment Co. reports payments in five years of $95,000 and initiates formal inquiry with outside legal counsel and independent auditors. Tanaka released on bail along with four others of Marubeni Corp.

August 19: Ralston Purina admits making foreign payoffs, called "isolated."

August 20: All Nippon Airways president indicted in Lockheed case. Lockheed gets British order for twelve long-range jobs; no foreign commissions or agents used. Ernst & Ernst urges LIFO accounting method to adjust for inflation. U.S. industry cuts overseas investment, according to McGraw-Hill survey.

August 22: *The New York Times Magazine* features article on Dutch entitled "Innocence Lost." *The New York Times* reports on competitive practices of Boeing and McDonnell for Air Force contract of $4 billion. *The New York Times* features article on Japanese scandals.

August 23: *London Daily Telegraph* features article on "Bernhard Bribes." Rebates of U.S. Lines Inc., subsidiary of Walter Kidde & Co., investigated by Federal Maritime Commission and two grand juries; other shipping lines also involved in Justice Department's antitrust investigation. Japan arrests ex-aides of Transport Ministry in Lockheed case, involved with All Nippon Airways, accused of "shaping ministry policy to industry needs."

August 24: FTC reverses stand and agrees to study Lockheed payoff effect on competitors, under law barring bribery as unfair competition, with penalties up to $10,000. General Tire and Rubber Co. involved in suit for payoffs in Morocco.

August 25: Ex-Firestone aide accused of contempt in SEC action for refusing to supply data on payoffs to aid audit committee's continuing investigation. Four Schlitz Brewing Co. executives granted leaves of absence in investigation of payoffs, involved in Emersons inquiry; also postponed

$50 million public offering of debentures. Hercules Inc. reports foreign payments supplementing SEC report.

August 26: *The Wall Street Journal* features article on "The Morality Issue." Accounting dispute continues in court case by Andersen, with briefs being filed by other firms to support SEC. Prince Bernhard ordered to give up business life and resign from all public functions; removed as inspector general of Dutch armed forces to avoid constitutional crisis.

August 27: Dutch leaders oust Prince Bernhard to protect monarchy from disgrace (he is forced into retirement from all public and private offices due to Lockheed involvement). *The Wall Street Journal* features article reviewing Prince Bernhard and Lockheed connections.

August 28: *Manchester Guardian* features article on Prince Bernhard, disclosing several handwritten letters to Lockheed asking for $4 million.

August 29: Continuing reports on Prince Bernhard's Lockheed and other business connections (he is called "top-dollar Dutch salesman"). *London Times* features article on Lockheed connections in Germany involving $12 million payment to Christian Social Union through Swiss bank account. Sunday *Times* features article on Lockheed connections with Prince Bernhard, entitled "The Big Squeeze."

A Final Note: Selected Bibliography

In an area as dynamic as business and society, student and practitioner require up-to-date information and analysis. Current daily business newspapers such as *The New York Times, The Wall Street Journal, Barron's,* and *Forbes* are indispensable for such knowledge. *Business Week, Newsweek, Time,* and *U.S. News & World Report* add a weekly time perspective. In-depth analysis is provided by the monthly or quarterly reviews, of which the following are outstanding: *Academy of International Business Review, Academy of Management Journal, Business Horizons, Business and Society Review, California Management Review, Challenge, Columbia Journal of World Business, Harvard Business Review,* and *Fortune.* More infrequently, *Review of Social Economy* and *MSU Business Topics* deal with topics related to economics and ethics.

The Bureau of National Affairs and Prentice-Hall publish continuing series of reports on a variety of subjects related to social responsibilities of business and, of course, Commerce Clearing House *Tax Service* is invaluable for financial accounting, as is BNA *Securities Regulation and Law Report* for shareholders.

Bibliographies proliferate, but the time-honored *Business Periodicals Index* still provides the most useful variety of sources for business-oriented subjects. The problem remains, not too little, but too much. The well-read executive must be a decisionmaker in this area also and establish priorities. Hopefully, we have assisted in this process. We have deliberately omitted professional journals, such as in accounting or law, except for a few well-chosen examples. In these areas there is no substitute for consultation with a competent professional.

The selections listed in our bibliography have been classified as follows: books, periodicals, special studies and documents, and corporate publications and speeches.

Books

Ackerman, Robert W. *The Social Challenge to Business.* Cambridge, Mass.: Harvard University Press, 1975.

Anshen, Melvin, ed. *Managing the Socially Responsible Corporation.* New York: Macmillan, 1974.

Anshen, Melvin, and Bach, George. *Management and Corporations, 1985.* New York: McGraw-Hill, 1960.

Barnet, Richard J., and Muller, Ronald E. *Global Reach: The Power of the Multinational Corporations.* New York: Simon and Schuster, 1974.

Baumhart, Raymond, S.J. *An Honest Profit: What Businessmen Say About Ethics in Business.* New York: Holt, Reinhart & Winston, 1968. Chapter 1, "The Many Meanings of 'Businessman' and 'Ethics'," pp. 10-17; Chapter 4, "Pressures That Disturb Businessmen," pp. 26-37; and Chapter 16, "Codes of Ethics," pp. 153-71.

Baumol, William J., et al. *A New Rationale for Corporate Social Policy.* Lexington, Mass.: Heath-Lexington, D.C. Heath, 1970. Committee for Economic Development, Supplementary Paper no. 31.

Bowen, Howard. *Social Responsibilities of the Businessman.* New York: Harper, 1953.

Carr, Albert Z. *Business As A Game.* New York: The New American Library, 1968. Chapter 13. "The Ethics of Bluffing in Business," pp. 173-89.

Chamberlain, N.W. *Enterprise and Environment.* New York: McGraw-Hill, 1968.

_____. *The Limits of Corporate Responsibility.* New York: Basic Books, 1973. Chapter 1, "The Corporate System," pp. 2-10; Chapter 8, "The Corporation and International Relations," pp. 154-78; and Chapter 10, "The Limits of Corporate Responsibility," pp. 201-10.

Clark, John W., S.J. *Religion and the Moral Standards of American Businessmen.* Cincinnati, Ohio: South-Western Pub. Co., 1966.

Cole, A.H. *Business Enterprise and Its Social Setting.* Cambridge, Mass.: Harvard University Press, 1959.

Committee for Economic Development. *Social Responsibilities of Business Corporations.* New York: Committee for Economic Development, 1971.

The Conference Board. *The Future of Capitalism.* New York: Macmillan, 1967.

Davis, K., and Blomstrom, R.L. *Business, Society, and Environment: Social Power and Social Response.* New York: McGraw-Hill, 1971.

Dierkes, M., and Bauer, R.A. *Corporate Social Accounting.* New York: Praeger, 1973.

Drucker, Peter F. *Concept of the Corporation.* New York: John Day Co., 1946.

_____. *Management: Tasks, Responsibilities, Practices.* New York: Harper & Row, 1974.

Eels, Richard, and Walton, Clarence. *Conceptual Foundations of Business.* Homewood, Ill.: Irwin, 1974.

Friedman, Milton. *Capitalism and Freedom.* Chicago: University of Chicago Press, 1962.

Galbraith, John K. *The New Industrial State.* Boston: Houghton Mifflin, 1967.

_____. *Economics and the Public Purpose.* Boston: Houghton Mifflin, 1973.

Garrett, Thomas, S.J. *Business Ethics.* New York: Appleton-Century-Crofts, 1966.

Gruchy, Allan G. *Contemporary Economic Thought.* Clifton, N.J.: Kelley, August 1972. Chapter V., Gunnar Myrdal, "Economics of Integration."

Hayek, Fredrick A. *The Road to Serfdom.* Chicago: University of Chicago Press, 1944.

Heilbroner, Robert L., et al. *In the Name of Profit.* Garden City, N.Y.: Doubleday, 1972.

Heyne, Paul T. *Private Keepers of the Public Interest.* New York: McGraw-Hill, 1968.

Hill, Ivan, ed. *The Ethical Basis of Economic Freedom.* Chapel Hill, N.C.: American Viewpoint, Inc., 1976.

Hocking, William E. *Types of Philosophy.* New York: Charles Scribner's Sons, 1959.

Jacoby, Neil H. *Corporate Power and Social Responsibility.* New York: McMillan, 1973. Chapter 5, "Multinational Corporation," pp. 94-125.

Knight, Frank H. *Ethics of Competition.* London: Allen Unwin, 1935.

Kolasa, B.J. *Responsibility in Business: Issues and Problems.* Englewood Cliffs, N.J.: Prentice-Hall, 1972.

Linowes, David F. *The Corporate Conscience.* New York: Hawthorn Books, 1974.

Manne, Henry G., and Wallich, Henry C. *The Modern Corporation and Social Responsibility.* Washington, D.C.: American Enterprise Institute for Public Policy Research, 1972.

Marx, Karl. *Capital.* New York: Charles H. Kerr, 1906.

McGuire, J.W. *Business and Society.* New York: McGraw-Hill, 1968.

_____. *Theories of Business Behavior.* Englewood Cliffs, N.J.: Prentice-Hall, 1964.

Nader, Ralph, and Green, M.J., eds. *Corporate Power in America.* New York: Grossman Publishers, 1973.

Papandreou, A.G. *Paternalistic Capitalism*. Minneapolis: The University of Minneapolis Press, 1972.

Petit, T.A. *The Moral Crisis in Management*. New York: McGraw-Hill, 1967.

Schumpeter, Joseph. *Capitalism, Socialism and Democracy*. New York: Harper, 1942.

Sethi, S. Prakash. *Up Against the Corporate Wall*. Englewood Cliffs, N.J.: Prentice-Hall, 1971.

Simon, John G., et al. *The Ethical Investor*. New Haven: Yale University Press, 1972. Chapter 2, "Responsibilities of Corporations and Their Owners," pp. 15-64.

Smith, Adam. *An Inquiry into the Nature and Causes of the Wealth of Nations*. (1776) New York: Random House, Modern Library, 1937 (reprinted).

Spurrier, William A. *Ethics and Business*. New York: Charles Scribner's Sons, 1962. Chapter 2, "Ten Commandments and The Golden Rule," pp. 10-17.

Steiner, George A. *Business and Society*. New York: Random House, 1975.

Towle, Joseph, et al. *Ethics and Standards in American Business*. Boston: Houghton Mifflin, 1964. Albert W. Levi, "Ethical Confusion and the Business Community," pp. 20-29.

U.S. Treasury Department. *Foreign Portfolio Investment in the U.S.* (Interim report to Congress), Washington, D.C., October 1975, 110 pp.

U.S. Department of Commerce. *Index to International Business Publications*, Washington, D.C., June 1975, 45 pp.

Votaw, Dow, and Sethi, S. Prakah. *The Corporate Dilemma: Traditional Values vs. Contemporary Problems*. Englewood Cliffs, N.J.: Prentice-Hall, 1973. Chapter 6, "Changing Corporate Patterns of Response," pp. 167-214.

Periodicals

Andrews, K.R. "Can The Best Corporations Be Made Moral?" *Harvard Business Review*, May-June 1973, pp. 57-64.

Arrow, K.J. "Social Responsibility and Economic Efficiency," *Public Policy*, Summer 1973, pp. 303-17.

Baumhart, R. "How Ethical Are Businessmen?" *Harvard Business Review*, July-August 1961, pp. 6-19.

Bell, Daniel, et al. "Corporations and Conscience: The Issues," *Management Review*, Fall 1971, pp. 1-24.

Berle, Adolf, et al. "Company Social Responsibility—Too Much or Not Enough?" *Conference Board Record*, April 1964, pp. 7-17.

Blodget, Timothy B. "Showdown on Business Bluffing," *Harvard Business Review*, May-June 1968, pp. 162-70.

Blumberg, Phillip I. "Corporate Responsibility and the Employee's Duty of Loyalty and Obedience," *Oklahoma Law Review*, August 1971, pp. 279-318.

Bremer, O.A. "Is Business the Source of New Social Values?" *Harvard Business Review*, November 1971, pp. 121-26.

Briscoe, R. "Utopians in the Marketplace," *Harvard Business Review*, September 1971, pp. 4-6.

Brook, Herbert C. "Director's Indemnification and Liability Insurance," *New York Law Forum*, Summer 1975, pp. 1-39.

Canham, E.D. "Management and Social Values," *Advanced Management Journal*, October 1967, pp. 12-17.

Carr, Albert Z. "Is Business Bluffing Ethical?" *Harvard Business Review*, January-February 1968, pp. 143-53.

_____. "Can An Executive Afford A Conscience?" *Harvard Business Review*, July-August 1970, pp. 58-64.

Carroll, Archie. "A Survey of Managerial Ethics: Is Business Morality Watergate Morality," *Business and Society Review*, Spring 1975, pp. 58-60.

Cassel, F.H. "Social Cost of Doing Business," *M.S.U. Business Topics*, Autumn 1974, pp. 19-26.

Christiansen, Jon P. (Note) "A Remedy for the Discharge of Professional Employees Who Refuse to Perform Unethical or Illegal Acts," *Vanderbilt Law Review*, May 1975, pp. 805-41.

Clutterbuck, D. "Displaying A Corporate Conscience," *International Management*, November 1975, pp. 33-35.

Cushman, Robert. "The Norton Company Faces The Payoff Problem," *Harvard Business Review*, September-October, 1976, pp. 6-7.

Davis, Keith. "Five Propositions for Social Responsibility," *Business Horizons*, June 1975, pp. 19-24.

Dittmer, R.W. "Corporate Social Responsibility—An Overview," *Crisis*, June 1975, pp. 215-18.

Dixon, Arthur J. "CPAs Face Their Responsibilities," *CPA*, June 1975, pp. 21-24.

Drotning, P. "Why Nobody Takes Corporate Social Responsibility Seriously," *Management Review*, March 1973, pp. 63-64.

Elbing, A.O. "Value Issue of Business: The Responsibility of the Businessman," *Academy of Management Journal*, March 1970, pp. 70-89.

Eells, R. "Beyond the Golden Rule," *Columbia Journal of World Business*, July 1967, pp. 82-88.

England, George W. "Personal Value Systems of Managers—So What?" *The Personnel Administrator*, April 1975, pp. 20-23.

Ervin, Sam J., Jr. "The Role of the Lawyer in America," *New England Law Review*, Fall 1975, pp. 1-6.

"Ethics in America: Norms and Deviations," *The Annals*, January 1966, especially "The Ethical Posture of Business and the Professions," pp. 52-136.

Finley, G.J. "Business Defines Its Social Responsibilities," *The Conference Board Record*, November 1967, pp. 9-12.

Fitch, H.G. "Achieving Corporate Responsibility," *The Academy of Management Review*, January 1976, pp. 38-46.

Frederick, William C. "Social Issues in Management," *Academy of Management Review*, January 1976, pp. 99-101.

Friedman, Milton, "The Social Responsibility of Business Is To Increase Its Profits," *The New York Times Magazine*, September 13, 1970, pp. 32 ff.

Fulmer, R.M. "Business Ethics: Present and Future," *Personnel Administrator*, September 1971, pp. 48-55.

_____. "Ethical Codes for Business," *Personnel Administrator*, May 1969, pp. 49-57.

Gerstenberg, R.C. "Corporate Responsiveness and Profitability," *The Conference Board Record*, November 1972, pp. 51-53.

Godwin, Larry B. "CPA and User Opinions on Increased Corporate Disclosure," *CPA*, July 1975, pp. 31-33.

Grether, E.T. "Business Responsibility Toward the Market," *California Management Review*, Fall 1969, pp. 33-42.

Harris, L. "Public Credibility of American Business," *The Conference Board Record*, March 1973, pp. 33-38.

Hay, Robert, and Gray, Edmund R. "Social Responsibilities of Business Managers," *Academy of Management Journal*, March 1974, pp. 135-43.

Henderson, H. "Should Business Tackle Society's Problems?" *Harvard Business Review*, July 1968, pp. 77-85.

Kugel, Yerachmiel. "How to Avoid Expropriation," *Academy of Management Proceedings*, August 13-16, 1972.

Kugel, Yerachmiel, and Gruenberg, Gladys W. "International Payoffs: Where We Are and How We Got There," *Challenge*, September-October 1976, pp. 13-20.

Lerner, Max. "Shame On the Professions," *Current*, December 1975, pp. 9-13.

Levitt, Theodore. "Why Business Always Loses," *Harvard Business Review*, March-April, 1968, pp. 81-84.

_____. "The Dangers of Social Responsibility," *Harvard Business Review*, September-October 1958, pp. 41-50.

Lorig, A.W. "Where Do Corporate Responsibilities Really Lie?" *Business Horizons*, Spring 1967, pp. 51-54.

McCall, D.B. "Profit: Spur For Solving Social Ills," *Harvard Business Review*, May 1973, pp. 46-48.

McGuire, Joseph W. "Perfecting Capitalism—An Economic Dilemma," *Business Horizons*, February 1976, pp. 5-12.

McNulty, Nancy G. "And Now, Professional Codes for the Practice of Management," *Conference Board Record*, April 1975, pp. 21-24.

Muller, Ronald E. "Globalization and the Failure of Economic Policy," *Challenge*, May-June 1975, pp. 57-61.

Parket, I. Robert, and Eilbirt, Henry. "The Practice of Business: Social Responsibility. The Underlying Factors," *Business Horizons*, August 1975, pp. 5-10.

Pounds, William. "The Process of Problem Finding," *Industrial Management Review*, 1969, pp. 1-19.

Preston, L.E. "Corporation and Society: The Search for a Paradigm," *Journal of Economic Literature*, June 1975, pp. 434-53.

Purcell, Theodore C., S.J. "A Practical Guide to Ethics in Business," *Business and Society Review*, Spring 1975, pp. 43-50.

Redlich, Norman. "Lawyers, The Temple and The Market Place," *Record of New York City Bar Association*, March 1975, pp. 200-06.

Ruch, William A., and Newstrom, John W. "How Unethical Are We?" *Supervisory Management*, November 1975, pp. 16-21.

Rupp, Carla Marie. "How Sports Editors Reacted to Ethics Code," *Editor & Publisher*, June 14, 1975, pp. 17-18.

Schlusberg, Malcolm D. "Corporate Legitimacy and Social Responsibility: The Role of Law," *California Management Review*, Fall 1969, pp. 65-76.

Schwartz, Kenneth. "How Social Activists See Business," *Business and Society Review*, Summer 1975, pp. 70-73.

Sethi, S. Prakash. "Dimensions of Corporate Social Performance: An Analytical Framework," *California Management Review*, Spring 1975, pp. 50-64.

Sherman, V.C. "Business Ethics: Analysis and Philosophy," *Personnel Journal*, April 1968, pp. 271-77.

Sherwood, F.P. "Professional Ethics," *Public Management*, June 1975, pp. 13-14.

Spencer, H. "Dangers of Social Responsibility—Another Perspective," *The Conference Board Record*, November 1972, pp. 54-57.

Stebbins, R.A. "Putting People On: Deception of Our Fellowman in Everyday Life," *Sociology and Social Research*, August 1975, pp. 189-201.

Steiner, George A. "Institutionalizing Corporate Social Decisions," *Business Horizons*, December 1975, pp. 12-18.

Stern, Duke N., and Klock, David R. "Public Policy and the Professionalization of Life Underwriters," *American Business Law Journal*, Fall 1975, pp. 225-38.

Vance, S.C. "Are Socially Responsible Corporations Good Investment Risks?" *Management Review*, August 1975, pp. 18-24.

Votaw, Dow, and Sethi, S. Prakash. "Do We Need a New Corporate Response To A Changing Social Environment?" *California Management Review*, Fall 1969, pp. 3-31.

Walters, Kenneth D. "Your Employees' Right to Blow the Whistle," *Harvard Business Review*, July-August 1975, pp. 26-34, 161-62.

Walton, Clarence C. "Critics of Business: Stonethrowers and Gravediggers," *Columbia Journal of World Business*, 1966, pp. 25-37.

Special Studies and Documents

Polls and Surveys

American Management Association, *The Changing Success Ethic.* New York, AMACOM, 1973.

Business Roundtable. *A Survey of Business Members on Business Conduct Guidelines.* New York, December 1975.

The Conference Board. *Unusual Foreign Payments: A Survey of the Policies and Practices of U.S. Companies.* New York, 1976.

Investor Responsibility Research Center, Inc. *The Corporate Watergate.* Washington, D.C., October 1975.

Opinion Research Corporation, Caravan Surveys (for Pitney Bowes, Inc.). *Executive Attitudes Toward Morality in Business.* Princeton, N.J., July 1975.

U.S. Congress. Joint Economic Committee. "Pollsters Report on American Consumers and Businessmen," *Hearings*, Part I. Washington, D.C., October 30, 1975.

Special Reports and Documents

American Bar Association. *Code of Professional Responsibility.* New York, 1970.

———. *Canons of Judicial Ethics.* New York, 1968.

———, Committee on Corporate Laws. "Indemnification," *Model Business Corporation Act.* New York, 1959, as amended 1967.

American Institute of Certified Public Accountants. *Proposed Statement on Auditing Standards.* New York, May 12, 1976.

Bureau of National Affairs. "Special Report on White Collar Crime," *Securities Regulation and Law Report* (SRLR), No. 348, Part II. Washington, D.C., April 14, 1976 (bibliography).

Securities and Exchange Commission. *Report of the Special Committee to the Board of Directors of Ashland Oil, Inc.* Washington, D.C., June 26, 1975.

———. *Report of Special Review Committee of the Board of Directors of Gulf Oil Corporation.* Washington, D.C., December 30, 1975.

———. *Special Report by Phillips Petroleum Company to the Securities and Exchange Commission.* Washington, D.C., September 26, 1975.

———. *Report on Questionable and Illegal Corporate Payments and Practices.* Washington, D.C., May 12, 1976.

———. Letter from Chairman Roderick Hills, answering Staff Report of House Subcommittee on Oversight and Investigation. Washington, D.C.,

May 21, 1976 (reprinted in *Securities Regulation and Law Report*, No. 352, F-4-6).

_____. "Partial Response and Solicitation of Comments" (request of Arthur Andersen & Co. re Accounting Series Release No. 193A), File No. S7-647, *SEC Docket*. Washington, D.C., August 18, 1975.

U.S. Congress, House of Representatives, Subcommittee on Oversight and Investigation. *Report on SEC's Voluntary Compliance Program on Corporate Disclosure*. Washington, D.C., May 20, 1976.

_____, Senate, Committee on Banking, Housing and Urban Affairs. "Corrupt Overseas Payments by U.S. Business Enterprises," *Report* No. 94-1031 to accompany S. 3664. Washington, D.C., June 2, 1976, pp. 1-9.

_____, Senate, Select Committee on Presidential Campaign Activities. *Final Report*. Washington, D.C., June 1974. (Pursuant to S. Res. 60, February 7, 1973, a resolution to establish a select committee of the Senate to investigate and study illegal or improper campaign activities in the Presidential election of 1972.)

U.S. Department of Defense. "Procurements for Foreign Military Sales," Part 13. Washington, D.C., December 13, 1975.

U.S. Department of Treasury, Internal Revenue Service. "Instructions to IRS Field Offices," *News Release*. Washington, D.C., April 7, 1976.

Congressional Hearings

U.S. Congress, Senate, Subcommittee on Multinational Corporations. "Multinational Corporations and United States Foreign Policy," *Hearings*, Part 12. Washington, D.C., May-September 1975.

_____, Senate, Committee on Banking, Housing and Urban Affairs. "Prohibiting Bribes to Foreign Officials," *Hearings*, Washington, D.C. May 18, 1976.

Corporate Publications and Speeches

Corporation Publications

AMF Inc., Rodney C. Gott (Chairman and Chief Executive Officer). "Social Responsibility." White Plains, N.Y., April 27, 1971.

Air Products and Chemicals, Inc. *Policy Statement on Conflicts of Interest*. Allentown, Pa., March 4, 1976.

Armstrong Cork Co., James H. Binns (President). *Annual Report* (President's Letter) "Statement of Principles and Objectives." Lancaster, Pa., 1975.

The Bendix Corporation, W.M. Blumenthal (Chairman and President). Speech at University of Detroit, Detroit, Mich., November 18, 1975.

Carborundum Company, William H. Wendel. "Ethics—The Many Shades of Gray," speech to Chemical Buyers Group, Purchasing Management Association, Niagara Falls, N.Y., October 16, 1975.

Castle and Cooke, Inc. *Proxy Statement to Shareholders*. Honolulu, Hawaii, March 1976.

Caterpillar Tractor Co. *Worldwide Code of Business Conduct*. Peoria, Ill., October 1974.

Continental Oil Co., Howard Blauvelt (Chairman and Chief Executive). *CONOCO '75*, December 1975. See also *The Conoco Conscience*. Stamford, Conn., March 19, 1976.

Corning Glass Works, Thomas C. MacAvoy (President). "Business Ethics—Black, White and Grey," speech at University of Notre Dame. South Bend, Ind., November 1, 1973. Also *Corning—An Attitude*. Corning, N.Y., March 1, 1976.

Cummins Engine Co., Inc., H.B. Schacht (President). Speech to Planning Conference. Columbus, Ind., June 1975. Also *Annual Report*. Columbus, Ind., March 11, 1976.

Diamond Shamrock. *Policy on Legal and Ethical Standards*. Cleveland, Ohio, March 1, 1976.

Dow Chemical Company, Carl A. Gerstacker (Chairman of the Board). "Garrett Lectures on Managing the Socially Responsible Corporation," speech at Columbia University. New York, November 21, 1972.

Emerson Electric Co. *Annual Report*. St. Louis, Mo., 1975, p. 29.

Exxon Corporation. *Policy Statement on Business Ethics*. New York, September 24, 1975. Also *Notice of Annual Meeting*. New York, March 31, 1976.

Gulf Oil Corporation. *Annual Report*. Pittsburgh, Pa., March 12, 1976 (includes SEC Form 10-K). *Statement of Business Principles*. Pittsburgh, Pa., February 27, 1976. *Notice of Annual Meeting of Shareholders and Proxy*. Pittsburgh, Pa., March 19, 1976.

International Business Machines Corporation, Frank T. Cary (Chairman of the Board). Speech quoted in *Business Roundtable Report*. New York, January 30, 1976.

Lever Brothers Company, David A. Orr (Chairman of Unilever, Ltd.). "Europe—Cooperation or Isolation," speech to Northern Ireland Branch of Institute of Directors. London, April 16, 1975.

Levi Strauss International. *Annual Report*. San Francisco, Calif., 1975.

Lockheed Aircraft Corporation. *Management Policy Statement*. Burbank, Calif., October 16, 1975.

Merck & Co., Inc. *Notice of Annual Meeting*. Rahway, N.J., March 26, 1976.

The Norton Company. *Code of Ethics*. Worcester, Mass., 1976. See also supplement in *1974 Annual Report*. Worcester, Mass., 1975.

Pitney Bowes, Fred T. Allen (Chairman of Board and President). Speech before Investor Responsibility Conference. Stamford, Conn., December 10, 1975.

Also speech before Swiss-American Chamber of Commerce. Stamford, Conn., October 16, 1975.

The Quaker Oats Company. *Annual Meeting Report.* Chicago, Ill., October 2, 1975. See also "Principles and Objectives," speech by Robert D. Stuart, Jr. (President and Chief Executive Officer). Chicago, Ill., September 1970.

Rockwell International. *Corporate Policy Standards of Business Conduct.* Pittsburgh, Pa., February 12, 1976.

St. Joe Minerals Corporation. *Annual Meeting Report.* New York, May 10, 1976, pp. 8, 13.

Standard Oil Company of Ohio, Charles E. Spahr (Chairman of Board). "Ethics and the Corporation." *Sohioan*, Fall 1975. Also "Government Regulation," speech before Financial Executives Institute. Cleveland, Ohio, May 11, 1976.

Stauffer Chemical Company. *First Quarter Report.* Westport, Conn., 1976, p. 12. Also *Annual Report.* Westport, Conn., 1975, pp. 4, 35.

Texas Instruments, Inc. *Policy on Ethical Conduct.* Dallas, Texas, October 1975.

Other Speeches

Evans, John R. "Truth or Consequences," speech before Securities Cooperative Conference. Denver, Colorado, May 15, 1975.

Johnson, Franklyn A. "Self-policing the Professions." *Vital Speeches*, November 15, 1975, pp. 89-93.

Parker, Wolcott C. "Bribery in Foreign Lands." *Vital Speeches*, February 15, 1976, pp. 381-84.

Schwartz, Harry. "Responsibility and Accountability in American Medicine." *Vital Speeches*, January 1, 1975, pp. 175-82.

Sommer, A.A., Jr. "The Limits of Disclosure," speech before AICPA Advanced Management Program. Philadelphia, Pa., June 24, 1975.

Index

About the Authors

Yerachmiel Kugel is professor of management sciences at Saint Louis University, where he also serves as associate director of the International Business Program. Since receiving the Ph.D. from Michigan State University, he has published numerous articles in professional and technical journals relative to multinational business behavior and serves as consultant to many organizations engaged in transnational operations.

Together with Dr. Gruenberg, Dr. Kugel is coeditor of two readings books, one to accompany the international payoffs text, the other (scheduled for publication in 1977) entitled "Ethical Perspectives on Business and Society." He is currently under contract with Oceana publications to write a book and to provide an annual update on the subject of legislation relative to business ethics throughout the world.

Gladys W. Gruenberg is an associate professor of economics at Saint Louis University. In addition to courses in economic theory and policy, she teaches business ethics and comparative labor markets. As an arbitrator and accredited personnel diplomate, she is interested in the impact of economic policies on human resources both in the United States and abroad. Professor Gruenberg is a member of the American and Southern Economic Associations and of the Association for Social Economics. She is currently chapter president of the Industrial Relations Research Association and associate director of the Personnel and Industrial Relations Program at the School of Business and Administration.